Smart But Stuck:
Resilience with
Learning Disabilities

"*Smart But Stuck* outlines significant and convincing connections between psychology and neuroscience as factors in the understanding of resilience. Most important, this lively and informative book is of interest well beyond the world of ULD. For any professional or lay person who has struggled to move beyond seemingly stubborn limitations, Orenstein's ideas about the interface of creativity and resilience will be a breath of fresh air."

Constance Goldberg
Faculty, Institute for Clinical
Social Work, Chicago

"Dr. Orenstein perceptively and sensitively describes the feelings engendered by learning challenges in adults with undiagnosed learning disabilities (ULD) and the ways that those feelings imprison intelligence. Liberally illustrated by excerpts of interviews with people who had ULD, she outlines in clear language the stages that they pass through as they discover the true cause of their learning difficulties and the dynamics that foster the resilience that leads to successful management of learning difficulties. The second part of the book contains the historic, theoretical, and pragmatic information that can guide professionals who intervene therepeutically. *Smart But Stuck* is important reading for anyone with learning disabilities and the professionals who work with them."

Nan Freund, MEd, BCET, FAET
Past President, Association
of Education Therapists

Smart But Stuck

Resilience with Learning Disabilities

Third Edition

Smart But Stuck

Resilience with Learning Disabilities

Third Edition

Myrna Orenstein, Ph.D.

For more information about this book and its author, please visit www.smartbutstuck.com.

Cover and interior design by George Reisch.

The Library of Congress has cataloged the earlier edition of this book as follows:

Orenstein, Myrna
    Smart but stuck: how resilience frees imprisoned intelligence from learning disabilities/Myrna Orenstein.—2nd ed.
    p. cm
    includes bibliographical references
    1. Learning disabled —Psychology. 2. Learning disabled—Mental Health. 3. Learning disabled—intelligence levels. 4. Learning disabilities. I. Title.

RC394.L37O7 2007
616.85'889—dc22

                                          2006035433

To my partner and editor of more than just this book

John Summerhays,

To my mentor and emotional nurturer without
whom this book would never have been written

Dr. Fred Levin,

and

To my granddaughter Rachel

About the Author

Myrna Orenstein, Ph.D., LCSW, BCD, ACSW, is a licensed clinical social worker and psychotherapist. She earned her Ph.D. from the Institute for Clinical Social Work in Chicago and her Master's degree in social work from the University of Chicago. Dr. Orenstein is a former instructor at Oakton Community College in Illinois. She is currently an allied professional with the Association of Educational Therapists and was on the board of the Mental Health Association of the North Shore in Illinois. She has presented at conferences and conducted workshops and classes on resilience and on the emotional consequences of learning disabilities in adults.

Contents

**Part Two: Psychotherapeutic, Historical,
and Theoretical Perspectives**

Foreword to the
Second Edition

By Joe Palombo

Recent developments in the neurosciences have put to rest the old conflict between the exponents of the position that environmental factors play a major role in personality development and those who advocate for the view that endowment dictates the course of development. Researchers now accept the premise that not only do brain systems affect the course of development but also that brain development is itself affected by the environment. In this new edition of her book, Orenstein not only accepts this premise but also applies it to our understanding of the problems of people with learning disabilities. With the addition of a new chapter, co-authored with the psychoanalyst Fred Levin, she undertakes to examine the role of resilience in overcoming the constraints that learning disabilities impose on a person's functioning. Orenstein's view of resilience highlights the complementarity between nature and nurture in overcoming these constraints.

We no longer need to think of resilience as either an attribute that people have, that is, with which they are born, or as a competence that people can acquire, that is, one that may be proactively enhanced with sufficient support from a caregiving environment. Both may occur. A person may possess such a mental faculty and may actively engage in attitudes and activities that enhance it. Resilience may then act as a protective factor against the development of debilitating shame or other pathological outcomes of having a learning disability. It may immunize a person against defeatist attitudes and act as an antidote to failure. In this sense, resilience may also be thought of as reinforcing what researchers in development call the self-righting ability that occurs during maturation. The self-righting ability is the ability to bend when buffeted by inclement events to which a person is exposed and then to spring back to regain the previous equilibrium. Orenstein considers this ability to be a component of resilience.

How then may we characterize resilience? We each have our own list, as Orenstein points out. Mine includes among others the following abilities:

- To have the drive to overcome adversity
- To persevere in the face of reversals and seemingly insurmountable obstacles
- To accept the constraints that endowment imposes and to use one's assets in the service of achieving desired goals
- To take in stride the narcissistic injuries that are an inevitable part of temporary failures
- To maintain faith in one's self and one's ability to tackle arduous tasks with a view to mastering the difficulties they present
- To take a proactive attitude that allows one to learn from past mistakes and avoid making them in the future.

These abilities cannot be exercised in a vacuum, as they require the support of others who can act as releasers—Orenstein's term—of positive emotions. These emotions are essential to the learning process that accompanies a person's struggles. This book offers people with learning disabilities concrete suggestions through which they may overcome the adversities to which they are exposed and provides hope that they may triumph and find their way to success if they remain resilient.

Joseph Palombo, MA
Founding Dean
Institute for Clinical Social Work (Chicago)

Author's Note

It is my opinion that some subjects are too complex for any single specialized area of knowledge to fully understand. For this reason, periodically, throughout my book, I have added interdisciplinary input to better understand the various experiences of people with learning disabilities (LD). This new material especially concerns how they adapt and work with their LD and how they use their resilience to master various problems.

Acknowledgments

Revising this book is like watching a child grow. Although the first edition is my creation, many kept me moving during the lengthy creative process.

First, Connie Goldberg and Joe Palombo's input was decisive and always thought provoking. In regard to the second edition, I would like to thank Fred Levin and Jay Einhorn for their thoughtful contributions.

A special heartfelt thanks to my friends and colleagues who were kind enough to read my original manuscript when I was feeling stuck and in my own personal chasm: Kenan Heise, Lois Roewade, Ruth Rootberg, Susan Sholtes, Jeanne Hanson, and Janice Wiley. Furthermore, my husband Al and my children have always been a source of support.

I wish to thank my editor, Cindy Pineo, who has stuck with me through two editions of this book. She has this remarkable ability to turn complicated ideas into elegant, easy-to-read sentences. Also thanks goes to David Block for his great ideas, contagious enthusiasm, and sociological insights.

A grateful thanks to George Reisch and John Summerhays, whose astute editing skills coupled with their capacity to work as team players made the creation of this third edition a pleasure.

Thanks to all the people at Haworth Press: Tara Barnes for her editorial expertise and also Amy Rentner, Kerry Mack, Jason Wint, and Marie Spencer for their helpfulness and support.

Thanks also to Sandy Sickels, Margaret Tatich, and Bill Palmer, who were instrumental in assembling such a remarkable crew. Their insight and vision helped this book live up to its potential.

Of course the participants in my research form the backbone of this book. Their ability to persevere in the face of many obstacles was the fuel that propelled the writing of their story. Much gratitude to Thomas Kenemore, Patrick Curtis, Amy Eldridge, and Dennis Shelby of the Institute for Clinical Social Work for encouraging and supporting my research.

Finally, heartfelt thanks to my mentor, and friend, Fred Levin, without whom this book would not have been written.

Introduction

Imprisoned Intelligence
in Resilient People

My curiosity about the experience of living with learning gaps led me into a world I could not possibly have imagined. It began with a simple question. I asked adults who finally learned about their previously undetected learning disabilities, "What's it like to know *now* that you lived with an undiagnosed learning disability?" Almost everyone interviewed answered with one word: "Frustrating." This was the tip of the iceberg.

Exploring this frustration became an adventure. As the participants shared their experiences, they described being stuck in "the chasm"—an impasse frustrating their desire to learn. They also described the exhilaration that comes from their resilience: the ability to persist against seemingly impossible odds. This success, unfortunately, barely clothes a secret world of shame and exposure. My reverence, therefore, for the courage and dignity of these individuals increased with each interview.

The story of overcoming the chasm needs to be told. Here is a snippet from one interview.

PARTICIPANT: They said it was a mild learning disability. I had trouble, they said, with certain decoding skills. I know the words, but I make little errors, or I'll leave a word out occasionally, or I'll skip over words a lot of times. What I know I do is, I'll draw a conclusion without reading it.

Interviewer: How do you mean?

Participant: I'll read a bunch of stuff, and I'll say I want to read this, and this is what I think, where I think it's going to go, you know? I'll do that a lot and [laughs] sometimes I'm right, and sometimes I'm not, although I'm right better than half the time. They said had I chosen some other line of work, it would have been [laughs] nothing! I might not have even noticed. But even though I've always been promoted at work, I've had to do more and more reading and my frustration level got higher and higher.

It is interesting that some very smart people:

- feel intrinsically flawed and fear being "found out"
- can be successful, yet feel stupid inside
- can be considered goof-offs rather than underachievers.

This book is about them—resilient people who struggle with frustrating learning gaps; people who are gifted in some areas but seemingly incompetent in others. It is about the absent-minded professor, the engineer who gets A's in math but fails English, or the gifted writer who cannot spell. It is about the paralegal who takes work home every night because she just cannot finish it at the office, and the secretary who uses the dictionary a thousand times a day.

People such as these shared with me what it is like "being stuck in the chasm," as they put it. They described the invisible nature of learning gaps and how this hidden problem constricts intelligence. They also shared reasons why the chasm can create serious emotional distress if one's innate ability is either overlooked or misunderstood.

This book shows the courage of those who have been willing to admit what is missing in themselves. This capacity to face one's deficits is, as we shall see, a hallmark of resilience. Their strength and perseverance let them find fulfilling outlets for their potential.

The participants in this study found that they had learning disabilities. Other factors, of course, can also cause learning gaps. For example, some people unfortunately missed out when certain skills were taught in school. Others may have emotional problems that constrict their learning. *But no matter what the cause, if intelligent individuals are missing skills vital for achievement, they may end up being left out in the cold.*

This book is about the emotional consequences of having undiagnosed learning disabilities. Life can be difficult for these people, because they suffer the emotional fallout of seeming very bright in some areas of learning and curiously "out of it" in others. These areas of weakness can interfere with using, or even knowing, one's strengths and even oneself. These discrepancies can imprison intelligence and constrict potential.

Many people struggle with this problem. One out of five children have learning disabilities; 20 percent of the population in the United States have suffered or continue to suffer (National Center for Learning Disabilities). The chances are, therefore, that there are individuals with frustrating learning gaps in most families.

In spite of how common learning disabilities are (diagnosed and undiagnosed), the literature about the emotional fallout of learning disabilities is surprisingly sparse (Gazar, 1992). While there are many books and articles about how to educate people with learning disabilities, there are few books or articles about the emotional world of these people. Especially when the learning disability is undiagnosed, the learning disability commonly creates a baffling inability to learn certain kinds of material. Other people will often tell the person that he or she is either stupid or lazy, and it is tempting to believe it. The purpose of this book is to describe these emotional consequences of learning disabilities and to offer insights into how to resiliently and most effectively meet these emotional challenges.

Learning disabilities and the problems they create differ from person to person. Here are some examples.

Musically, Mozart was incredibly gifted. In fact, according to historians he wrote music the way one eats ice cream. It was easy for him. Yet, as seen in the movie *Amadeus* (which by all accounts accurately depicts this aspect of Mozart's personality), he could never figure out how to act around people and ended up alienating himself from everyone.

These discrepancies are quite common. A mechanic I once knew could hardly read, yet he was extraordinarily gifted. When a car broke down, he was the man of the hour. His ability to solve difficult mechanical problems was uncanny. And it was usually inexpensive. Obviously it would have been tragic if this mechanic ended up writing music or if Mozart's only option was to fix cars. Everyone needs to find a niche in life, and many are not as lucky as Mozart and my mechanic. Each could use his intelligence without always tripping over his weaknesses.

For people with learning gaps, strengths can often be hidden by weaknesses. Teachers, bosses, or family members may not be able to see their strengths because their deficits get in the way. This problem of discrepancies (unless one is very lucky) is no trivial matter.

As a music major in high school and college, only the bare necessities in math and science were required of me. My geometry teacher even called me the most inept student she had ever passed. Yet this was not a deterrent for me in a professional career as a singer where no one cared about biology. When earning a Ph.D. in social work, however, I discovered that "getting around" learning gaps was indeed challenging. A tutor, for example, was a necessity in order to deal with statistics.

To this day, my areas of weakness continue to confound me. It is not only math. I lack of a sense of direction and this causes me difficulties. New environments are especially troublesome. Driving alone across the country is not even possible. If a crisis required reading a diagram or building a bicycle in five minutes (or even five hours), trouble would be afoot.

Think about the bright people in this country who are floundering in school. How many of us have heard: "How can someone as bright as you flunk this test?" or "You must not care," or "You're lazy."

To those who struggle with these problems, this book is not a hand-holder. The focus of the book is how to handle the emotional side of learning disabilities, to enhance resilience in the face of learning disabilities. It will underscore the importance of (1) taking responsibility for one's strengths and weaknesses, and (2) recognizing and defending oneself when others inadvertently sabotage one's motivation.

Clearly, as the research in this book shows, undiagnosed learning disabilities (ULD) can cause Imprisoned Intelligence. I interviewed twenty people with ULD. Each interview was detailed and focused in-depth on what it was like to grow up with this problem. Participants invariably described how their uncomprehending teachers failed to notice their abilities. As the details unfolded, it became clear that their problems created a tapestry that wove together intelligence, creativity, ULD, and shame. This unfortunate combination created an environment of victimization for innocent people. I believe this same tapestry can describe others with learning gaps as well. It is tragic when one straddles high intelligence and serious weaknesses because destructive shame is often the result. How does this happen?

To answer this question, it is necessary to discuss shame. Shame can be helpful or toxic. Constructive shame facilitates learning. It stops people from making fools of themselves. Individuals can get the hint, pull back, and learn to behave more effectively. This is how we learn everything from table manners to the best way to talk to the boss. To learn, healthy doses of shame are a necessity.

However, like too much food, too much shame can stifle. Those who are subjected to shame too often, and without the opportunity to learn new information, feel enfeebled and even flawed. When there is too much shame, it is difficult to fix what is wrong because people simply withdraw. Too much shame interferes with one's ability to be curious.

This sense of "flawedness" happens in smart people whose wish to learn is frustrated by invisible obstacles. However, the shame does not necessarily spring from the learning gap itself. Bright people can learn to compensate for, or get around, learning gaps in very, very effective ways. But if the obstacle is unrecognized or undiagnosed, then attempts to learn can be blocked. They do not know why they can't learn, and so they become disappointed in themselves and ashamed.

Although those of us with learning disabilities often develop "compensations," the chances of finding effective compensations often decrease the more the problem is hidden. When people find themselves blocked over and over again by this invisible obstacle, they tend to accept blame and to perceive themselves as "stupid." No other explanation makes sense. Their self-esteem suffers, and then, it becomes difficult indeed to learn.

Those who inhabit our academic environment (teachers, parents, and peers) need to see and accept how learning gaps can cause Imprisoned Intelligence. Then, with appropriate interventions, those properly diagnosed could have more fulfilled, dramatically enhanced lives. In short, Imprisoned Intelligence is a challenge that has to and can be faced and surmounted.

You are reading the third edition of this book. The first edition focused on shame, in particular, the shame that people experience when for unknown reasons, i.e., for reasons that have not been diagnosed, they cannot learn what is expected of them. The second edition added new material discussing resilience. Resilience is the capacity to find alternatives when normal approaches don't work, which can be a pathway to hope and success. The third edition adds the results of recent research regarding our primal urge to explore. This urge, carried in our brains by what researchers call "the seeking system," gives us a powerful urge to try out alternative approaches if the normal approach isn't working, and thus to have a resilient response to challenges such as those posed by undiagnosed learning disabilities.

This book will examine how growing up with Imprisoned Intelligence created emotional difficulties and continues to cause problems for many individuals. It is divided into two main sections: Section I includes eight chapters and is written for the individual who struggles with Imprisoned Intelligence, and for his or her family, friends, supervisors, colleagues, and teachers. Section II shifts the focus to more conceptual psychological perspectives and includes seven chapters for laypeople and clinicians alike. A brief description of the individual chapters follows.

Chapter 1 will give an overview of how people with undiagnosed learning disabilities struggle, survive, and achieve.

Chapter 2 is an introduction to shame, seeking compensations, and resilience, an experience central to the psychological landscape of ULD sufferers. By providing some background on shame, seeking, and resilience, the stories of the participants will make more sense.

Chapters 3 through 6 are the heart of this book. The painful problems of ULD are defined and described in depth. It is from these experiences, with their details, that an accumulated body of material can be built. When adults discover, deal with, and finally accept their learning disabilities, they walk a similar path that changes over time. It is a difficult path that begins with a bewildering sense that something is wrong and ends with reconciliation. Along the way, they learn fortitude and flexibility. If the parents, teachers, or psychologists of the study participant I call "True Grit" had access to this information, his life would have been changed immeasurably!

Chapter 3 specifically highlights the chasm: the fundamental problem caused by ULD. The chasm is an experience of being stuck with no way out of being frozen in time. It involves excruciatingly shameful humiliation, exposure, and despair and occurs when people cannot live up to internal or external expectations. They then must struggle not only with ULD, but also with its emotional consequences. For example, a very bright boy may have poor motor coordination, and he may fail tests because he cannot write fast enough to finish them in the allotted time. He then suffers from both his own disappointment and ridicule from peers; the combination creates a huge emotional burden.

ULD itself does not cause Imprisoned Intelligence. *It is the emotional aftermath that hinders the flowering of potential.* Many people with ULD never know it and never need to know. They have created successful coping strategies. For example, a poor writer can live a fulfilling life as a truck driver, actor, or salesperson. A poor speller can use a spelling checker. However, a brilliant scientist who can answer complex questions but cannot write well will find that scholarly work is difficult (unless he or she has the money to hire a good editor). To repeat, emotional problems unfold when ULD prohibits us from meeting the demands of our world.

Chapter 4 describes how it feels to be tested, while Chapter 5 discusses the painful aftereffects of learning about this problem. People grieve for what they now know they will never have.

Chapter 6 shows how resilient people can and do triumph over this previously unrecognized learning problem. Although there is often not a lot a child can do to treat LD without help from caregivers, adults have the capacity for self-nurturance because of the capacity to seek out and provide for their own needs. The participants in the study took action that allowed them to fulfill their potential. They showed a determination to free their intelligence in the face of frustration and despair. The book shows how they made peace with this old enemy.

Chapters 7 deals with possible solutions and explains how to help oneself and find assistance from others, while Chapter 8 revisits shame and seeking. Section I concludes with Chapter 9 that highlights the necessity for academic institutions to face and deal with the emotional aspects of learning disabilities.

As stated earlier, Section II shifts focus. It is directed to the clinician and layperson alike. Chapter 10 considers whether psychotherapy is necessary and what one can expect and learn. Chapter 11 explores the psychotherapeutic ramifications of working with individuals with undiagnosed learning disabilities. Chapter 12, authored by Jay Einhorn, discusses how the chasm manifests itself within different learning disabilities and examines the neuropsychological foundations of the chasm, while Chapter 13, coauthored with Fred Levin, looks at resilience from a neuropsychological perspective. Chapter 14, "Learning to Be Resilient: What's Needed When We Have LD" is also coauthored with Fred Levin and applies these insights to the task of becoming resilient.

After an epilogue, I offer two addenda. The first describes how self psychological theory provides concepts that enhance the understanding of imprisoned intelligence. Addendum II provides a historical overview of the field of learning disabilities, looking at the state of research as well as academic controversies. Finally, a list of recommended readings provides resources for those who wish to read further.

Part One

What Everyone Needs to Know About Learning Disabilities, Imprisoned Intelligence, and Resilience

Chapter 1

Imprisoned Intelligence: How Does It Happen?

Work hard and you'll succeed.

If you don't succeed, try and try again.

Our culture assumes that success comes to those who are intelligent, motivated, and hardworking. However, for many, hard work is followed only by the frustration of being stuck in the chasm.

This book is about such people. It's about Imprisoned Intelligence that occurs when adults are restricted by frustrating learning gaps due to undiagnosed learning disabilities (ULD). They, for the most part, are resilient survivors who succeed despite this adversity.

They are uneven learners who accept and live in two contradictory worlds: (1) the world of success where learning is easy and fun, versus (2) the world of struggle and failure where learning is embarrassing, painful, and difficult. A girl with great verbal skills, for example, might be able to read like an adult, but because of visual motor problems she may be unable to comfortably hold and manipulate a pencil. If so, she will be unable to transfer what she sees to the written page. The youngster therefore enters the chasm because she cannot learn to write. Her intelligence cannot be expressed in written assignments. The learning disability, in other words, interferes with and blocks her potential to achieve. These are the kinds of obstacles that create what I call Imprisoned Intelligence.

The words of the participants form the basis of this book. For the many individuals who struggle with ULD, the following stories will be an eye-opener.

TRUE GRIT

To help understand how learning disabilities have impact on real people, the reader might look to a participant in the study whom I have nicknamed "True Grit." His resilience in the face of overwhelming odds is a story repeated over and over by others.

True Grit, the first person interviewed, had vulnerabilities, brilliance, and a painful isolation that reflected the experiences of almost everyone in this study. He provoked an almost missionary zeal to right a serious wrong. His story needs to be told. In essence, that first interview launched this book.

When True Grit walked into the room, his charisma and commanding presence created an energy that was almost palpable. Few would ever suspect that he had learning disabilities. This articulate, good-looking, well-dressed twenty-five-year-old was successful, having started a small business that had quickly become a multinational enterprise. Clearly, he was making his way in society just fine. This had not been the case when he was in school. In fact, the differences between his current success and his school failure demonstrate his resiliency.

In his early school years, loneliness and isolation were not yet a problem. True Grit was not aware of any differences between himself and his classmates. He felt himself to be part of the class even though he also knew that he made mistakes. At that time, he viewed them as simply a part of the learning process.In fourth or fifth grade, his world changed dramatically. As a result of the testing that is given to all fourth graders in his state, True Grit was found to be a "poor reader" and was placed in a painfully boring "slower" reading group and was given "silly books with bigger print" to read. He hated it! Not only was he bored, but he felt separated from other intelligent students. He felt demeaned and was ridiculed by both teachers and students.

> They just said, "We're going to help you improve your reading. You're going to be in reading group B, and that's it." They'd sit you in a big classroom, and the substitutes would be given the project to work on. . . . They'd sit at their desks, and then reading group A would be in the back of the classroom. She'd rotate us, okay? Like inventory. . . . And, you know, this reading group B, which is the one I was in, was the worst and the lowest one. You were given silly books to read, bigger writing.

Because he felt patronized, demeaned, and ridiculed by both teachers and students, his performance continued to decline.

> The teacher always treated the more intelligent students with more respect. Didn't patronize them. Didn't put them in the remedial reading group. Let them have more liberties to do what they wanted. And then while I was told to be in the remedial reading group, I was treated with what I thought was contempt, not only by the teachers, but by my peers. And I wasn't given the same privileges as everybody else was.

His performance continued to decline but he was "just promoted along" from grade to grade in deference to his well-educated, well-respected family. True Grit recalls, "I just knew that school was harder for me than them [other students]."

He also felt invisible sometimes. For example, in his parochial school, True Grit was consistently passed over as a reader in chapel:

> It's a big thing to be appointed to be a reader in charge, you know? Because we had school Masses. The best readers would be asked to read from the Bible or something like that. I did that once for ten seconds, and that was the end of it.

Furthermore, his motivation was consistently challenged. Teachers and principals would criticize him for not working hard enough even though he always completed his homework. Since he knew he was doing his best, his anger and frustration level were enormous.

> She (my mother) helped with my algebra. The homework
> was done all the time, on time. Everything. I handed every
> assignment in. I think I missed two assignments or stuff like
> that, which I lost . . . and I still flunked . . . every assign-
> ment. I still got Ds and Fs and still flunked. She helped with
> spelling. And I memorized the entire list of spelling, and I'd
> still flunk.

True Grit's biggest problem was not his undiagnosed learning disabilities per se. Rather, the problem lay in the fact that no one saw them. Except for his mother (who valiantly did the best she could), no one was there to help him. This oversight created an experience of aloneness, and struggling with this alienation was extremely difficult. "Nobody had any idea of what I was going through. I was completely and totally on my own."

True Grit felt himself at the mercy of his peers when he could not live up to class expectations, particularly when tests were being passed back to the students.

> The test would be passed out around the room. You know,
> they'd say, "Take your test and pass it along." Okay? Well,
> everyone would know my grade, you know? I'd be sitting in
> the back of the room somewhere. . . . There would be com-
> ments made. . . . "That was the easiest test on the face of the
> earth. How come he couldn't do that?"

True Grit's home life was also rapidly deteriorating as a result of his school performance. He was the fourth of five children born into a family with a strong tradition of medical careers. He was expected to become a doctor. True Grit's siblings were extremely high achievers and were outstanding students in school. One brother was a straight-A student and considered a genius. His siblings began to tease him mercilessly. To make matters worse, his father felt that being tough would improve the situation. He received countless lectures.

> They were always telling me to work harder. That I was
> going to be a garbage man. I'd never be promoted. Grades
> and everything were always very important in our house. I
> constantly got Cs, Ds, and Fs. And every time report-card
> time came, it was very traumatic at our house. I mean, any-
> time I got my report card, there was always hell to pay.

His father would bring the subject up at dinnertime in front of the rest of the family, pointing to True Grit as a model of failure and his brother as a model of success.

Although this heavy-handed treatment was difficult to swallow, the covert denigration was even worse. His siblings would repeat cruel remarks his father made about him (or he would overhear them himself), compounding his feelings of alienation, worthlessness, and shame. "I was stupid. And that was all there was to it. Very low self-esteem."

True Grit's parents sent him to several psychologists in hopes of curing his problems. But since learning disabilities were not common knowledge at that time, the psychologists attributed his problems to lack of intelligence or motivation:

> My parents decided, "We don't know what's wrong with this kid. It's time to send him to a psychologist." And that was when I hit sixth grade. I saw at least about four different kinds of learning experts—psychologists or something like that. And so I went to all these psychologists. And they couldn't find anything. They just thought I was beneath average intelligence. That's all there was to it. "The kid's a moron. Live with it." That's about all it boiled down to.

In the meantime, his father's fuse was becoming shorter and shorter, and True Grit was starting to withdraw from his family:

> I lived in a lot of fear. I separated myself from my family. I was completely autonomous. When we went on vacation, like at skiing and water skiing, where you start very young, I would always do it on my own. I was completely separate. I would have to go outside of my family for support of things because I realized . . . I'm just totally different from everybody else, in terms of the ways I talked, my interests, everything. I was like the fifth wheel in this family.

In seventh or eighth grade, True Grit just gave up. Tired of being battered by constant accusations of not trying, yet trying his hardest and failing, he no longer had the strength to continue caring about academic success. The incongruity between his inner reality and others' perceptions was both discouraging and angering. Suffering from destructive, chronic shame, True Grit reasoned that if everyone wanted him to be dumb he would indeed act that way:

> I did not think highly of myself. I thought I was dumb. I just started agreeing with everybody else. I rolled over and died. That was it.

His life began to change in high school. For one thing, he began to realize that he had artistic talent. Since his family did not see art as a moneymaking venture, they did not respect it. He learned, however, that he had an eye for design and strong three-dimensional skills. As a sophomore, he began to visit art museums and to watch public television. "It was like a heaven in the middle of a hell."

He also taught himself to play several instruments. His family derided these behaviors as snobbish and foolish. When others outside his family discovered his activities, they were surprised that a "dummy" would be doing these kinds of things. This earned him a certain grudging respect.Also during this time, True Grit experimented with his design talent in the landscaping business. During the summers, in his basement, he created his own landscape contracting business. He served as a wholesaler of landscaping supplies, installing and designing the jobs himself. He worked with real estate developers who would sell the building and his landscaping job together.

True Grit was able to go to college—if only to a small, mediocre liberal arts college. At college, however, he reached an important turning point. A thoughtful English teacher noticed that this bright student was flunking her class. She referred him to the director of education, who administered some intelligence tests. These tests showed that he was of above-average intelligence. However, the tests were not sophisticated enough to tell much else. They shed little light on what his real difficulties were because they could not isolate his specific learning problems; that is, they could not explain why his performance was so poor. The director told him that he had some sort of learning disability that she was incapable of diagnosing. However, she offered to serve as a personal tutor and did so for the two years of his education there.

Although True Grit struggled for his grades, he was also bored. Paradoxically, the institution in which he was failing was just not challenging enough for him! Recognizing this, the director lobbied on his behalf for acceptance into a more prestigious institution nearby.

Counselors at his new school encouraged him to get tested at the school's Center for Reading and Learning. However, he resisted during his first year until he realized that he was in danger of flunking out. Sometime in his junior year of college, True Grit finally went for testing. He discovered that he had dyslexia—not severe, but enough to hamper his learning.

After testing, he failed to deal with his dyslexia. He majored in finance and then continued to make poor choices. Upon graduating, he took a job as a clerk that involved adding up numbers with a calculator. Although this would be child's play for most finance majors, it was a disaster for a dyslexic who reversed numbers as he keyed them into the calculator. True Grit was fired. At the time, he was still living with his parents, who responded with deep disappointment.

In this instance, shame served a positive function: It "reset" True Grit. It showed him that his current approach was not working and afforded him an opportunity to rethink his strategy. This flexibility is a hallmark of resiliency.

> I was afraid that this was going to like completely destroy any future hopes of me getting a job . . . and it did for about two weeks. But I got back up on the horse and went out and, you know, pursued my own business.

Remembering his high school landscaping success, True Grit decided to create his own display company. He approached hotels and restaurants and began to sell, design, and install holiday displays. Soon he landed an account with a large, successful restaurant chain. Building on this success, he began importing his supplies directly from Asia, where display items are typically manufactured.

Over time, True Grit developed savvy work habits that compensated for his learning disability. He now relies on his computer and spelling checker for any correspondence and always rewrites each letter or email several times. To avoid any embarrassment because of his atrocious spelling, True Grit carries an electronic pocket spelling checker. In his own words:

> It [the learning disability] is part of me, and I accept it as part of me. It's a problem I've got to deal with in the business world. . . . I cannot be a financial consultant. I cannot be an accountant. I cannot be any of those things. It has to be all qualitative. And if it involves quantitative support, it's got to be done on the computer. But I've got to be sure my entire career is not based on a financial background.

Unable to live up to school standards, True Grit found the outside world's standards more to his liking. His success became a source of pride. "This is no longer school, school is way in the background now [and] no one even cares about that." In fact, True Grit pinpoints his watershed experience—the point at which his talents were able to take off—as the time when he was finally able to "become detached from the standard."

Furthermore, as he began to comprehend and reconcile his life with his dyslexia, he not only forgave himself but he also began to forgive his family. In looking back over his life True Grit is very grateful to his mother. She never lost hope. Although she had no idea he was learning disabled, she encouraged his intellect and perseverance. **"My mom . . . knows that I wasn't lazy."** (As will be seen in chapter 11, having someone "rooting" for you is an important component in the growth of resilience.) His relationship with his dad began to heal over time and his family has been forced to recognize his success.

True Grit now realizes that Imprisoned Intelligence is not just failure to make the grade. *The by-product of these failures is alienation and loneliness, and it is these emotions that lead to Imprisoned Intelligence.* To free Imprisoned Intelligence, he says, one must confront the inevitable aloneness and alienation that can go hand in glove with ULD:

> First of all, you've got to identify it. I think that's the important thing. Aloneness is when you're not getting support for what you want. You've got to identify the aloneness to

> see if you're not getting it [support] from your core group
> of people, which is usually your family. Okay? And if you're
> not being supported, then you recognized that aloneness.
> You're alone.

Only then, after one has struggled and identified this problem of aloneness, can one consider alternatives:

> Once you've identified it, then you've got to act on it. . . . I
> mean no one's an island in this life. You've got to go get it
> from somebody else because if you don't have support, or
> you're completely alone, you've got to have encouragement
> for when those rough times come around. Because when
> life got rough for me . . . I had to go to turn to some of my
> friends and stuff like that.

To free intelligence, True Grit has these words of advice to offer parents of a learning-disabled child: "Pay attention to the things that are influencing him [or her] positively. [For example,] if the child is an artist, make sure attention is given to those strengths."

This is how True Grit achieved his own victory. He incorporated his artistic talents and people skills in the context of business. By capitalizing on his strengths, he conquered his shame about his ULD and was able to accomplish great things. His family began to express their pride in his success and to respect his abilities. Now, he has a solid sense of self-worth. He knows he is valuable. He found his place in the sun by incorporating his artistic talents and skills in a meaningful business pursuit.

WHAT SORT OF PEOPLE HAVE UNDIAGNOSED LEARNING DISABILITIES AND LEARN RESILENCY?

Throughout history, many successful people have had LD. Since testing for LD is a relatively modern phenomenon, there is no proof that the individuals discussed below had or have ULD, but the evidence strongly suggests it.

When Thomas A. Edison was diagnosed as "mentally ill" by his teacher, his angry mother withdrew him from school and taught him at home. In his later recollections, he said that he found it impossible to learn English and arithmetic by rote. He found it necessary to "do things" or "make things" in order to learn. His interest in reading was piqued only when his mother began reading books aloud to him. His early writings display a marked difficulty with written language. And yet Edison was the brilliant mind who brought us the light bulb, the phonograph, the motion picture camera, the ticker tape, and many other inventions.

Auguste Rodin, the famous French sculptor, had similar difficulties with reading, spelling, and arithmetic. Despite early indications of a gift for drawing, Rodin's father forbid further exploration of this talent, insisting that his son learn reading and writing to secure a better future. His father was disappointed when Auguste was expelled from two schools because he was "ineducable." Although his failure was ascribed to "poor eyesight," his later production makes this an unlikely explanation. Dyslexia historically has often been ascribed to eyesight problems.

When considering the great intellects of the modern age, Albert Einstein's name will surely come to mind. Yet as a boy he was considered slow. While excelling in mathematics and physics, he experienced great difficulty with language. He failed his first attempt at college entrance examinations, yet he formulated the theory of relativity in his mid-twenties.

Cher, a successful recording artist and actress, became aware of her LD only when her daughter, Chastity, underwent similar experiences. Throughout Cher's own schooling, teachers would remark that she seemed to have the ability, but failed to apply herself. Since she was working as hard as she could, her teachers were likely observing not a lack of effort, but the discrepancy between potential and achievement that characterizes LD. Despite her difficulty in reading and writing, Cher reports that she can often memorize a script in a single reading.

Failure in the classroom caused by dyslexia pushed Olympic gold medal winner Bruce Jenner into the sports arena. There, he found he could earn a pat on the back for his hard work, instead of frustration. Eventually he was able to bring the confidence he gained in sports back into the classroom so that he could achieve there as well.

The list of successful individuals who have struggled with undiagnosed LD is enormous. I mention these examples only to demonstrate that an intelligent mind can be imprisoned by LD; it is the individual's tenacity and inventiveness that allow him or her to exceed the expectations of others and to excel.

Once a problem is identified, solutions are always possible. A *Time* magazine article noted that Ennis Cosby, the son of entertainer Bill Cosby, grew up with an undiagnosed dyslexia. As a result of his experiences, he was working toward a graduate degree in education and helping LD students. Tragically, he was murdered before he could contribute his gifts fully. About his learning disorder, he said, "The happiest day in my life occurred when I found out I was dyslexic. . . . I believe that life is finding solutions, and the worst feeling to me is confusion" (Chuaeoan, 1997, p. 25).

DEFINITION OF LEARNING DISABILITIES AND RESILIENCE

Research for this book led me to others like Ennis Cosby: people who did not find out that they had a learning disability until adulthood. The research clearly indicates that (1) ULD constricts potential and causes Imprisoned Intelligence, and (2) creative alternatives are possible.

One serious problem, however, involves how learning disabilities are defined. Many people have a vague notion that "having a learning disability" means "having a learning problem." Perhaps the term "stupid" even comes to mind. Most people, asked whether a person with a learning disability could have above-average intelligence, would probably answer "no." This is just one of the many misunderstandings. Even if a person is deficient in certain areas, she or he may be brilliant in others. A bright, creative, literate person, for example, may have a terrible problem with math, or vice versa.

To understand the emotional problems caused by undiagnosed learning disabilities (ULD), some short introductory definitions are in order. (More precise academic definitions of learning disabilities are given in Addendum II, Historical Review.) According to a February 13, 1996, *New York Times* article, "learning disabilities are the unexpected failure to learn, despite adequate intelligence, motivation, and instruction; reading disorders like dyslexia are the most common" (Lewin, 1996, p. 1).

Learning disabilities, then, are disorders that, in contrast to an individual's intelligence, *interfere* with his or her ability (in one or more areas) to listen, look, think, speak, read, write, spell, or do mathematical calculations that could otherwise be done very well. Learning disabilities can disrupt normal academic or social functioning. They are presumed to result from a hardwired problem in one's brain.

An undiagnosed learning disability—the focus of this book— is one that is invisible or overlooked. It is covert. So, how can learning disabilities remain invisible when they clearly disrupt functioning and achievement in school? Testing for learning disabilities, it turns out, is a relatively new procedure. (The term *learning disabilities* was not even coined until 1962.) For many who discovered their learning disabilities as adults, testing was not available to them in the 1960s. Although they had the same learning disabilities that some school children had, they did not have the benefit of testing and identification of their difficulties. From their point of view, they simply felt frustrated because they knew that their performance did not live up to their potential. They may have been average students, but they were not average thinkers. Take, for example, a student who has an outstanding grasp of mathematical concepts but is dyslexic and cannot read or reproduce numbers accurately. Unless the disability is known, the dyslexia can prevent this person from excelling in advanced math classes.

You might ask at this juncture, "How do I know if I have ULD? What does it feel like?" It is difficult to describe the frustrating experience of wanting to learn and not being able to because some unknown "something" gets in the way. Interviews with adults suggest that an undiagnosed learning disability is experienced as the wish to succeed and the belief that one can succeed—yet without the ability to do so. Smart adults with ULD have an expectation that academic problems can be mastered if one tries hard enough. And yet, the problem is perceived as a permanent, invisible gap in one's brain that creates mysterious impasses that prevent learning. Here is how some of the participants in this study defined ULD.

- Learning disabilities mean taking longer to learn.
- I can receive information but I can't put it out.

Why is ULD so difficult to identify when one is an intelligent adult? Complicating identification is the fact that bright people often learn to compensate for their deficits; however, since the problem is unidentified, they must do this, more or less, alone. Usually, they creatively learn to get around the problem. One person in this study who could not read well asked great questions in her high-school classes because somehow she knew she had to learn by listening. She was always considered an outstanding student, and this way of acquiring knowledge worked beautifully. In college, however, she was sunk. Professors were not interested in her questions because there was too much material to cover.

The core of the problem is not the learning disability itself. It is the lack of diagnosis and clarification. Once a problem is identified, solutions become possible. By definition, ULD is invisible or overlooked. Because it is not identified, it is misunderstood, and the individual may not realize that help exists. The problem and the pain are magnified by impossible expectations from the world and from oneself.

INFORMATION ABOUT THE RESEARCH

All my information about Imprisoned Intelligence was acquired from interviews. Being a member of the very large tribe of those who have learning disabilities was an advantage. The knowledge that I was "one of us" seemed to allow the participants to feel more comfortable sharing their experiences. Because there are so many different types of learning disabilities, an objective stance could also be retained so that curiosity about the participants' own subjective experiences could unfold. My clinical training allowed me to keep the focus on experiences.

What criteria were used in selecting participants? Individuals had to be over seventeen years old before they received their learning disability diagnosis. A total of twenty participants from the ages of nineteen to sixty-one were involved. One was Hispanic. The others were Caucasian. There were six men and fourteen women. Their socioeconomic status ranged from poor to wealthy. Most lived in the Chicago area. Two lived outside of Chicago, one in Boston, and another in a small town in South Carolina. Twelve were in college at the time of the study, although not all for the first time. Their occupations are or were as follows: college student, social worker, artist, college professor, massage therapist, certified public accountant, meter collector/actor, contractor, secretary, and full-time mother.

Participants were recruited in a variety of ways. Several students attended local universities or a community college in the Chicago area. A call for participants was placed in the boxes of all students who were working with counselors in the learning disability departments. Many were referred word-of-mouth by other participants. Participants were not selected by random sampling.

The initial interviews took place on the phone, when information was elicited to determine the participant's eligibility. Prospective participants were given the opportunity to ask questions regarding my qualifications, educational background, and so on. Almost everyone was enthusiastic about the project.

The face-to-face interviews were usually held either in a private room in a local college or in the privacy of the participant's or my home. Exceptions were the interview in Boston, which took place in the home of a mutual friend, and the interview with the participant living in South Carolina, which was done by telephone.

Initial interviews ranged from one and one-half to three hours. As the information became redundant, however, subsequent interviews were limited to one and one-half hours. Member checking was done by phone. (Member checking is a procedure in which the researcher shares the data and findings, which are then corroborated by the participants.) These follow-up sessions took from forty-five minutes to an hour. Most face-to-face interviews were taped. Notes were substituted for the few people who were uncomfortable with being recorded. Notes were also used during member checking.

A release of information was signed by both participant and researcher. Each kept a copy. This release was in both a short and long form to help those participants who did not read well to understand its essential nature. Also, I used code names for my own identification purposes. In this way no real names were attached to the notes, thereby ensuring confidentiality.

SOME REFLECTIONS

The story of True Grit in this chapter reflects the experiences of almost everyone in this study who experienced similar contradictions in their lives. They have suffered the painful alienation and isolation that often accompanies ULD, but they were also resilient and achieved a high degree of success in their areas of strength. These discrepancies were eventually managed by learning to recognize and deal with learning gaps. Why is this important and what makes this mastery so difficult? Here are three possible reasons:

First, a learning gap, one that has not been understood, can interfere with the growth of potential. Picture, for example, a would-be mechanic who reads very slowly but has always been able to "get by" through high school. His love for cars and his intrinsic understanding of the inner workings of automobiles would make him a master mechanic. However, he may never achieve this goal. Because he reads slowly he may fail, for he may not have the time to understand the manuals and therefore cannot pass necessary exams. With such a problem, his first attempts in school to pass preliminary classes might end in failure. He may never get hands-on practice because either he or his teachers will quickly become discouraged.

Second, undiagnosed learning disabilities can stifle an individual's ability to compensate for overlooked handicaps. Since ULD has never been recognized, teachers or parents cannot understand the problem and cannot help the child figure out ways around it. The child, for example, who simply needed more time to write, but had no advocates because no one knew or understood, is simply left to fend for himself.

Third, ULD can stunt the growth and enhancement of self. Without adequate self-esteem, it is difficult to stay motivated. How does this happen? When bright students have trouble learning and cannot understand why, they tend to blame themselves. Parents and educators often attribute a learning problem to lack of effort; so they may blame the student as well. Learning becomes much more difficult because excessive blame assaults one's motivation. When this cycle of blame is repeated many times, the consequences are traumatic, long-lasting, and far-reaching.

Chapter 2

Shame, Seeking, and Resilience: A Brief Introduction

This chapter is an initial attempt to give you a framework from which to view the next four chapters in this book. These chapters tell the stories of people who were helplessly shamed due to the invisibility of ULD, and yet they sought other approaches to learning, thereby finding a resilient response to their ULD. I believe keeping shame, seeking, and resilience in the back of your mind will bring an additional coherence to the following pages.

Then, after reading how these people suffered and survived, Chapters 7 and 8 will provide some background about the highlighted concepts of shame, seeking, and resilience. For those of you who want more information, there will be an extensive discussion about these concepts in Chapter 8 on resilience.

The stories you will read about will take you on a path from helplessness to struggle, to survival. The people you will meet in the following pages traveled a path from shame to seeking to coping, leading to a place of achievement, and even more important, resilience. People with imprisoned intelligence because of ULD somehow found in themselves creative novel ways to deal with the shame and struggle of ULD. Because many were able at first to count only on themselves, they discovered their inner strength, ingenuity, and creativity to survive somehow and also achieve.

This book is about people whose experiences of shame did not stop them, and who "somehow" found creative ways to achieve.

How do people get from point A, a frozen feeling of shame, to point B, overcoming those feelings? What drives people to keep on trying, to keep looking for solutions, even when the temptation is to give up?

Recent research tells us that we all have a drive to explore, a drive to learn new skills and try out new experiences—just like we have a drive to learn new computer skills when we buy a new computer. Researchers have now identified the parts of our brain that work to fulfill this exploratory urge: They call it the "seeking system." I believe that the seeking system, and the associated exploratory urge, help explain why, when shame strikes, people eventually find the urge "somehow" to try out new approaches. Propelled forward by the seeking system, people "somehow" find alternatives that are less shame inducing.

My hat is off to them. They are to be saluted.

Now it is time to listen to—and learn from—their stories.

Chapter 3

Something Is Wrong with Me:
A Chasm in Learning

SPARKLY: Well, by the time that I found out that I had a learning disability, I was nineteen. When I was in grade school I
knew there was something wrong when I read as opposed
to the teacher speaking. I could understand when he or she
spoke, but when I read, it was impossible. There was no mention of anything—not learning disabilities, dyslexia, nothing.
I hadn't even heard of it, but I knew that I wasn't stupid. So
I knew there was something that was getting in my way. At
those moments when I was really frustrated, I would blame
it on stupidity. And when I would rationally think about it, I
knew that there was something. I didn't know what it was, but
there was something that was just standing in my way, and
that I wasn't stupid.

INTERVIEWER: But that was always the struggle for you.

SPARKLY: Right.

When people are faced with a gap in their intelligence that they
cannot explain, they are left with the uneasy feeling that "something is wrong with me." Despite wanting to learn and believing that they can learn, actual achievement hovers out of reach.
Something indefinable is missing.

I experienced that something was shamefully wrong with me.
I experienced myself internally as being unusually bright, unusu-

ally capable, perceptive beyond how my peers seemed to be. But, in the concrete experience of what was happening in school, I couldn't learn the way they did.

This chapter (and my research) focuses on this frustration. It describes how people with ULD experience a painful failure to learn, how they struggle to learn and reconcile a belief in their own intelligence with their lack of success.

Bright people have high expectations for themselves and enjoy acquiring knowledge. Just as they begin to feel excited about learning something new, however, they may experience an unexpected obstacle—the undiagnosed learning disability. The result is an inexplicable failure. Since their learning disabilities are undiagnosed, they can find no reason for their lack of achievement and consequent shame. Lacking a logical explanation, they end up blaming themselves and questioning their own motivations.

The individual with ULD experiences learning failure over and over, first as a child, then as an adolescent and an adult. This quickly begins to take on a pattern with several repeating elements. Of course, no two individuals experience this in quite the same way, but the participants in the study had certain emotional experiences in common, which tended to occur in a particular order.

The diagram below summarizes the pattern of feelings that accompany a learning failure.

bewilderment → the chasm → struggle → resignation

These domains of experience* are laid out like a musical composition—*bewilderment* is the prelude; *being stuck in the chasm, an unbridgeable learning gap,* is the central theme; *struggle* and *resignation* are the postlude—all set to the overwhelming counterpoint of the repeated refrain, "What's wrong with me?"

The first domain, bewilderment, emerges when academic expectations cannot be met for reasons unknown, and confusion

---

* Daniel M. Stern (1985) employs the term "domain" to describe infant development of self in *The Interpersonal World of the Infant.*

sets in. (Unlike the other domains, bewilderment does not reoccur later.) This is the individual's introduction to shame. Next, the chasm occurs when unpreventable and recurrent failures in school cause an individual to experience hopeless exposure and isolation.

As discussed in Chapter 2, constructive shame stops us from making fools of ourselves. We get the hint, pull back, and learn to interact with the world in a different way. Although everyone needs a healthy dose of embarrassment, too much of it can lead to a chronic condition, an attachment of shame *to the self* rather than *to the situation* that leads to failure. Since intelligence fosters interest in learning and ULD causes mysterious failure at it, this combination is a natural setup for self-destruction. In this domain, chronic shame has begun to take hold.

Third, struggle develops as individuals attempt to solve their learning problems with coping strategies or diversions of their own device. Sometimes these interventions are successful, but since they lack knowledge of the true cause of the problem (the learning disability) often the interventions are not. Resignation sets in as an uneasy acceptance of these unnamed problems is adopted as a long-term viewpoint. Here, shame becomes firmly attached to the self.

BEWILDERMENT

All my life, I knew something was wrong,
but I never knew what it was.

Bewilderment occurs in a state of innocence and reflects the initial confusion that results from faltering performance. An individual who succeeds in some areas or some of the time will suddenly fail. Specifically, bewilderment results when people experience a radical departure from the expectations they build based on their perceptions of their own intelligence. Thus, failures occurring in specific subject matters or tasks are all the more poignant because they are set against the backdrop of sporadic success:

- I could understand when, you know, she spoke; but when I read, it was impossible.
- I know I'm smart, and everyone tells me I'm smart, so this doesn't make sense.
- They figured that since I was brilliant in math, I should be able to apply myself and do well enough in English.

A person experiences bewilderment when academic requirements become impossible to meet. Concepts or tasks that seem easy to others are beyond his or her grasp. Despite pedagogical advice or attention, there seem to be no intervening steps—no learning "tricks"—that solve the problem. The individual seems unable to learn *how to learn* in this area. As a result, simple problems become confounding and embarrassing, leading to feelings of internal confusion, chaos, and shame:

- I'll never forget my father trying to teach me, when we had math problems in school, how come minus and plus become even. Both of us couldn't figure out why I couldn't get that.
- When it comes to math, I've always felt out of it—you know, out to lunch.
- I just can't concentrate.
- It's not clicking.
- Nothing makes sense.
- It's like having the information on the tip of my tongue, but not being able to write it down.
- There were these mysteries about how people learned. If the teacher says, "Go home and memorize the multiplication tables" and there's nobody to tell . . . how in the world are you supposed . . . what does that mean to *memorize* something?

Bewilderment is (primarily) a reaction to intellectual disparities. It is impossible for an individual with an undiagnosed learning disability to understand how his or her intelligence can work so effectively at times and yet seem to stop working altogether at other times. The assumption underlying the traditional educational system holds that an intelligent person can achieve academic success as long as he or she is willing to work hard. Since the child with ULD exhibits intelligence and yet experiences inexplicable academic failures, it seems to others that the child must not be working hard enough. The child experiences shame and, in seeking to find a cause for the shame, finds only the self. Parents begin to encourage the child to attach the shame to the self by calling his or her motivations into question:

- You're lazy.
- You're only interested in your friends.
- You just don't pay attention.
- You daydream too much.
- You're not interested in school because of your sports.

Educators do not seem to have the answer either. They cannot see the obstacles inhibiting learning. So, like the parents, they attribute a lack of academic success in a seemingly intelligent individual to a lack of effort. Also, like the parent, they compound the child's growing sense of self-shame:

- The principal said, "I know you can do better, so try harder."
- The teacher said, "If you had cared more and been less messy, I would have given you credit on your homework."
- "This would have been an A paper if I wouldn't have had to stop so often to correct your spelling."

Over time, myths are created. Poised against a backdrop of success in certain areas, achievement in other areas is impossible despite effort. As the surrounding world continues to attribute poor school performance to lack of effort, the child begins to accept blame and to question his or her own perceptions. A world of chronic shame is born. Once convinced of his or her intelligence, the child now turns to stupidity and lack of motivation as feasible explanations for academic failure. Although these two explanations are in direct conflict, the lack of any other explanation binds the child in this catch-22. If children believe themselves to be smart, then they must be lazy if they fail to learn. If children believe themselves to be trying hard at learning, they must be stupid if they fail to learn.

In time, the child with an undiagnosed learning disability becomes accustomed to living with the baffling variations of doing both well and poorly. As the child is receiving internal and external messages of stupidity and academic apathy, he or she gradually incorporates self-blame into an internal belief system and accepts them as factual. Confidence and self-esteem drop while reactive feelings of chronic shame surface. As a result, it becomes increasingly difficult to learn:

- I always felt as though it was my fault because I didn't apply myself.
- Every time I lost my homework, I would tell myself it's because I was dumb.
- I would beat myself on the way home from school because I upset the teacher because my paper was so messy.
- I figured they were right: I must be lazy.

There is no longer a question that something is wrong: It has become a fact of life. These myths of stupidity and academic apathy, internally digested and externally reinforced, set the stage for two subsequent domains: chasm and struggle. These represent attempts to adapt to the now-accepted reality that something is wrong.

BEING STUCK: THE CHASM

Inside of me, there's a chasm which—that's huge. There's no way you can get from one side to the other. And that's where the learning disability goes. When there were things that I just couldn't explain when I was a kid, I just thought, "Oh, it's just going into that chasm."

As stated earlier, Imprisoned Intelligence results when the standards and goals set by academic institutions cannot be consistently met by the person with ULD. Although achievement in some areas or at some times is possible, failure is both unpredictable and inevitable. This bewildering experience can cause a temporary cognitive paralysis, a feeling of being frozen or "being stuck in the chasm." This concept is a central focus of this book. Often, this inability to proceed is seen as an unbridgeable gap.

The term "chasm" attempts to capture what it feels like during the *moment* when one expects to learn but there is a gap in learning. "Being stuck in the chasm" is a phrase that embodies the following stepwise progression of feelings that seem to connect with this momentary freeze: People feel confused, helpless, alienated, shamed, and disappointed in themselves because of an assumed lack of initiativeThe participants in this study describe this "being stuck in the chasm" as a serious obstacle in their attempts to learn. Why do people get stuck when trying to learn? One explanation might be that chronic shame, triggered by a recent failure, "freezes" the individual from going forward *in order to prevent augmenting or restimulating* the shame experience. Just as individuals who have been hurt in a love relationship may fail to fall in love again, ULD children may stop themselves from proceeding into further shame once a learning crisis has evolved:

- It feels like a painful invisible emptiness inside my brain.
- Other people knew things. And I had—and I think this is accurate—that I had a "chasm" of—of no knowledge . . . but then it was just this place inside of me that, you know, was an emptiness. You know, like, if you were to draw a picture of my body, that there was this great space that other people had filled up, that I didn't.
- My brain wouldn't work.
- Nothing would happen.

The chasm is not only a vacuum that precludes academic achievement. It also expresses the individual's increasing distance from the surrounding world. This cognitive freeze is characterized by a sense of being shamefully overwhelmed by time as well as by physiological signs of alienation and anxiety:

- I sat there all those hours . . . I couldn't start. I had no middle. I had no end.
- The teacher would be talking, and I would understand her. But then, I couldn't anymore, and I knew that I would be stuck in this place of nothingness what seemed like forever—or until the bell rang.
- At times, it was as though I was watching myself trying to speak, watching my mouth trying to form the words.
- It's like having a button, but not being able to find the buttonhole.

The person with ULD has also, by this point, established that he or she can harbor no realistic expectation that effective help will be forthcoming. Since no one has been able to understand what is wrong, solutions seem out of the question. The tools needed for accessing intelligence are unavailable. Furthermore, since there is no understanding that other tools are possible, people appear stupid to themselves and to others. Shame, which should be a signal to the individual to try another method for success, is not a help, but an intractable burden. Hope is lost, leaving the trap of Imprisoned Intelligence, where futility becomes the reality. The idea of being stuck in a chasm encapsulates the experience not only of futility, but also of acute shame.

The never-ending pit of the chasm is both a source of and a symbol for shame. This cognitive gap and these painful feelings feed on each other and become intertwined in a single dance. The intellectual freeze is accompanied by feelings of exposure, fear, shame, and humiliation. One's feelings stand out in relief against the success of others, further intensifying the original feelings:

- I would stand out like a sore thumb.

- You have this totally helpless feeling that's like everyone else is getting it and you're not.
- I hated getting my exams back because I would have to hide them from the rest of the class because the grades would be lousy.

Sometimes, a person would be able to determine that certain events or situations precipitated experiences with the chasm. When this happens, a special event might be greeted with a sense of foreboding instead of joyful anticipation. Certain school subjects or other activities could also become associated with the chasm, their occurrence and the anticipation of their occurrence filling the individual with dread:

- Passover would always make me afraid. . . . I would have to read in front of the family. . . . It was terrible.
- If I would have to go to a restaurant and read the menu, it was terrible. Then I wouldn't be able to hide from other people.
- If she announced that it was reading time, I would be in trouble.
- It's a horrible memory, sitting in class and then going around, each kid reading. You have a book and each kid reads a paragraph or sentence. I knew, probably after the first time I did it [laughs], that I wasn't going to be very good. And kids would just be going through it without any problem. And I'd have to read ahead, so that I'd know my sentence, and then I'd get to it, and I wouldn't know the words.

Once this lonely chasm becomes an intrinsic part of one's psychological world, an underlying mild to severe anticipation of doom follows, accompanied by fears of humiliation and exposure. There is a sense of foreboding that a chasm will unexpectedly appear and one will be shamed. Continuous fear of an unexpected shame event creates a pervasive sense of insecurity. Because there is no consistent pattern, one never knows when the deficits will be exposed or when the teacher's agenda will move into the areas of deficits. An overarching fear of shame events pervades one's life:

- I never knew when I would look stupid.
- I would have this lurking sense of doom that followed me around.
- I felt as though I was skating on thin ice.
- I was always waiting for her to ask me a question.

This pervasive sense of shame can swallow up or contaminate even the successes experienced by a child with ULD. The individual has become so totally convinced of his or her inability to learn or succeed, because shame is attached to the self, that a success is interpreted as a fluke. Since this fluke could potentially be exposed, the child's feelings of impending doom and concealment are heightened. People with ULD live in constant fear that someone will "find them out"—that even their small successes will be exposed as mistakes:

- I always felt that he couldn't have given me that A if he knew that I didn't know how I did it.
- I was always afraid that I wouldn't pass, and when I did pass it was because someone let me get away with it.
- I never did figure out why I got so many votes to be class president because I was terrified that I'd make it, because then I'd be given responsibilities that I couldn't deal with.

The individual with ULD now lives in a world of shame, embarrassment, pain, and insecurity. The anxiety that the chasm is looming ahead is constant. Emerging from this situation is the struggle, in which the child tries to find ways to cope with the disability and the resulting shame.

STRUGGLE: IMPASSE AND BYPASS

As time goes by, the reality of the undetected learning disability does not change: Being stuck in the chasm and the accompanying shame is a familiar problem. With the chasm in place, there is no longer a sense of bewilderment. The paradoxical intelligence of the ULD individual, however, causes an unquenchable desire for learning. This desire leads him or her to break the chronic tendency to avoid shame and to continue the lonely struggle to achieve. In this struggle, the ULD child employs two main strategies. The first is to continue behaving like the other children who are learning successfully, hoping that this time will be different. This strategy is called *impasse* because the result is the same repeated deadlock: a repeated strategy leading to repeated failure. The second strategy involves seeking a way to get around the difficulties the child is experiencing, creating a *bypass*. In this domain, the individual employs ingenuity and creativity to overcome an as-yet undiagnosed problem. Here is where resilience is nourished. It's the impasse that facilitates resilience by creating such difficult challenges.

Impasse

> *I was told that whatever you work for, you can get.*
> *I worked for it, and I didn't get it.*

The yearning in the ULD person to put her or his intelligence to work cannot be permanently quenched. Motivation is often high, producing repeated attempts to persevere in the face of continuing defeat. With each new semester or school year, the belief resurfaces that *this time* hard work will produce success. Out of the seemingly illogical past of intermittent learning failure, they seek logical, consistent reasons for past failures. After all, if the failure can be attributed to a specific cause, there can be hope of correcting it. So, the individual with an undetected learning disability seeks to correct a past behavior that may be responsible for failure:

- Each semester, I would buy fresh notebooks and come to school with new hope.
- I would stop thinking of something else when the teacher

was talking.
- I would stop daydreaming.
- I will work harder and get better grades.

The results, unfortunately, are not altered, and disappointment arises again and again. Shame accompanies each failure:

- I was very diligent . . . I would complete my homework, and I failed tests. That's how it went.
- I could handle myself in class. . . . You know, when she called on me, I knew what was going on because I could work out problems. But I would go home and not be able to do the assignments and hand in the work.
- I would say to my instructor, "How can I increase my reading scores?" He said, "I don't know. You're just too slow."

Repeatedly, the same shame events appeared to greet the individual in his or her born-again enthusiasm. For instance, time continued to pose difficulties. Many people with learning disabilities need to work at a slower pace. Despite their ability to do the homework or papers, they might therefore fail timed tests. Interwoven with time difficulties, then, is a fear of time. This anxiety can impose further burdens since fear can interfere with recall, inhibiting memory. Once again, fear of shame and shame avoidance impede performance:

- I was a good student in class, but I flunked a lot of exams because I couldn't finish them.
- Exams did not test me for knowledge, they tested me for speed.
- Because I knew I'd never get through, I gave up before I even got started.

Another element of the impasse is that some strategies which may have produced positive results in the past may not continue to work. For instance, if an individual was able to devote more time than others to learning in elementary and high school, the increasing academic demands of college might prevent success. The additional workload forces a ULD individual to budget time in a way that prevents him or her from achieving success:

- I never had enough time to play because of all the work.
- I was always under this time pressure to get things done quickly.
- If I knew there were a lot of things I wanted to do, I might feel just overwhelmed by what I was going to do first.

Bypass

I just knew that I could do whatever I wanted to do.
It just took a lot longer time to do it in.

Bypass is the domain in which the resilient person with undetected learning disabilities seeks a way to get around his or her cognitive problems. The individual learns to compensate, sometimes without any help from others, by employing ingenuity and creativity to overcome an as-yet undiagnosed problem. To express their Imprisoned Intelligence, people with learning disabilities rely on the combination of their strength, intelligence, creativity, and ability to persevere. This section discusses the roles of determination, diversion, intuition, cheating, and personal relationships in this domain.

For some participants, spending additional time and effort promotes resilience and creates a bypass around areas of failure. Driven by positive feedback, hard work and tenacity become necessary to gain success:

- I loved getting good grades, and after a while I demanded that of myself. . . . Nothing short of perfection would do.
- My mother was so proud that I worked so much harder than the rest of my brothers and sisters.
- My grades became a source of pride for me.

Effort heightens the individual's sense of competence. So, no matter how time-consuming or difficult, he or she continues a push to learn:

- I would simply refuse to give up.
- I would put one foot in front of the other, and say to myself, "I'm gonna do it."
- It took me seven years to get through undergraduate school. I repeated a lot of classes. And I'd tape everything and listen to it over and over and over again.

Not all bypasses are of a positive nature. Some are simply shame techniques, such as creating a diversion. By rerouting conversation or distracting the audience, the person with ULD can shift the classroom focus to an area of comfort so that his or her strengths will be validated and a shame event avoided:

- I was known as the class clown, and I loved it.
- Talking was for fun and for avoidance of class work.
- Distracting teachers worked better in elementary school than in college.
- Doodling kept my mind focused.

Shame avoidance could take the form of removing oneself from class participation. Not being able to concentrate could create discomfort or boredom; therefore, daydreaming or sleeping could produce a needed escape:

- The class was so boring, so I fell asleep.
- I didn't understand a word of it.

Many students with ULD rely on cheating and lying to survive their academic experiences. They cope by mastering these tactics and employing them with discretion:

- I always knew when I could get away with lying and when I couldn't.
- I had this sixth sense as to what people would believe.
- I always thought of myself as a con artist.

For some, trusting one's intuition can become the only viable option and a way of life. An individual will often feel his or her way through an examination, guessing and relying almost exclusively on intuition. Answers seem to come out of nowhere, rather than as the result of memorization or logic. ULD often causes a sense of estrangement from one's work. Papers also seemed to emerge from nowhere and turn out to be acceptable:

- If I did well, I figured it was a lucky guess.
- I never really knew when I wrote a paper whether it would be an A or an F, but somehow, somewhere, I trusted that it was okay.
- It wasn't like I knew I had memorized something.
- I never knew how I got things right.

Other people also can become important resources in bridging learning gaps. Friends can provide the help necessary to circumvent learning difficulties, sometimes through swapping strengths with a ULD classmate:

- I knew from third grade that I was pretty and attractive, and I would make friends of the boys. I would be sweet and engaging, and they would do my homework.
- She would come over and fix my spelling; I would give her tennis lessons.
- The teacher let us work in pairs. . . . I talked and she wrote. . . . We got good grades together.

Parents, particularly mothers, often play a crucial role in providing a bypass to success. In addition to helping with schoolwork, they can function as emotional supports by soothing the shame or counteracting others' denigration. Parents might also fulfill the crucial role of locating better instruction or learning situations for their children and often find a way to "reconnect" with their children who experience the disconnection of shame:

- He drilled me on my multiplication tables until I finally got it. . . . It took a long time. . . . He never gave up.
- Everyone was on my back . . . but my mom always believed in me. . . . She knew I was smart, and I knew that she knew I was smart.
- My mom was on the school board just because she knew she would have some clout about getting me a good teacher.

Finally, tutors can also help find ways around a problem. Although not all experiences are positive, tutoring often provides an environment that a child with a learning disability finds more conducive to his or her abilities. For instance, those who are readily distracted will find less to send them "off track" in a one-to-one experience. Tutoring can have a greater effect when the student feels he or she is special, particularly because the classroom experience is providing negative feedback. The experience of having a tutor believe in him or her can counteract chronic shame and can help the student learn coping skills:

- Somebody else believed in me. You know, then I wanted to reach for another step and yet another step.
- I could work at my own pace.
- I had her undivided attention.
- I learned that if there is something I can't learn in a group situation, I have a better chance to understand it on a one-to-one [basis] at my own pace.

RESIGNATION

You've only got a limited number of choices, and I could only think of one. "So," I said to myself, "as long as I pass, it will be good

enough. It will get me through once I get out in the world. Just don't
open those grades because grades don't mean anything anyway."

The final domain, resignation, comes about when an individual comes to grips with the fact that the learning problems are here to stay. It occurs when people learn to think about, live with, and make some accommodation to their "invisible shackles." Despite the fact that they do not understand the cause, people affected by an undetected learning disability form conclusions about their "problem areas." They decide that either they will give up trying to succeed in these areas, or they must accept that certain academic pursuits will be an eternal battle with continuing shame and only sporadic victories. In either case, the individual learns to live with the pain and, with some variation, to accept the fact that one's Imprisoned Intelligence will remain unexpressed.

The individual with ULD often finds unempathic responses from important people. Although he or she feels intelligent and understands that something is wrong, the outside world continues to blame and accuse. The result is continuing shame:

- No one was interested. No one cared.

To deal with their disappointment and shame, individuals build a front. The driving force behind it is anger because the world cannot validate either their intelligence or the cause of learning failure. This protective facade can manifest itself as offensive behavior, which is used as a weapon against the world they find so frustrating:

- If somebody makes fun of you, the next time someone makes fun of you and the next time and the next, and it's all about the same stuff, you build up a front to that. And if someone's going to do it, you're going to attack eventually.
- I was sarcastic and angry.
- I was snotty and forceful.
- I was arrogant.

Sometimes, fear of retaliation could also drive the attacks underground rather than against the outside world—that is, the attacks might be expressed internally, not externally:

- And I would think, "You show me what you've got, I dare you."
- As I got older, I got sick and tired of my father saying to me, "Shape up or ship out." And I learned, very well, how to look respectful while I was imagining not nice things about him.

At this stage, people become resigned to living with what they perceive as a shameful problem. As they realize that no solutions will be forthcoming, they become disheartened and consider giving up:

- As I got older, I just realized that I couldn't verbally, I couldn't really get my ideas or my thoughts in a clear manner. There was nothing I could do. There was a relative in the family who was mentally retarded and close to my age, and my mother would push me to play with this child. Since I had trouble in school too, I would take this to mean [that] she thinks I'm retarded too.
- I finally believed that it wasn't important to be smart. All I needed to do was to look pretty.
- My father always said to me, "If you can talk, you can write." And on some level, I always believed that, but the outcome was utterly unusable. . . . In time, I stopped trying to understand this phenomenon.

Accepting that certain areas will continue to pose difficulties, the individual begins to employ heightened tactics of shame avoidance. He or she might make a conscious decision to stay away from the problem, whether it be academic situations in general or certain subject areas. (Sometimes the holding pattern is a way of waiting until opportunities for growth arise.) The ability to make this sort of decision differs markedly from the earlier domains in which the student continued to struggle with the learning deficiencies:

- I just wouldn't go to school.
- After some thought, even though my teacher urged me to apply for college, I decided not to do so at that time because I knew what kind of work was involved, and I would fail.
- I would make myself invisible . . . no classes in algebra or geometry, no language classes.

Unfortunately, acceptance of the problem is often accompanied by the acceptance of the world's labels. Individuals begin to accept the conclusion that they are dumb. This is a hallmark of chronic shame:

- Something was making me have to work harder and work slower. . . . It was a fact of life. . . . I considered myself stupid.
- I usually knew the answers in my head, but I thought I was stupid because I couldn't repeat them out loud.
- I was stupid because I couldn't spell.
- Being smart and being dumb was just the way I was.

To tolerate the situation, individuals begin to develop short-term personal incentives. They rationalize to get themselves through the class, the paper, or the program. One prevalent thought is, "All I have to do is pass." Or they might build a reward/punishment schema, such as "Mom will be so happy if I pass this" and "I'm gonna get it if I screw this up":

- When I graduate, I'll never look at a book again.
- I'll never punish my kids for not passing tests the way the folks are punishing me.
- If I can pass, I'll never have to see this teacher's face again.
- When these methods fail and the shame can no longer be tolerated, they may decide to give up:

- I decided it was easier for me to simply accept a failing mark than to be told I was lazy or I wasn't meeting, you know, working to my potential, or whatever the thing was. I decided that from now on I was going to design my own system which meant that I would not be judged.
- I simply could not hand in inappropriate or inadequate work. It becomes somewhat of a pragmatic issue.

Resignation differs from the earlier domains because chronic shame has taken firm hold, and the surrender to the learning disability holds a sense of permanence. In essence, hope is dead. The individual with ULD, not having the concept of a learning disability, believes that there will be no change to his or her condition—an intelligence imprisoned forever because it cannot be expressed adequately. While all the domains share varying degrees of shame and pain, this domain adds a dimension of sheer hopelessness.

Chapter 4

Discovery: The Diagnosis

"Brilliant" is an articulate middle-aged woman who did not find out about her learning disabilities until she was in her forties. Here is her story.

BRILLIANT: The reason that I entered school again as an adult was that I came to a place in myself where the fear and trembling and the demons, as I call them, which kept me from school all these years, needed to be faced. So what I did was to place myself in an untenable position. I enrolled in summer school at [a local community college] and registered for a first-year algebra class, anatomy, and a physiology class.

I remember thinking at the time, you know, that this is a matter of grit [laughs]. I wasn't sixteen years old anymore. I was a grown-up, and I had children. And I knew what it was to work hard. And, you know, my children were old enough so that I really could put my nose to the grindstone. No excuses! I could do this.

Well, it was an accelerated program because it was summer school. In other words, they were attempting to put a year's amount of learning into an eight-week course which I thought was wonderful. You know, I would just get it over with quickly.

And, you know, all I had to do is pass, except really I was

thinking to myself: No, that's not true, I really need to get an A. At any rate, I went into this with a vengeance. I mean, my family didn't see me during this period of time. I just gave it my all.

In the algebra class, I very quickly discovered [laughs] that an absolutely horrible thing was happening. I mean, it was truly like a revisitation of, you know, ghosts from the nursery or something like this. I relived, in the most excruciating way, the difficulties I thought I had put behind me when I left school at sixteen. And it was terrifying. I mean, soul-wrenching, terrifying. . . .

I'll start by just trying to describe what happened. I would sit in algebra class, and the teacher would explain the algebra lesson. And, you know, I was in class with eighteen-year-olds. These were all young kids. And I had the advantage, or so I thought, and truly felt, that I had the advantage of being an adult. I wasn't having to flirt with my neighbors, or worry about how I looked, or any of these other burdensome things that these eighteen-year-olds [laughs] have to deal with.

I could concentrate on algebra. And she [the teacher] would explain to us the process and the particular algebraic problems or formulas for it. And I would take it in, and I would understand it. Instantly! I mean, really instantly! And it would be very gratifying.

INTERVIEWER: You really enjoyed this.

BRILLIANT: Oh yes, first, you know, do this, and then you do that, and it's a six-part process, and, you know, you follow the format, and you'll get the answer. Right? And I understood the format.

But then, I would go to follow the format. And, I would get the wrong answer. Every time. And I would do the problem over. Gee, I've done something peculiar here, you know, I must have done something peculiar here. And I'd start at the beginning, and yes, that's the right step, step one, two, three, four, five, six—get me to the end. Hmm! Wrong answer.

Each problem was taking me a half an hour to do. And on an individual assignment, in an accelerated algebra class, there might be five pages of two hundred problems to do. It was taking me an inordinate amount of time. And my frustration level was reaching the breaking point.

This was like my proving ground now. Right? So the grade was very important to me. I really wanted to get an A in the class and was not handing in work unless I knew that I would get a 100 percent. I would not hand it in! And I definitely got an easy mouth on me, and was participating in class. She would ask a question, I would have the answer. When she called on me, I knew what was going on.

I was handing in all my work on time, so the teacher didn't have a clue what was going on with me until she walked around one day, and saw me working out the problems. She took a look at my work and she said to me: "Oh, I see you've got the formula, but you've mixed up your signs." And then she said, "Oh, wait a minute, I see what you did: you wrote a 6 when you meant to write an X."

You know, I mean, it was like a light bulb going off in my brain cells. My daughter had, two years earlier, gone through testing for learning disabilities. So, I had, it was still fresh in my mind, what learning disabilities was all about. And there was something about her telling me [laughs] that I had not only reversed my symbols, but that I had written a 6 when I meant to be writing an X, that went . . . that went, Bingo! You know, if this isn't a classic form of dyslexia, I'm not [name] [laughs]. And she [the teacher] said, you know, this is something to go and find out about. Because you've clearly got the mathematical ability, but there is something going screwy here. No adult, no person in my entire life had ever said that to me. You know, that there was a discrepancy between ability and function.

Eventually, many who suffer with ULD will become aware that such things as learning disabilities exist. This new knowledge, that there is a legitimate discrepancy between ability and function, can be a revelation. The period of *discovery* begins with the discovery of learning disabilities, continues through the testing experience, and ends with the person's first thoughts and feelings about the testing results.

Discovery has four domains. "Awakenings" occur when one first encounters the concept of learning disabilities. Then comes the testing experience, which itself evokes conflicting emotions as the hopelessness of the past is challenged. This process is described below in "The Test: Pleasure" and "The Test: Pain." Finally, the individual receives the confirming diagnosis and experiences "The Aftermath: Making Sense" as newfound potential and future possibilities and struggles begin to come into focus.

AWAKENINGS

Awakenings begin when someone learns that he or she may have a learning disability. Once the concept of learning disabilities is introduced, the individual begins to make sense of what seemed to be chaos. Learning problems may, after all, have a valid explanation. The feeling could be epitomized as, "I might just not be crazy (or stupid or lazy) after all."

This new concept (ULD) can help many people understand the split inside themselves: feeling intelligent yet unable to do what smart people do. Once an individual understands that his or her intellectual development may have been impeded by a ULD, the old wish to make sense out of the chaos re-emerges—this time, with more hope that a solution can be found.

For many, awakening is a dramatic experience that validates past feelings. They remember well the relief they felt when they first heard about learning disabilities:

- My professor was a very kind lady. One day in class, we were discussing something in life span development, and, all of a sudden, the topic came up . . . learning disabilities. And about ten minutes out of the class, I was hysterical in tears. . . . I went to [my professor's] office, and all I could say

to her at the time was that I wondered if that was what was wrong with me. . . . She managed to get me tested.
- I met a girl who said she got special testing privileges for taking certain tests. I ran over and asked, "What do you mean, special testing privileges? What is this about?" I was like: "What is this? Tell me. Tell me." And she said, "Don't you know about the disabled student services at [this university]?"

For some, this dramatic moment is not altogether heartening. It may strike an uncomfortable blow by reviving memories of shame and exposure:

- I was humiliated when my professor suggested that I get tested. He pointed out my inability to pass the tests even though I knew the material.
- When she said my performance didn't make sense, I almost died.
- My academic counselor in college suggested it [testing] after she looked at my reading score. She knew something was up. Now she even thought I was disabled.

Awakenings do not always come as a sudden jolt; sometimes they grow over time. A common scenario is for adults with ULD to find their children experiencing learning difficulties. As they learn about their children's learning disability, they realize that they too might have been affected by learning problems:

- My younger son has a learning disability. And as I was fighting the battles for him, I recognized that I had a learning disability too.
- I had the same spelling problems as my son, so this sneaking suspicion began to grow in me.
- I realized that I lost all my papers when I was a kid too.

As their parents were, the children of those with ULD are ashamed when their learning disability hinders their efforts at school. When adults observe a child's pain, sometimes they must relive their own feelings of shame that they have long tried to bury:

- I re-experienced so much of my own long-buried pain when I saw my brilliant son not being able to keep up with the class in script.
- I felt so helpless because, until the school pointed out the problem, I could only suffer with him.
- I knew how bad she was hurting because I went through the same thing. But I didn't know what to do.

The need to investigate this new idea—that their childhood difficulties may have stemmed from a learning disability—leads individuals with ULD to undergo the testing procedure.

Testing includes quite a number of tests (when I was tested, they gave fifteen tests plus an interview) and often takes several days. Some of these are standardized achievement tests similar to those given yearly to public school children. One function of these tests is to identify discrepancies in ability. For instance, a high score in math and a low score in reading comprehension might indicate a reading disorder. Subjects are also given an IQ test to pinpoint discrepancies in scores on different sections of the test, and to see if IQ scores are commensurate with achievement test scores. There are tests specifically for motor skills, reading, short-term memory, critical thinking, auditory learning, visual learning, and other areas, as the LD specialist sees fit.

You may wonder, if one is done with school and has found a career that suits one's strengths, why get tested? After all, the test is long, stressful, and most likely expensive. Yet even participants who had already finished their education chose to be tested. Some wanted to confirm that they have areas of giftedness as well as weaknesses. This consoling knowledge can boost self-esteem and clarify one's abilities. Testing was also used to satisfy the outside world, or at least to provide some ammunition for dealing with others who are critical. Many simply wanted to know the truth about themselves:

- I wanted to have a better understanding of why I had this peculiar mix of abilities or lack thereof.
- The thought of the test as a means to give me a reason to deal with their anger was energizing.
- I had something to say to my friends when they would wonder what took me so long.

Some individuals are still completing their education and want new information to help them tackle specific problems. They hope not only for an explanation, but also help:

- Maybe I can figure out how to write papers faster.
- Maybe I can get some extra time for tests.
- When I was in graduate school at [an academically prestigious school], the field of thinking about dyslexia had moved on quite a bit and lots had been accomplished in seven years. [But] I was still getting grief from my professors because I couldn't spell. And my father and I agreed that I should get tested.

THE TEST: PLEASURE

The testing experience evokes both positive and negative reactions. Individuals with ULD perform very well in some areas and poorly in others; therefore, some parts of the tests are exciting and intellectually challenging. For some, the sense of mastery achieved during the testing experience boosts self-esteem:

- It was gratifying to see that I could finish before the time was up.
- It was like doing crossword puzzles—only even more fun.
- It was fun to figure out things.
- I felt like I was in grammar school again—when I felt smart because I did well on tests.

Often, for those who need more time, untimed tests are most gratifying. Freedom from the clock puts success within grasp:

- The way a lot of these tests work is that you go until you can't anymore . . . and then you've reached your level. I enjoyed this.
- I was surprised—for once I didn't have to worry about the time—how quickly I did the test.
- I liked being able to do this as slow as I wanted to.
- The person conducting the test can contribute to the feeling of accomplishment. Those tested by an empathic tester feel comfortable enough to perform well.
- I was really able to concentrate because I knew she was with me.
- I knew she was rooting for me.

THE TEST: PAIN

Testing is not invariably fun. For some people, LD testing brings back the pain of school exams. When a person runs into familiar stumbling, he or she can panic about the inability to follow very simple instructions, solve simple problems, or make simple drawings. The person may feel ashamed and defeated even before the testing is finished:

- I felt as if I would die within this space of temporary nothingness.
- My concentration was just, you know . . . I could feel my whole body tighten up and focus on this, and there was this kind of pit-in-the-stomach feeling.
- To sit there and go through the things she had me go through . . . I didn't know the answer. . . . Maybe the answer was that I should have driven a truck like my father.
- Some things I simply couldn't do. . . . I just couldn't do it.

An individual with ULD might feel trapped or panic. In school, some developed their own special ways to succeed in exams, such as looking at problems and finding unorthodox solutions. For example, simple geometry problems can be solved without knowing the formulas by drawing pictures to scale and measuring the sides. A pupil gifted in art but bad at memorizing might get away with this for a while. However, LD diagnostic tests are designed to prevent such loopholes by, for instance, providing only out-of-scale diagrams and not allowing rulers in the testing room. The test-taker's usual artillery is taken away, and this can be scary and frustrating.

- I was used to figuring my way out of things. . . . In life, one can usually come at a problem from different angles. But with these tests, it was like coming to a dead end with no way back.
- I felt like my back was against a wall, and I could not go around it.

Some of the tests are timed. Some people feel that the time limit is like being trapped in a box. Sometimes, a person reaches a point in the tests where he or she cannot do any more, but time is not up yet. In these situations, a certain time limit still has to be waited out, effectively trapping the individual with ULD in a time warp of powerlessness.

- The clock seemed never to go forward.
- I had one half hour to understand and rewrite that page, and I could not do it. . . . It was the longest period in my life.
- I hope time never gets that long again.
- Some things I just couldn't begin to do, so I had to sit there for three minutes. . . . It was one of the longest three minutes in my life.

When people feel powerless, they are subject to intense feelings of shame, exposure, and humiliation. As test-takers find themselves unable to work around obstacles, they are dumped back into the chasm of shame that they knew as children. Some were surprised that the testing situation could evoke such emotions in their adult selves:

- I had forgotten that this was the way I suffered in elementary school . . . good Lord.

- No matter if I had finished the last section in record time and with minimal mistakes, when it came to drawing a face or remembering the lines I drew, I bombed it.
- I wished I could die.
- I couldn't believe not doing such a simple little exercise could humiliate [me] so much.

Shame is frequently amplified because the person knows he or she is observed by another person, the tester. Some testers have been trained only in technical aspects of evaluation and have not been taught how to deal with their subjects empathically. Consequently, the testers seem cold and distant. The test-takers sense that lack of warmth; they feel uncomfortable and encounter further intellectual "cramping" while taking the tests. The test setting itself can cause alienation and isolation:

- I felt like a fly on the end of her pin.
- Her face was impassive throughout the whole three days. . . . I guess that was part of the testing. . . . I felt so alone and isolated.
- Different people came in and tested me for different skills. . . . They were students, and I knew that there were supervisors watching behind that one-way mirror. . . . It didn't help my thinking process.
- When I couldn't get something. . . . I could see those two women look at each other like, "Oh, look."

THE AFTERMATH: MAKING SENSE

Sparkly: So when they told me I had dyslexia, I was almost relieved. It's like when you don't know, sometimes, it's real difficult to get through it. But when you find out, "Okay, I have dyslexia," then I could take this path to further my education. I could take this path to learn how to read, or whatever it may be. It was so reassuring. What I think it goes back to, again, is that I just . . . I just was worried. Now, there was a reason why I had such difficulty in school. It wasn't because I was stupid, or that I just couldn't understand it. Now there was a good reason!

People experience a sense of confirmation when they receive their results: "So *that's* what's wrong with me." Individuals with ULD can finally understand the "why" behind their lifelong struggles. For many this knowledge brings a profound sense of relief and clarity. They feel free to finally stop blaming themselves for their performance difficulties:

- Two parts of that exam for me made sense. One was, I knew now why I get lost. And then I knew that I focus on the same thing: a small area. So, what I learned was to step back and try to observe a large picture.
- It was really good to separate out my strengths from my weaknesses.
- I always knew I couldn't help it.

Others find the results dispiriting. The knowledge they gain confirms their worst fears and simply reminds them of their short-comings:

- It only made me feel worse.
- I knew I had learning disabilities. But until I got tested, I didn't know how bad.
- I'm disabled.
- I knew I was different, but I don't like it.

But even for those who are at first depressed by their results, the new knowledge that testing provides often benefits them in the long run. They gradually begin to see the myths that they have lived with, and how these myths have fostered shame and self-blame. One day they can begin to forgive themselves for things outside of their control:

- I wasn't lazy.

- I'm not getting even.
- I'm not acting out.
- I remember coming home from the testing and telling my mother through the tears . . . that I could finally forgive my younger self. That child that I had just been so abusive to inside of myself for so long was finally, sort of, laid to rest. And I could feel infinitely kinder toward this child as a consequence of this knowledge.

An important result of testing is increased access to help: Laws have been passed mandating services for learning disabled individuals. This knowledge brings comfort to those who have ULD and can empower them to make important changes. They begin to understand that they have a right to ask for help and, in some cases, a relaxation of the rules:

- The thought that I could take my tests untimed was a wonder to me.
- [I found out that] I needed to use a typewriter if they wanted to find out what I had learned on a test. . . . Even if I wouldn't be able to do so, at least I would know that the test would be more difficult for me.
- To understand that I would need a note taker and a tape recorder gave me a new determination to try harder.
- I think what it did for me was to have this piece of paper, this document. And it gave me some other way of working and gaining the ability to get tapes from the Library of Congress. So it [the diagnosis] gave me more tools.

Discovery changes people. It creates milestones along life's path. Gaining a new understanding of self is a riveting experience, yet memories of this period seem dimmer than those from the periods directly preceding or following. Perhaps the testing experience fades in the memory because of the intensity of the period to follow. Whatever the reason, the results are clear: hope and understanding are the new tools individuals carry away with them from these discoveries. Chapter 5 shows how people integrate into their lives the knowledge gained from the LD testing.

Chapter 5

Learning to Live with It:
After the Diagnosis

SPARKLY: It was the first class, or it was the second class after I got diagnosed. I looked at this man, and it was the first time I was going to be putting into practice this new "[Sparkly], the Student." You know? I said to him "Well, what does correlative imperative mean?" And I remember saying the sentence and thinking, "I don't want to do it," but I did it. He looked at me, and he laughed at me condescendingly. [He said] "It was in your book. Why don't you know?" Oh, gee! And I thought . . . . I'm telling you, right there, I lost it. I almost left the room. In my mind two billion things were running, "That's it! School's out! I don't care! I'm going to get my real estate license! I don't care about this anymore! The degree's out the window!"

And, you know, that's just something that I have to learn: not to take offense. I don't have to take it so personally. I look at the man today, and I think, "Well, the guy's just condescending, and that's how he'll teach his class. And I've got four more weeks of him, so I'll get through it," and blah, blah, blah. Which is something that I'm learning how to do.

After testing, one is relieved to find a diagnosable problem. One hopes that finally a solution to long-endured learning difficulties is forthcoming. However, this relief is only the beginning of an evolving psychological process. A person who now understands that he or she has a learning disability must begin fresh attempts to resolve it. Unfortunately, despite the advantage of having a defined problem, struggling with LD is still a lot of work. Here is where the opportunity to discover and enhance one's resilience unfolds. There are still no simple answers. Though perhaps less harrowing than ULD, LD remains hard to treat. Furthermore, many continue to feel ashamed of their now-apparent weaknesses.

After receiving a diagnosis, one must begin to wade through the regrets, sadness, and grief that inevitably accompany learning that one has a disability. In time, grieving will give way to a healthy understanding and respect for personal strengths and limitations. The individual can then begin to take responsibility for coping with the learning disability. Armed with more information, he or she can now sift through problems, separating a "hard-wired" and often permanent disability from emotionally driven problems, such as the shame cycle. As this happens, the person may find it easier to ask for and accept help from others.

Five processes are involved here. Although they are presented in a sequence, often one experiences these domains simultaneously or vacillates between them. The section "Facing the Music" describes the painful struggle of confronting the learning disability and developing new ways to work around it. In "Grief: It's Here to Stay," an individual accepts the fact that the learning disability and its shame-producing ramifications are permanent. "Identifying Helpers and Hinderers" explores the uncomfortable task of seeking help from others with varying degrees of success. In "Avoiding Pitfalls" individuals with LD continue to treat and accept their learning disability; their they also learn to fine-tune their ability to prevent shame incidents. Last, "Taking It In" describes the attempts to reconcile, in one's mind and heart, the fact of one's learning disability with one's innermost feelings and internalized messages from the past.

FACING THE MUSIC: BECOMING RESILIENT

I can't do what I've been doing. I have to learn all over again.
And I'll tell you, it's very difficult.

Facing the Music involves replacing comfortable but less-than-effective methods of achieving with unfamiliar but far more effective approaches. This capacity for flexibility is one very important component of learning resiliency. It can be distressing to give up familiar, comfortable methods of learning even when these techniques fail again and again. For adults, study habits are tough to change or give up; they have had many years to solidify.

Trying new ways of compensating for one's learning disability can stimulate familiar feelings of shame. As before diagnosis, the shame cycle drives people to avoid the disability and therefore to fail to develop innovative ways around it, compounding the problem:

- I am adaptive. But I'll tell you—I get very tired of it.
- I now know that if I want to get A's I must start papers early. And that means that I will suffer for a longer period of time.
- It was very difficult for me to stop using my mouth and now try to listen in class.

Educational consultants (also called learning disabilities specialists) can be a tremendous help to a person with LD. Their training gives them access to the most effective strategies for fighting LD. However, carrying out their suggestions is easier said than done. (Bringing oneself to ask for their help in the first place is another issue; this problem is discussed later in "Identifying Helpers and Hinderers.") The disability seems impossible to surmount and may even prevent the individual from absorbing the new ways of learning that the consultant is trying to teach:

- No matter how much help I get, nothing is going to stop me from getting sleepy when I read.
- I can't remember what my tutor told me.

- Since I'm so disorganized, I can't keep my notes straight.

The hope engendered during testing is tempered by the difficult reality of finding appropriate tools with which to learn and work. Slowly reality sinks in: no magic formula will fix a learning disability.

- I need to research every damn thing that comes up . . . nothing stays in my head.
- I can't break down things into steps.
- I resent having to work so hard.
- How can I write papers when I can't think in a clear, organized fashion?

Time, a familiar enemy, returns. Both teachers and bosses value the ability to work quickly. However, many of the necessary steps suggested by educational consultants involve restraining oneself, taking more steps, or repetition. The techniques slow down the LD person when they may already feel "too slow." These new, time-consuming steps generate frustration. The slow pace of work in the area of disability contrasts painfully with quick success in other areas:

- I'm a hard worker and I love school . . . no matter how badly I do. I do my best, but why does it have to take so long?
- Sure, good for her [the tutor]—she can casually say, "Tape the class and then listen to the tape and take notes from the tape." But this is only one of our four classes, and it takes forever. Not only that, I have to listen three or four times before it clicks in.
- Every time I look at an article or a book, I first look at how thick it is. . . . The longer the article, the more hours and hours of painful work ahead of me.
- I can't read something, digest it in a reasonable period of time, and give it back in an appropriate way.

Seeking ways to work around a learning disability may again raise the specter of the chasm. As an individual tackles old problem areas once again, the familiar paralysis and isolation of shame may hinder the effort. These feelings must be overcome to bring success within reach:

- It's so painful to know that the first four or five times I try to memorize something, absolutely nothing—*nothing*—will stay in my head.
- It's as though I were back in first grade again being asked to read with the bluebirds.
- I feel I'm up against a brick wall. . . . There is no place to go.
- I feel degraded. . . . Why should I have to have it so special? Why can't I do it normally?

To summarize, soon after diagnosis, people must replace familiar ways of achieving with what at first seem to be harder, inefficient, and confusing methods. As difficult as this learning is, this process of tackling and mastering what is difficult promotes resilience. One learns not only the material at hand, but also *how* to become more adaptive and hence more resilient. What complicates this process is that in confronting the familiar areas of difficulty, one can feel stuck in the chasm—an old and unwelcome feeling. The shame instinct to stop, coupled with the educational consultant's instructions to proceed doggedly forward, can make the learning experience almost unbearable. As the enormity of the task of compensating for a disability becomes clear, the grieving experience begins.

GRIEF: IT'S HERE TO STAY

> *It's always there. I knew it in my head,*
> *but then I knew it in my heart.*

People go through a grieving process not only when a loved one dies, but when anything dear to them is lost. This can include a cherished dream, a valued relationship, or an idealized picture of who they are and how they fit into the world. One step in any grieving process is to accept the loss as permanent. In the case of newly discovered learning disabilities, an individual comes to a sobering realization: after years of fighting learning difficulties, then years of not really dealing with them, one must finally face the fact that he or she can do certain things, if at all, only slowly and deliberately. This will not change. Although there are tools and tricks for dealing with a learning disability, they cannot make the disability itself go away:

- No matter how much therapy I have, I'll always need to tape things and then have to slow down the tapes. I think that's a problem that's just there and that I have to learn to live with it.
- I was born this way.
- It's never going to go away. So as long as I live, it will be there.

Part of the grieving process also involves regrets. An individual with now-understood LD regrets lost opportunities and unnecessary suffering:

- So much that could have been learned has been lost.
- Because I was labeled a behavior problem, I never had the opportunity to learn from and like other bright kids.
- You can't erase all the trauma I've had because nobody knew why I wasn't learning.

Regret can also take the form of jealousy. Comparing oneself to others often leaves the individual feeling isolated and unfortunate. This experience echoes earlier feelings of "Why me?"

- Why do I have to start my papers early in the semester when people in my dorm have lots of time to do other things together and then finish their papers anywhere from one night to, at most, a week?
- It's not fair that I work so much longer and harder than other people and they get better grades.
- This guy frustrates me because he looks at something one

time and he knows it. . . . It's not right that I should have to work so hard.

Once the individual really accepts the disability and grief has run its course, the person can begin to seek help.

IDENTIFYING HELPERS AND HINDERERS

Following diagnosis, an individual with LD will often decide that it is necessary to seek help. Apart from making use of the help once it is received, asking for help in the first place runs counter to the strain of independence that has helped a person with ULD survive thus far. In the past, working around these invisible problems was a lonely endeavor. Success depended on an individual's own ingenuity, creativity, and initiative. These self-governed strengths, therefore, enhanced early self-esteem. Now, asking for help from the world evokes feelings of exposure and is understandably difficult:

- I figured out how to get by myself.
- I've always stood on my own two feet.
- I don't like putting myself on the line like that.

Since the diagnosis—perhaps even the knowledge of learning disabilities—is new, a person may be unsure whether it is appropriate to seek help. The ensuing feeling of dependence can become even more humiliating. It seems as though one is asking for help one does not deserve:

- Maybe I was asking for something special. I really didn't know.
- I was told I had the right to ask for this, but it felt as though I was taking advantage of the situation. . . . Now I know better, but at the time it was difficult.

Of course, once the person with learning disabilities overcomes these roadblocks and seeks help, he or she does not necessarily meet with success. The two main sources of help are LD special-ists, who give one-on-one consultations, and educational institu-tions or teachers, who have the power to grant special privileges. It is generally easier to ask for help from the former than from the latter. For one thing, since it is their job to be well informed about LD, specialists rarely fail to understand and cooperate, while schools and teachers might have little information or experience. Also, seeing a specialist does not feel like asking for a favor, but seeking help from a school often has that meaning, even though such assistance is a legal right. Consulting a specialist, therefore, might be a somewhat less daunting task—although not all spe-cialists are consistently supportive:

- Asking for someone to be my note taker is embarrassing. I feel like an idiot.
- I hate asking the professor for more time.

Hinderers are those who meet requests for help with annoy-ance, misunderstanding, and accusations. Some who are asked for help intensify the discomfort of the person with LD by react-ing with insensitivity or ignorance. In this case, asking for help can be disconcerting. When attempts to communicate a need for assistance fail, the paralysis and despair of the chasm re-emerge:

- I told one instructor I had dyslexia, and she said I should go to an optometrist for new glasses.
- She [the professor] accused me of manipulating her and de-manding extra attention no one else gets.
- He [the professor] said, "This is college, you know."
- The first time I did it [asked a question], I knew I wasn't making much sense to him because his eyes glazed over. I could see it, and I sort of gave up.

Eventually, many persons with learning disabilities become quite adept at seeking and receiving aid. In some instances, how-ever, this process can somehow still feel dishonest and deceitful, requiring furtive behavior:

- I say, "I've heard that you know this stuff. What should I look for?" And they won't tell me what I should look for; they'll tell me the answer. . . . I've always thought of this as cheating.
- If I need something to read or something checked over, I know how to finagle people to get what I need out of them. . . . Not that I'm doing this in a deceitful, mean way. It's just called survival.
- The better I make them feel, the more complete their answer is to me.

Receiving needed assistance engenders a new set of feelings. First, the person with LD can feel validated: another human being listened and accepted his or her disability. It may be that the solution is simple; a slight bending of the rules will suffice. Most important, the door of achievement is finally opened. The person may find success in subject areas that had previously caused tremendous pain and difficulty. The Imprisoned Intelligence begins to experience its first taste of freedom:

- If someone can understand the difficulty—even if they won't change the date due, for example—it helps so much.
- He can see my artistry and my disability, both.
- If I'm heard, I can switch to another way of learning. I can move to another direction and find the way through.
- I don't need sympathy. I just need a place where I can type my exams.

Some individuals can also have their own semisuccessful coping methods validated when competent professionals and understanding educators show them how to build onto these approaches:

- Since the normal ways didn't work, I felt like she and I were working together to figure out creative ways to free my intelligence.
- I could be a computer operator because I did not learn from

the books. . . . I walked into the lab and said, "Show me."
And they showed me, and I graduated.
- She started with what I had and then helped me learn a better way to organize.

As individuals with newly discovered LD begin to ask for help, they encounter both hinderers and helpers. In the former case, they may re-experience the shame and paralysis of the chasm. In the latter case, they begin to experience personal validation and learning success. Over time, an individual will try to limit experiences with hinderers by developing proactive strategies.

AVOIDING PITFALLS

> I was at Passover, and they wanted me to read a portion. . . .
> Now, I can't even read regular English words, let alone Hebrew translations. And I went up to somebody and said, "Do you know what that word is?" They said, "You don't know how to read?" It felt like I was back in third grade again. It took me longer [to read], people started blurting words out, and I was nervous. If I go to a Passover reading, I will not read in front of the group unless I have rehearsed it. But I will not go point blank. I won't do it.

The incident illustrates an embarrassing situation that exposed a learning disability. It also illustrates an individual with LD drawing the line—he has decided that a certain task is not worth the grief and will not let himself be pushed. By avoiding such pitfalls, one protects oneself from recurring painful experiences.

One important pitfall individuals often face is prejudice against learning disabilities. They come to realize that, while some people can be approached as helpers, information about the disability is often best kept secret. Not only could knowledge of the disability result in a loss of respect from colleagues, teachers, supervisors, and friends, it could compromise future career and academic success:

- I've never said I have a learning disability at work because I wouldn't have gotten to where I've gotten if they knew.

- I didn't tell anyone I had learning disabilities because I had tried that once over there [at a major university] and it was a big flop. . . . So I learned to be very careful and disguise it.
- When I told the dean of students because I was behind in papers, she was just fine. But this is not the air we're breathing in. There aren't many learning disability people out of the closet. They may not even know they are in the closet.
- I need a reference from that lady. . . . Do you think I want to give her a reason not to think highly of me?

TAKING IT IN

> *Even knowing what I know, I can't help it.*
> *Blaming myself is like a habit I can't break.*

After testing, an individual has the information that the learning disability is most likely physiologically based. This intellectual knowledge is often accompanied by a nagging inner voice: *It's your fault. You're lazy and stupid. You're not fooling anyone with these excuses about LD.* Because these childhood voices are powerful, individuals must struggle to integrate what they know to be the truth with what they *feel* to be the truth.

From testing, people understand that parts of their intellectual functioning differ from the norm. They struggle between blaming themselves and accepting the learning disability as a product of physiology and/or development:

- I still think the conventional way—that I should be able to pick up a book and read it.
- I still think that there's something wrong with me and I must be stupid.
- I can get it, but I feel humiliated because it took me too long.
- Sometimes I think I'm failing because I'm lazy and sometimes I know that I'm stuck and need help. . . . It's hard to know which is which.

Most realize that they are having a hard time integrating their knowledge, as these quotes show. In some cases, however, blaming the self has become so ingrained that it is difficult to stop. They continue to place blame on personal behavior or traits rather than on the disability:

Part of knowing that I'm LD now is not good because of wanting to use that as an excuse—and like, not working hard or something. But maybe if I worked a little harder at it, I might get it. But because I know I'm LD in that area, it's kind of like, why do it if it's not going to work? So part of that—part of me wishes I hadn't found out. Maybe I would try harder. But part of me is glad that I did because I stopped beating myself up for not getting certain things.

The acceptance of the physiological nature of the problem can be enhanced when individuals with newly discovered LD realize that others in their families probably suffer from similar disabilities: This knowledge transforms what we knew into what we now know as we re-examine memories and past perceptions.

- My brother suffers from the same problems, but he never did anything about it.
- My father is just like me. It takes one to know one.
- My mother said she couldn't read because she didn't know English. But now I know she can't read in Spanish either.

Suspicions about the genetic basis of the learning disability can be bolstered by similar diagnoses in the family:

- My sister was diagnosed before I was, and she was younger.
- When my daughter was diagnosed, I knew I suffered some of the same problems.

The individual learns to confront the learning disability, grieve over what cannot be changed, find appropriate ways of seeking help and avoiding hinderers, and begins to integrate the knowledge into the ingrained message he or she had previously accepted.

Chapter 6

New Reflections:
A Different Mirror

"Scholar" is a successful academician who discovered his learning disability in late adolescence.

INTERVIEWER: Has learning about your learning disabilities been helpful in understanding your own development?

SCHOLAR: Oh yes. You have a lot more flexibility in dealing with the educational world. At the earlier levels, I didn't have a mechanism for dealing with the teachers who wanted to see me as stupid, who found me frustrating, who reacted very negatively to my inability to spell and to write well. And to be honest, I think there are an awful lot of anal compulsive people out there who see their job to get Johnny to *spell it right* but they don't have a particular model on how to help kids learn to *think.* So it would have been very useful [for] me and my parents to have this rhetoric to deal with these teachers.

INTERVIEWER: Has it helped you now, in your day-to-day living, to know about your LD?

SCHOLAR: Oh sure. Absolutely. The more you know, the more you can make sense out of it, the better off you are. I'm in a profession now where the whole question of how bright you are and how good a scholar you are is endemic; I mean, this is a professional liability. No one in a top research university doesn't spend a certain amount of energy worrying about just how good their work is; and having an understanding of my history as dyslexic means that it's helpful in dealing with these problems. The initial response [in academia] is to evaluate people according to volume; how much they publish. But on the other hand, I think over the long term, people look at the quality and the impact the piece of work has. [For example,] the guy who just got the Nobel prize in economics, he only published twelve articles in his life. Period. They were just twelve great articles [laughter]. Enormous impact. If you look at his life, the lack of the number of articles published must have caused him a lot of grief. But if you look at the *quality* of what he did, it resulted in his getting the Nobel Prize.

INTERVIEWER: So, in this sense, one's learning disability gives one time to think more creatively. Why do you think this is so?

SCHOLAR: Well, it's like the experiments with rats about how you get feedback. If you want to make the rat most persistent, you give him intermittent feedback. If it's just regular [feedback] they do reasonably well, and if it's not regular, they won't perform at all. But, if it's random, you get the most positive behavior on their part. They will be the most aggressive at pursuing something.

Well, if you look at my life, sometimes [I] got lots of positive feedback and sometimes [I] got negative. It was random and this keeps one tenacious.

Coming to terms with a newly diagnosed learning disability requires a great deal of psychological and practical effort. One has to work both to change oneself, by reconstructing learning skills, and to accept oneself, by realizing that the disability is a physical fact and not a malleable character flaw:*

> I've accepted my learning disability in my heart and in my mind now . . . I'm smart. I'm gifted. I'm talented. And even though the learning disability frustrates me, I just have to accept it.

---

* For more about how new information about learning disabilities impacts on our old memories, see chapter 14.

Chapter 5 explored the struggles involved in learning to live with LD. This chapter will discuss what happens when the struggle is reconciled.

Reconciliation has four domains. These domains will overlap, and an individual may oscillate between them. In the first, *personal definitions* evolve for the individual. Then *acceptance* slowly emerges. The painful events of the past are resurrected and resolved as *personal history is reinterpreted.* This capacity to shift and enlarge upon our own internal story is a hallmark of the flexibility that resilient people with LD seem to acquire after the diagnosis. The world's standards lose their awesome power to define the individual, and *personal perspectives* can be developed.

PERSONAL DEFINITIONS

One part of reconciliation is developing a personal definition of learning disabilities. This is quite different from parroting an expert's technical or legal definition. Creating a personal definition involves encapsulating and articulating a lifetime's worth of learning experiences and therefore requires considerable insight and self-knowledge. Some of the following definitions are deceptively simple. Their elegance resides in their capacity to transform what was once ineffable and mysterious into an explicit and comprehensible problem:

- Learning disabilities are like a short in the system.
- [Having] learning disabilities means taking longer to learn.
- [Having] learning disabilities is like watching TV and you're blind.
- Imprisoned Intelligence is the sense of myself as being intelligent, but outward expression becomes excruciatingly difficult.
- Imprisoned Intelligence is being able to hear better than I can see, but having to learn by reading.
- Imprisoned Intelligence is the opposite of the goodness of fit.

If evolving a personal definition answers the question "What?" then accumulating a knowledge base about one's LD answers the question "Why?" Knowing and accepting the causes of one's constrained learning can be a great source of comfort:

- Now when I hit the "chasm," at least I have a "because."
- I have an auditory processing problem, so sometimes I can't retain what people are saying.
- Now I know why I couldn't read a book no matter how much I wanted the information in it.
- My brain works in slow motion, but I know that two hours from now something will kick in.

ACCEPTANCE

There is no one moment when an individual "accepts" her or his disability. Acceptance develops only with time and experience. It grows out of day-to-day involvement: dealing with frustrations as they come up; gradually learning to be resilient; working with what one can and cannot do. Acceptance allows one to set realistic goals and standards for oneself:

- I'm not a whole, perfect person, and I've got some missing parts, so that feels bad. And then I say, "But you've got all these other talents and skills, and a lot of people have missing parts." . . . I say to myself, "You know, you're not going to ruin your life over this. You just can't."
- I finally became detached from the standard of the school.
- I don't think I'll feel fully comfortable in school because it's just not my element.

The emotions connected to the learning disability may never disappear, but they do become bearable and under control. Another hallmark of resilience is that painful feelings are not as overwhelming as they were in prediagnosis days:

- It's like dipping into the pool of pain and pulling up a bucket as opposed to falling into the pool and being drowned.
- I've done so much to make myself not feel so bad that, when I talk about it more at this level, it makes me understand why I feel so bad about this learning disability.
- The feeling never gets so overwhelming that I really fall into a deep depression like I used to.

LD sufferers learn to tolerate their own imperfections. Like every other human being, they are flawed and will sometimes fail. This no longer seems like an unforgivable sin:

- I'm handicapped here, vulnerable here. And I need some help.
- I could finally forgive the younger self in me that I had been so abusive to.
- Now I could finally lay it [the learning problem] to rest and feel infinitely kinder toward that self as a consequence of this knowledge.

Because their disability can now be separated from their intelligence, these people are free to examine their intelligence objectively. Without the distortion of ULD, they can know and appreciate their strengths. They begin to take pride in their gifts, talents, and accomplishments. Indeed, acknowledging the disability enhances self-esteem, as they recognize the tenacity and resourcefulness that it took to survive all those years:

- My dyslexia forced me to learn to think for myself.
- My strong suit had been tenacity, and that usually pulled me through.
- I did not take the advice I was receiving from the rest of the world, and I'm glad I didn't because I'd be sitting in a mental institution if I had done that. I just kept on fighting.

Individuals can now use their intelligence and talents with confidence. A newfound feeling of empowerment* allows them to seek out appropriate alternatives and to make good choices for themselves. They take charge of their own learning environment:

- I am learning things about myself. And I can say, "I don't learn that way; this is the way I learn."
- I can choose the necessary tools to help me learn another way.
- I will decide when I want to take tests untimed and when I don't.
- I don't need to tape all my classes, just a few of them.

Another indication of acceptance is the ability to joke about one's disability. Previously, the learning disability was too painful to be humorous. With acceptance comes an ability to make light of the situation:

- I don't need sleeping pills; I just need a book.
- I just pick up a boring book, look at a page, and I'm sleeping.
- Every time I give my wife a paper to read, she begins groaning.

PERSONAL HISTORY REINTERPRETED

Armed with new information, individuals can look at their past and make new sense of it. They can reinterpret events that their confused, younger selves did not understand, and debunk old myths. In other words, their memories get modulated. (For more information on memory modulation, see Chapter 14):

- I can look back with some sense of hindsight. I mean, it really was like, you know, having my life as a jigsaw puzzle with two-thirds of it missing.

---

* Please see chapter 14 to learn more about empowerment and personal power.

- I wasn't lazy.
- I don't hate my mother.
- I'm not getting even.
- I'm not acting out.

Grief and despair over what might have been evolve into a more benign wistfulness. The note of anger and desperation fades:

- I feel I wish I could have done this a long time ago.
- If I had known, if they had known, if there had been help, what if?
- I saw a Montessori school program recently, and I thought to myself, "Geez, I wish I had that."

One re-examines past relationships. Realizing that no one knew about LD then, the individual is able to accept the ineffectual attempts of parents and others to help as well-meaning. After all, how could anyone offer much assistance when they didn't understand the problem? One can forgive former nemeses:

- My mother has been very hard on herself now for what she said to me then. We fought a lot.
- No one apologized to me. And I guess, maybe I expected them to, but then later on I thought to myself, "Look, your parents aren't people that hate you. They tried to help you."
- I know now that my father was trying to motivate me into being a better person. It didn't work, but now I can forgive him.
- I have the sense that people who reacted negatively to me were either professors who gave up hope and thought I couldn't learn or maybe, I don't know, people who have undiagnosed learning disabilities themselves.

PERSONAL PERSPECTIVES

Many individuals with ULD are especially interested in scrutinizing the practices of the schools they attended, since the classroom was where they experienced their first learning failures and consequent shame. With the knowledge they now have, they can identify specific practices that stopped learning in its tracks:

- Sometimes, it wasn't the teacher's fault, it was the system.
- In kindergarten I learned to read quite well using phonics, but then we transferred to another school where they taught reading using sight. And being a dyslexic, I was dead, right there.
- When she spoke, I learned everything easily, but when I had to read, I failed.
- When I was in high school, I was the world's worst French student and a lot of that had to do with the fact that French was taught in an almost exclusively auditory way and I just couldn't process it. And this was in contrast to my being one of the very best Latin students in school. In Latin you had to read and translate.
- I failed the test because I couldn't write it. But when he asked me all the questions, I knew every answer.
- I spent a semester at [University #2]. It was so enormously different than [University #1]. It really pretty much blew me away. The emphasis [at University #2] was so much on neatness, getting it right, having it said correctly, so on and so forth. I did very well at [University #1], Phi Beta Kappa and honors and all sorts of things. And, I have to tell you, I didn't work too hard. I had a good time. And it was really clear to me that if I had gone to [University #2] on a permanent basis, which I think is not nearly as good a school, I would have done much worse.

Out of this re-evaluation of school standards comes a concern for others with ULD who might still be at the mercy of an unyielding educational system. Many emerged from their experience with a feeling of group solidarity and an interest in LD as a social issue:

- I think teachers should be aware of learning disabilities or shouldn't be in a position where they can't help students.
- I think about all the kids who never get a chance to use their brains.
- I guess they just gave up . . . it's so sad.
- In fact, many of the individuals who participated in this study did so to reach out to others who might be suffering in ignorance:
- I think this is very valuable research. It's information that is not really easy to get at and that's not well reported.
- This message needs to be spread.
- I'm only doing this so you will teach others about this when you finish.

Reconciliation is the final acceptance of living with an undiagnosed learning disability. How people incorporate the information about their disability, modulate their memories, and use that information to enhance their flexibility and resiliency is a testimony to our creative capacity for maturity and wisdom. Over time, one develops new perspectives and views of the self that provide some degree of meaning and comfort. Reconciliation, however, is ongoing, a process that will continue for the rest of one's life. By and large, the individual grows increasingly comfortable with the disability as time goes on. Even so, this comfort never overlooks the fact that early diagnosis could have mitigated the pain of growing up and vastly improved one's academic and intellectual careers.

Chapter 7

Resilience and
Fulfilling Potential

INTERVIEWER: Since this problem was unknown, others could not be there for you in the most effective way. Can we talk about how you helped yourself?

SCHOLAR: My reputation is a person who produces very high [-quality] work but not fast. People complain about the fact that I don't produce fast enough. Well, I know something about why I don't produce fast enough: it takes me a lot longer for me to craft the paper into a top work than it does for most people and it has to do with the dyslexia. When I write papers it's easier because I understand why I have this problem, and so I have to work harder to compensate for it. And to think about that problem as being dyslexic as opposed to "you're stupid" is a lot easier.

People with disabilities enhance their resilience as they fulfill their potential. Because the disability can interfere with the unfolding and flowering of mastery in areas of strength, they are propelled to use their creativity to get themselves unstuck from the chasm. This adaptive process creates a stage where potential can grow. Adaptation, grounded in resiliency, is part and parcel of how people with LD overcome and master. Resiliency, creativity, and adapting to risk go hand-in-glove. In essence, the disability itself forces people with LD into creative modes. Scholar tells us how he did it.

Scholar: When I write a paper, I get my wife to go through it, I get the secretary at work to go through it, I mean I find other kinds of compensating mechanisms now. When I go to the university, I'll say, look, I need a secretary that doesn't have to do a lot of work, but she has to be brilliant in spelling and grammar, because that's what I need. The world out there sees me as extremely well organized, extremely proactive. I tend to keep a fairly rigid calendar. When you go into my office, there's a spot for everything. I'm very big on lists and am always asking, "What do we have to do today?" I tend to always have things in on time, but I must!

Scholar has, obviously, over time, figured out ways to help himself succeed. This is what resilience is about: the ability to figure out what's wrong and how to fix it. How do people do this? In the first place, living with learning disabilities gets the sufferer's attention. If nothing else, people learn what to stay away from. There is nothing like the humiliation of being stuck in the chasm to highlight the problem and force one to adapt. It's just too painful to feel stupid. Some people use avoidance as a way of adapting. They cut classes or stay away from work. But others find that using their creative juices is an exciting, pleasing activity that creates a storehouse of motivation for other parts of their lives, as well.

Let's take the example of the class clown: Some students with LD have learned that they can enhance the connection with others by making them laugh. So, when the teacher asks a question and the student deflects the answer by responding with a joke, the attention in the classroom shifts from not being able to answer a question to a "behavior" problem. Being labeled a behavior problem is easier to manage because the student knows that his behavior is under his control. Also, as a byproduct, he has learned how to endear himself to others. This interactive gift can hold him in good stead for the rest of his life. In essence, the capacity

to creatively adapt to an impossible situation (like being humiliated because of one's LD) can transform feelings of stupidity into
a mutually enhancing interactive experience among peers.

This kind of creative transformation and release of potential
is enhanced once the learning disability is identified. The diagnosis can interfere with the previous self-blame or denigration to
which people with ULD automatically subject themselves. People
like Scholar cannot routinely call themselves stupid anymore now
that they know their "stupidity" is a hard-wired glitch and not
their fault.

Once a person's attention is on the problem (the LD), the adaptive processes can begin, and potential can be unleashed. How
does this process begin?

Intelligent people with learning disabilities live with great
strengths and weaknesses. Some parts of themselves are fruitful
and function beautifully. The great college quarterback who is
dyslexic and has trouble reading can perform with agility and
grace on the field. However, in the classroom he can look and feel
like a dunce. It's the distance between these two experiences that
make life so problematic.

Let's look at another example: When one easily meets the demands of the world (as a bright math student does in a math class),
one assumes that learning will be relatively quick and painless.
And it is. But when the demands of the world cannot be met (the
bright math student does poorly in English class) the same assumption, that learning is easy, makes it more difficult to succeed
in these areas. In other words, the part of one's mind that learns
easily is impatient when learning is not comfortable. At the same
time, the nonachieving part that learns with difficulty is painfully
ashamed, because in difficult areas, it's not only hard to learn, but
there is exposure in the face of inner critical impatience (Levin,
2003; Trevarthan, 2003).

What can be done about inhibiting internal criticism? *Learning about our emotions is critical here. Understanding our feelings through
emotional attention can create the bridge between strengths and weaknesses.*
Becoming aware, or paying attention to this "voice" (as opposed

to simply reacting) gives one the opportunity to develop and nurture a benevolent observing negotiator inside one's own mind. This inner mediator can attempt to look at all sides of the problem and can negotiate between one's demands and expectations for mastery instead of simply living with the humiliation of being "stuck." This capacity to pay attention to and modulate negative inner voices enhances resilience.

A person suffering with ULD, however, might declare, "I cannot simply create a benevolent internal negotiator inside myself out of the blue; how am I supposed to do this?" Well, it will be neither simple nor out of the blue, but this problem *will* respond to intuition, curiosity, and introspection.

Becoming aware and respectful of the feelings that flow from discrepancies in cognitive functioning enhances resilience by allowing for compassionate self-exploration. Individuals can then wonder about when, where, why, and how they feel accomplished or incompetent. Understanding their deficits nonjudgmentally helps people learn to view their learning disabilities from a responsible, yet nurturing, perspective. By taking responsibility for both strengths and weaknesses, one's strengths can be used to *help* weaknesses.

Taking personal responsibility is the overarching message behind this chapter because it is a foundation for resilience. It will suggest four ways to begin to learn the flexibility one needs in order to fulfill potential: (1) facing the problem; (2) facing the chasm; (3) finding support; and (4) finding appropriate professional help.

FACING THE PROBLEM

Facing the Problem involves two components: (1) identifying strengths and weaknesses, and (2) finding appropriate compensations.

Identifying Strengths and Weaknesses

People with ULD know themselves best. Not all learning disabilities are problematic. Let me be clear about this: *ULD matters only if it interferes with fulfillment.* Many people have created comfortable niches where their intellect is challenged and their learning disabilities bypassed. The brilliant computer programmer, for example, does not have to worry about spelling because of spelling checker programs. But, if a person's world changes and demands are made to learn in a way the person finds difficult, it might be very important to know about this possible hidden dimension of undiagnosed learning disabilities. Imagine, for example, a successful person who, after being laid off from a comfortable job, suddenly finds it difficult to learn; a previously successful student who inexplicably cannot learn from a new teacher; or friendly people who have always lived in the same place but cannot seem to make friends after moving. If goals are waylaid by unknown factors, ULD is a possible problem.

However, before getting help (and in order to get help) it is very important to honestly evaluate strengths, because then motivation for further investigation will be enhanced. This will help determine how to proceed. This sounds easy. It is not.

Most smart people are proud of their intelligence. Pride takes a beating when one admits that, in some areas, learning does not happen. Recognizing one's weaknesses is painful and individuals try to create a world in which they feel wholly competent. The problem is that this comfortable world is a fiction that cannot be maintained. Sooner or later, school or work will make demands that call upon areas of weakness, and people are rudely and painfully shocked. This shock, and the subsequent descent into the chasm, can be prevented if there is an awareness of weakness that then can be addressed and treated. An internal bridge is needed to bring strength and weakness into contact.

One factor that prevents this bridge from developing is prolonged shame. Sporadic but chronic feelings of stupidity can cause individuals to be caught in a cycle of destructive shame (see Chapter 3). Once it starts, shame is difficult to stop. It becomes almost impossible to keep from berating ourselves or to remember our intelligence. This may sound like a catch-22: If people do not understand their weaknesses, they become acutely ashamed, and if they are acutely ashamed, they will not be able to understand their weaknesses. This is why ULD is neither easy nor simple to treat. However, gradual awareness of the shame cycle will help curtail its effects. This chapter will suggest ways to foster such self-awareness, as well as other methods for straddling strengths and weaknesses.

One of the participants in this study learned that the reason she cannot read maps or easily find her way in new situations is a visual-spatial learning problem. After diagnosis she could more readily understand her husband's frustration when she was lost and late so often. She could also be more self-forgiving because she knew this was not her fault.

Without a diagnosis, however, analysis of one's strengths and weaknesses is complicated and requires self-observation over time. It helps to focus on taking a broad enough view to *encompass* both intellect and deficits. This keeps us from falling into the shame/blame cycle. Then when strengths and weaknesses become more familiar, it can be helpful to seek out more technical information about learning disabilities and about your particular diagnosis. (For further reading, see the "Recommended Reading" at the end of this book.)

Learning disorders are idiosyncratic; they occur in a wide variety. Unless an individual is that rarest of creatures, the "textbook case," a list of learning disabilities will not be specific enough. *One's own perception of learning discrepancies, on the other hand, will tell a great deal.* The fundamental question is: Are individuals very good at some things and very bad at others? For all intents and purposes, this is a defining characteristic of learning disabilities. The goal of diagnostic tests is to find such discrepancies between ability and function that indicate a possible learning disability.

Two other broad questions may be helpful. First, how did the person do in school? Second, how is she or he functioning now?

School

A history of repetitive difficult experiences at school can be an indicator of learning disabilities. Of course, there can be other reasons why people have trouble in school, but if there seems to be a pattern, learning disabilities can be a possibility to consider. Individuals who were labeled overachievers, for example, may have been compensating to hide the fact that it took longer to study or finish assignments.

Was the person an overachiever who never had time to play with other kids because of diligently *always* working on homework? Did he or she excel but somehow think and/or feel like a cheater? Was the person considered an underachiever? Was there trouble getting started? Did the person get A's in some classes and fail or nearly fail in others? Was there boredom in school but fascination elsewhere? Could the student learn from some teachers but, independent of effort, fail to learn from others? These are questions worth considering.

Current Functioning

The following may serve as markers for possible undiagnosed learning disabilities. Some people may be:

- Competent at some things and hopeless at others.
- Good in math and bad in English or vice versa.*
- Sloppy.
- Consistently late.
- Fond of reading but bored listening to lectures, or vice versa.
- Delighted to watch the educational channel and bored reading a book.

Other possibilities, in terms of current functioning, might include:

---

*There is an argument about this. Some feel that learning discrepancies such as this are really simply learning differences. Perhaps this is so, but if it is, schools still need to radically alter their curricula so that they do not prevent students from learning in their areas of "difference." Teachers must expand their teaching methods and find alternative educational materials that address a multiplicity of learning styles.

- Feeling the frustration of sporadic failures in the face of high achievement at work.
- Feeling that one's weaknesses and not strengths are being exposed. (Sometimes this is manifested by high achievers who think they are fooling everyone.)
- Struggle with variation in performance: some days people can function like greased lightning, while on other days they function like a car with a flat tire.

Conditions at home can also be problematic:

- Organizational problems may create a messy household.
- Tardiness may prevail.
- Being unable to help one's children with seemingly simple homework may provoke frustration.

Are there other explanations for these discrepancies? Functioning can suffer, for example, if people are worried about losing their jobs, are suffering from depression or, in particular, if they are grieving. It is difficult to know. It is important to foster an inquiring attitude.

One's intuition is important. In certain areas, does it feel almost impossible to learn or achieve, no matter how hard the attempt? Some people persevere no matter how many times they fail but never achieve their goals. (One participant, for example, wanted to be an engineer but eventually realized he could not conquer the mandated math courses.) One marker is consistency and time. If these problems have always been present, it is more likely that the problem may be an undiagnosed learning disability rather than a reaction to stressful situations. If there is stress from a breakup, an accident, or a depression in one's life, the ability to use one's brain effectively can temporarily diminish. In other words, it may be ULD or it may be something psychological. By paying attention to *both* possibilities a person will benefit. Essentially, the most important clue is a sense that, irrespective of intelligence, something is permanently wrong.

Finding Appropriate Compensations

Compensations help avoid exposure and embarrassment. Individuals will go to great lengths to avoid feeling embarrassed. It is amazing how children can figure out how to hide or modulate their deficits even when teachers and parents do not understand the problem. However, a child's capacity to strategize or get around unrecognized learning problems muddies the waters considerably because identification becomes more difficult.

Take the class clown. In many cases, class clowns are inordinately clever underachievers who entertain their peers and drive their teachers crazy. This role can be a form of compensation for students with ULD. For example, a smart boy with ULD becomes embarrassed when he cannot excel, and he hates to think of himself as dumb. The class clown does not put his head on the desk and cry because he cannot achieve. He compensates for his inability to learn by deflecting attention to his clever antics. Even though he may not be able to do academic work, he can still show his peers he is smart—even if he irritates the teacher in the process. The reasons underlying his lack of achievement are concealed by his seemingly psychologically based misbehavior.

The participants in this study compensated in very creative ways to subvert the invisible "something" that kept getting in their way. Some could talk their way out of any situation and managed to do quite well until the written work in college overwhelmed them. Others who could not listen or articulate comfortably would find themselves doing a great deal of written work for extra credit. It is interesting that, for the most part, the "writers" had an easier time in college than the "talkers."

The capacity to compensate can enhance growth and development. It creates pride in one's creativity and independence and is the hallmark of resilience. Children with ULD have their feet to the fire. Because no one understands their problem, they must figure out how to get around the "something" that keeps them from learning. Consider, for example, the participant who asked questions that got teachers to talk at length because she could not learn by reading.

However, compensations present their own problems. Children are left to rely on their own devices, and the techniques they employ may compromise their sense of self; the class clown is a case in point. Although idiosyncratic strategies may allow a child to function adequately, treatment could provide more effective methods and increase mastery and self-esteem.

To further complicate matters, compensations can fail when one's psychological world is in jeopardy. Those who can hide their deficits may live fairly comfortable lives until something in the environment throws a curve ball. For example, adults with hidden dyslexia have learned that qs are really gs. So, when they read, they convert each q into a g. This extra step is a part of their coping in normal times. But, when they become extremely emotionally distraught, fatigued, or ill, this extra step may not be possible.

This can be very confusing. How are individuals to discern when (1) they are just being lazy and not trying hard enough, (2) they cannot excel because of ULD, or (3) their compensations for ULD fail? Here is where responsibility enters the picture. It is necessary to determine whether one is struggling with motivational problems or whether new ways of compensating need to be learned. Fundamentally, each individual person knows best what *feels* psychological and what *feels* innate.

A boss is picking on an employee because expectations are not being met and the employee is not working up to snuff. If the inability to produce is emotional (suppose, for example, the employee hates the boss) then the problem is psychological in origin. But if the employee (1) truly cannot figure out what the supervisor wants and (2) has the feeling that something invisible, permanent, and immovable is getting in the way, the problem could be ULD.

Curiosity about the problem can be effective if people take a moment to wonder whether their intelligence is imprisoned. Is there some block to explain why performance is under par? ("I can't get organized"; "I'm always losing things"; "I really can't read directions fast enough"; "There's too much commotion around me and I can't concentrate"; and so forth.) Questions such as these can then help people figure out if there is any creative way to get around the problem.

Sometimes compromises have to be made that are not pleasant. Individuals may have to acknowledge problems such as this:

OK, I'm different. Even though everyone else can finish their work during office hours, I cannot. So, even though I resent it, I guess I'll have to take work home with me.

Some of those interviewed said that they had trouble, at first, asking for help without feeling that they were compromising their pride and independence. It is difficult to admit deficits. They also had learned that, at times, confiding to others was *not* to their advantage. It is only sensible to hide your deficits if people will think less of you.

FACING THE CHASM: THE BIGGEST CHALLENGE

Facing the chasm is the hardest part. It is difficult but necessary because without recognition, how can there be change? The chasm, as explained earlier, is the place of nothingness; an experience of being stuck where all thinking stops. This "being stuck in the chasm" causes people to feel frustrated and ashamed. A person who expects to learn but cannot becomes humiliated, and the humiliation stops thought. It's not surprising that experiencing shameful failure when a person expects to achieve can cause withdrawal. People will do anything to avoid these nonfunctioning moments. The chasm makes people afraid to try to learn. But after testing, and armed with different strategies for learning, they have better tools for confronting this fear so that resilience can begin to grow.

Although it is difficult, one can stop running, turn around, and look at what makes one's mind freeze up. For some it might be math, for others spelling, and so on. This can be very painful. The chances of experiencing self-shame in one's own critical eye will be very high. This is where the "internal negotiator" comes in, talking to the self like a good parent. It says, for example:

• It's OK, the shame will pass.

- Others can help.
- This is a treatable problem.
- I'm transposing numbers—it's not my fault.
- Do something for ten minutes and then come back and try again.
- How can I make this better?

In the chasm, we see learning failures with an unforgiving eye. Optimally, the chasm is trying to give us a message: "Get out of the situation now. Wait until later to think and regroup." But when there is *only* an inner dialogue of judgment and contempt, the chasm is prolonged and takes on a life of its own. Those who break this cycle do so by cultivating empathy for themselves.

Reacting to and *not* recognizing shame is what a person is doing (and doing far too much) while in the chasm. In the chasm one feels frozen and controlled by shame. In fact, an individual is trying so hard *not* to feel shame that he or she cannot think about it or learn from it. Recognition is the key. Allowing oneself to experience shame can help identify its cause and allow for new possible alternatives.

One man, a learning disability teacher, evokes miracles in children with serious learning disabilities. He, however, cannot read aloud. One day, while attending an in-service training, the facilitator asked the participants to read from the material. This gifted instructor almost died from the anticipated embarrassment of having to expose his learning disabilities in front of uncomprehending people. "After all, I am the learning disability teacher. Surely, I should know how to read." Because he knew that reading out loud only leads to his chasm, he excused himself before it was his turn and went to the bathroom. It worked!

It is sobering when people face their undiagnosed learning disabilities, and this knowledge can cause both anxiety and depression that further contributes to Imprisoned Intelligence.* The

---

*This is why learning disability specialists cannot do it all. Learning disability specialists can automatically cause anxiety because their primary focus and training involves confronting the learning disability itself. Having a psychotherapist to help with emotional issues frees the learning disability specialist to do his or her job more effectively.

feelings diminish in intensity as people learn to get help and live with this. Over time, with help, the feelings will fade.

FINDING SUPPORT

The next two sections of this chapter deal with finding mentors and friends who can help. Each serves a different purpose.

Finding a Mentor

Mentors are people of wisdom who can eventually be trusted to respect both an individual's strengths and weaknesses. Usually they are successful in the areas of the learner's potential. The best are ethical human beings who have excelled in their fields of expertise. Learning from them can be most rewarding because no matter what mistakes are made, they can keep the potential of the learner in mind. Within this framework, the learner feels free to share what is unknown or what feels impossible to accomplish. One can learn without the hovering presence of shame and fear of being patronized. Finding mentors, then, becomes vital for people with LD and ULD.

Mentors can see potential, accept weaknesses, and foster growth. While good college professors are famous for this, mentors can be found in all walks of life. Many participants in this study said that finding mentors made all the difference in their efforts to overcome difficulties. They began with areas of interest and found individuals who excelled. Students, for example, who loved writing found professors who became enthusiastic about their papers. One vital criterion is the need to look up to one's mentor. Admiration becomes a key ingredient that allows one to tolerate the internal shame that can occur when learning is difficult.

Finding people who can understand deficits without disregarding potential is essential. One can send out feelers to rule out intellectual snobs. One participant was careful to protect herself against her department chair for precisely this reason. Instead, she found someone in another department who was glad to be of help.

Finding mentors can be frustrating, but they are out there. Often people who are successful like to help others get their start; they may have had a mentor themselves and want to "give something back." A good mentor gets a thrill out of someone else's growth. Although the mentor may tell you things you do not want to hear, it is with the goal of propelling learning.

In the process of finding a mentor, however, protecting oneself from the judgments of those who do not understand LD is paramount. One young man talked about a teacher who was excited and interested in his discussions in class. After the student turned in his first paper, however, organizational problems were obvious and the professor's disappointment became quite clear.

Protecting oneself in a case like this does not mean dropping the class. It means realizing that some people do not know how to accept both strengths and disabilities. Looking for clues early on is helpful. Some people, despite their success, may shoot down others to boost their own self-esteem. Supervisors or professors who become impatient easily or are excessively critical may indeed be wonderful teachers and have much knowledge, but trusting them with one's vulnerabilities could lead to unnecessary shame and humiliation.

Pragmatically speaking, sometimes it is necessary to put up with impatient people who make subtle or unsubtle fun of others. A supervisor, teaching someone new computer skills, may be annoyed by the way that person learns. It is difficult to face such judgment but when push comes to shove, the supervisor has the skills necessary for the learner's advancement. Criticism can be tolerated if it's time-limited and the rewards are meaningful. (One participant remembers getting barely passing grades on papers he struggled to complete and saying to himself, "After three more months, Professor, you're out of my life.")

Furthermore, well-intentioned people sometimes truly believe that their denigration is helpful: "I'm doing this for your own good." Their intent may be honorable (or perhaps not) but one needs to accept that learning from them will be more difficult. In other words, expectations need modification. Learning from some people will be easy and from others difficult. But finding mentors that can teach what an individual is yearning to learn is indeed an exhilarating experience—and an important factor in the growth and development of resilience.

Finding Supportive Friends

Friends are not mentors. They are trustworthy people who can make significant connections with others. Friends, in the context of this book, are those one turns to when shame imprisons intelligence or when Imprisoned Intelligence creates shame. Family members can also serve this function. The antidote to shame is reconnection with others. Individuals with ULD need friends who have the potential for understanding their plight. They will be there when a person is struggling to learn. They can, for example, be called when one feels discouraged, and they have the capacity to inspire in the face of defeat. Friends do not teach, nor do they necessarily make suggestions. But they must be willing to listen.

Even though many participants reported having serious trouble in school, their friends were very bright and academically successful. During the interview as people reflected on this, they realized that their friends recognized their intelligence, and were often more than willing to offer practical aid. One participant who was a superb tennis player spoke of how she gave a friend tennis lessons in exchange for help with her math.

This benefit can hold true at work, as well. People do find friends on the job. Deals can be made. In fact, making deals is one way to acknowledge both strengths and weaknesses and clearly adds to resilience. For example, a worker with first-rate math skills can help a trusted math-deficient coworker who has good organizational skills. The thinking process might be: "She'll make sure I understand directions and I'll check her math." In school, someone who cannot take notes but understands concepts through listening might find a good note-taker who needs tutoring with concepts before exams.

FINDING APPROPRIATE PROFESSIONAL HELP

ULD and Psychotherapy

This study clearly indicates that ULD creates a world of anxiety and emotional distress. ULD is traumatic because expectations about the ability to succeed are frustrated by factors beyond one's control. Motivation, then, can be attacked as parents, teachers, or bosses conclude, "You didn't try hard enough." *Attacks on well-intended motivation sabotage self-esteem.* By the time people are adults they have learned to compensate, but the specter of shame lurks. This is one reason why the learning disorder and psychological problems are intertwined like a tightly knit fabric.

The idea of an orchestra with all the instruments representing different aspects of one's self is a good analogy. ULD is the horn section and the rest of the instruments are psychological factors. Each section has its own properties, and when combined, the results can range from delicate music to unbearable noise. If the horns are too loud, they will block out the most sophisticated aria of the flute.

Instruments in orchestras can be separated from one another. But ULD and the psychological consequences of shame are not quite so easily separable. That is why psychotherapy can be very helpful in unraveling innate learning disabilities from psychological factors. A psychotherapist who understands the emotional consequences of ULD will not try to change a client's personality or disregard his or her learning disabilities. The therapeutic focus here is understanding the influence of one on the other.

Finding a Therapist

People with ULD are caught between two disciplines: psychology and learning disabilities. The field of learning disabilities is part of education, and its focus is on academic achievement. The field of psychology focuses mainly on motivation and behavior. Falling between the cracks, a person with ULD needs a psychotherapist who is aware of how learning disabilities influence emotions or a learning disability specialist who is psychologically attuned.

In a perfect world, psychotherapists and learning disability specialists would consult. Schools training psychotherapists, however, do not generally provide courses on how LD influences psychological development. In time, this interface will happen more and more, but for now the field is too new.

The person with ULD is really the expert, although this may sound incredible. No one knows more about these experiences than the survivor. There are therapists who are eager to learn from their clients. These therapists can then use their expertise to help the clients gain a new understanding of how ULD affects on one's emotional life.

Finding a therapist who can suspend his or her beliefs in order to learn about ULD is a necessity. There may be disagreements but *the client's point of view must be respected*. For example, sometimes people find themselves saying "uh huh," thinking how smart the therapist is, when nothing is really making sense. Although the client looks interested, confusion and stupidity reign. In essence, the client is in the chasm and this experience needs to be discussed. Without this input, the therapist is in the dark. Alternatively, discussion about the chasm may then open the door to understanding more about ULD. Therapists who become patronizing in the face of the chasm need to be confronted. Lack of change in the therapist would indicate the necessity for a different clinician.

For example, a therapist was treating a client with "New Age beliefs." LD testing found that undiagnosed learning disabilities had caused great discrepancies between the client's intellect and his achievements. The metaphysical differences in philosophy between these two were quite apparent, but the client was willing to teach the therapist about his worldview. The client believed energy was entering his body from outside sources. He and the therapist could work with this belief system, and the client eventually came to understand how his ULD interfered with this free

flow of energy and blocked his wishes for success. From his perspective, recognizing his ULD allowed him to understand how
the energies in the world interfaced with his ability to learn.

Is testing beneficial? If so, when? First of all, there is no need
to hurry. If problems mostly involve emotional adjustment, putting off testing and finding a psychotherapist might be the first
priority. Much can be understood from memories about how one
learned and did not learn. In fact, many people have more than
adequately compensated. Help in understanding how this hidden
dimension of ULD affected emotional life may lead to the conclusion: "If it ain't broke, don't fix it."

A therapist, however, may feel that undiagnosed learning disabilities are constricting potential and that testing could be beneficial because testing:

- corroborates intelligence, which can give self-esteem a
  much-needed boost;
- isolates and defines strengths and weaknesses, which can
  give one a handle in working on more readily understood
  problems; and
- allows a person to develop a more understanding and for-
  giving view of him or herself.

If testing is indicated, a qualified specialist who understands
adult LD testing will be needed. People who test for LD are either educational psychologists or learning disability specialists.
Interviewing the person with the following questions in mind can
be helpful:

- Is the tester empathic?
- Has this person tested adults? If so, how many? Can she or
  he understand and verbalize the difference between testing
  adults and children?
- Does he or she know how to test for learning disabilities as
  opposed to psychological problems?

These questions help deal with the gaps within each discipline. For example, the field of learning disabilities provides a great deal of training for testing. Most of that training, however, focuses on children. Information on how to test adults is scant. The training, furthermore, focuses more on testing procedures than on the emotional consequences of being tested.

The psychologist, on the other hand, may not have specialized knowledge about LD. She or he might not have the ability or inclination to provide the extensive tests necessary to tease out complicated learning disabilities. Educational psychologists (EdDs) are an option, because they are often trained to test for LD.

People with ULD have had the picture of their intelligence obscured by some overall *average* score. When scores are averaged, strengths and weaknesses are combined into a total score. This means nothing. This final score is useless because intelligent, uneven learners need to understand the *difference* between strengths and weaknesses. Then, once it is determined where one's intellectual strengths lie, creative strategies can be employed to deal with newly understood weaknesses.

Resilience is usually understood as a counterpart to risk because it involves the capacity to adapt in the face of risk. However, there is another way of looking at resilience. In conclusion, I want to suggest that people with LD incorporate resilience in a different light—not just in reaction to risk (or as a form of protection against risk) but as a way of *looking for* risk, because figuring out how to navigate in a world with challenges is enhancing and is a perpetual form of pleasure. Dealing with risk continually (as some people with LD have to do) changes or transforms people.

Resilience in this context, then, is a form of learning that only comes about when people become competent in dealing with challenges. Many with LD have walked this path. They are stronger and more resilient because *learning* how to adapt to challenging circumstances is transforming. They look for risk because there is pleasure in the process of dealing with challenges. The mountain climber doesn't take risks to just protect herself. She loves the *experience of the challenge*.

Chapter 8

Revisiting Shame and Seeking

Now that you've heard the experiences of these valiantly brave people, this chapter will take a deeper look at how shame and seeking influenced these experiences. For those who are interested, this chapter will give more background and information on shame and seeking, while Chapter 13 will go into even greater depth to explore the history and neuropsychology of the seeking system.

Let's revisit one of Sparkly's experiences of feeling shame, and use this episode as a springboard for a deeper discussion about the nature of shame.

SPARKLY: You know, even now, knowing what I know, I still get so embarrassed when my learning disabilities stick out like a sore thumb. It's really terrible. I feel really embarrassed when I make a mistake reading . . . like over Christmas. You see, I was playing charades with my family. When it was my turn, I read my instructions, but I read them wrong. I read the whole thing wrong! So, I acted out this whole thing, and they guessed the title. But of course, the title was not what was written on the slip of paper I drew. They said: "This isn't it.". . . And I was so embarrassed. I made this joke, and everybody laughed, and my sister won. And I sat down, and I thought, "I wish I wouldn't have done that," you know, because I thought,

"This is my family. They don't care if I can't read." I was still . . . I was overwhelmed with embarrassment. "How did I read that wrong? Why did I read that wrong?" It was very strong.

I was humiliated. And it was so . . . I mean, the perfect stage setting. There I am, standing up there by myself, doing all this crazy stuff. They guess it. (What she read but not what was written.) I'm standing there, and there's silence in my . . . then my cousin goes, "That's not the title. You read it wrong!" And my finale was the big joke, and then, oh, my gosh! It was awful. It was unbelievable. [silence] But that's how that went.

Sparkly's experience of shame was shared by everyone in this study. People describe the shameful feelings of being shackled by inexplicable learning failures. The memories of these repeated shameful learning failures can seriously interfere with our desire to learn and master. So respecting and understanding the importance of the concept of shame can help us learn to circumvent the possible long-term influence it has on our sense of self and self-confidence.

To begin, and to help the reader understand the particular variety of suffering that Sparkly describes, I will give an introduction, definition, and description of something that we all know well but tend to avoid like the plague. This is shame.

SHAME

Shame is a painful emotion caused by an awareness of deficiencies or impropriety. The feeling creates a heightened sense of painful exposure that can cause a freezing response and withdrawal from others (Cozzolino 2002). It can be public or private. Public shame is triggered by external forces in our world such as the painful feelings experienced when being ridiculed or scorned by teachers, classmates, or family. Private shame is triggered by our memories of public shame. Once these feelings go into long term memory, our confidence can be undermined because it's too easy to believe that public condemnation is deserved. Of course, not all shame is bad. The feeling can help us become introspective so that we can figure out how to do or engage differently. There will be more discussion of good and bad shame later in the chapter.

In order to put shame into the proper context, let's look at a theory of its origins. The theory is an explanation of human emotions called "affect theory." Affects are innate biological responses that all humans—even six-week-old infants—have toward their environment. As people grow, their original affects evolve into complicated adult emotions (Basch 1988). Affects, then, are building blocks for an entire range of human emotional complexities. The phenomenon can be compared to a giant sixty-four-crayon box of Crayolas. There are only eight basic colors: red, orange, yellow, and so on. Most of the sixty-four are fancy colors, such as tangerine, raw umber, aubergine, and periwinkle. The fancy colors are simply mixtures of the original basic colors. Affects are our basic emotional colors.

Fundamental affects are never outgrown. Adults often have the same emotions as children. An adult can get as excited by learning to drive, fly, or ski as a child who has taken her first steps. To understand how shame fits in, and how it can constrict learning, knowledge about affect theory will be helpful. Let's begin with some background.

Psychologist Sylvan Tomkins videotaped children and infants to examine their feeling states and reactions to the world. By slowing down and observing the tapes, he discovered that every infant is born with nine instinctive "knee jerk" affects. What are these affects? Why are they important? Affect theory maintains that these "primitive" affects are, at bottom, what motivate all of us. The categories below each cover a range of emotion. These affects can be divided into three categories: (1) positive affects; (2) negative affects; and (3) other, or "auxiliary" affects.

The positive affects are:

1. interest that can increase to excitement;
2. enjoyment that can increase to joy; and

3. surprise that can increase to startle.

The negative affects are:

4. distress that can increase to anguish;
5. anger that can increase to rage; and
6. fear that can increase to terror.

The auxiliary affects are reactions to environmental stimuli:

7. dissmell (our tendency to withdraw from noxious odors);
8. distaste (our tendency to withdraw from unpleasant food);

and

9. shame that can increase to humiliation.

The intensity of the experience will determine the power of the reaction. It is similar to listening to music. If the volume is very low, we do not pay attention. If the volume is very high, it becomes painful. As children grow, they learn to think more complex thoughts, and these thoughts become integrated and can modulate these primary emotions. However, basic affects never lose their function. Obviously, adults still become startled, feel pleasure, and recoil from spoiled food. Adults and children may startle at different things, but the emotional reactions are built from the same basic elements.

This is particularly true of shame. Over a lifetime, shame feels pretty much the same, though as we age, we generally learn better ways to avoid it. The outward appearance of shame is lowered head and eyes and sometimes a blushing face. Inside, a person experiences intense exposure and heightened vulnerability. An individual feels cut off from other human beings and would like to "crawl into a hole."

Because of their painful experiences of learning chasms, people with ULD know all about shame. They never know when public shame will crop up, since it is a response to life's demands. For example, one participant who has a master's degree reads very, very slowly. She describes her exquisite embarrassment every time she eats out because she simply does not have enough time to scan the menu, so she enters a "reading chasm." When the waiter is hovering after everyone else has ordered, she experiences deep humiliation. Her way of compensating, if the restaurant is new, is simply to order the first thing she sees on the menu. If it is a familiar restaurant, she memorizes everything on the menu.

Why is shame needed? Shame is painful. To the human organism, however, pain is an important message. It prompts one to understand that something is wrong or that reacting differently to the environment is required. As Sparkly said in the first chapter, "I didn't know what it was, but there was something that was just standing in my way and that I wasn't stupid." Carl Goldberg puts it another way: "The constructive intent of shame is the realization that one does not know, and that which one does not know is knowable and should be known" (1991, p. 159). Shame can inhibit learning, but it can also propel learning. Thus, there are two types of shame: constructive and destructive. Let's begin with constructive or healthy shame.

HEALTHY SHAME

Constructive shame enhances resilience. It cues or alerts one to possible humiliating pitfalls, which can then be avoided. It is a protective device that keeps people out of trouble; it signals that something is not working, that we should stop and try something new. In this sense, the chasm is helpful because it prompts or forces us to look for alternatives ways to learn.

Shame keeps people on the right track, both culturally and as individuals. Without shame, social systems would falter because the specter of shame impels their members to follow cultural rules. On the individual level, healthy shame prompts withdrawal from a potentially hurtful situation by shutting down interest. In the case of personal relationships, it alerts people to rejection—perhaps someone did not move to shake an extended hand. In this case, shame propels the withdrawal of one's hand.

Another form of shame can occur within oneself, without anybody else around. For example, a woman may wish to have an affair with her best friend's husband. As she experiences shame over her forbidden wishes (as opposed to her guilt over how she would hurt her friend), she stops and "resets" her desires.

Healthy shame serves another critical function: it helps people reconnect with others. When an individual is ashamed, he or she pulls back and thinks about things. Then the person reaches out and tries again. The best example of this is pulling back, reflecting, and reaching out again to say, "I'm sorry." The outward expression of this disconnect/reconnection signals others that a friend or co-worker may need help.

So, healthy shame helps us know where we go wrong and when to stop and rethink. But not all shame helps a person grow. Leon Wurmser, speaking of excessively experienced shame, says "Shame is the degradation that has already occurred and the enduring sense of self-contempt and unreality that ensues from such humiliation and mortification" (Wurmser, 1987, p. 67). I call this destructive shame.

DESTRUCTIVE SHAME

Destructive shame is a private repetitive pattern of self-denigration. It is the outcome of this feeling experienced too intensely and too often. It occurs when healthy shame fails to do its job. When a person gets in an awkward situations such as learning chasms and feels ashamed, yet cannot solve the problem, the shame repeats itself again and again and plunges him or her further and further into a hole.

If shame becomes too repetitive, a chronic sense of shame develops. A child who is continually shamed by chasm experiences may eventually give up hope of reconnection. Then the child begins to attach the sense of shame not to the action or situation that triggered it, but to aspects of him or herself.

Clearly, shame plays a large role in children growing up with ULD. A student will become interested in a subject and tackle it. Suddenly, the rug is pulled out from under the child when the undiagnosed learning disability hinders performance. For example, a promising elementary math student may hit the chasm because she falters on multiplication tables, where memory skills become paramount. She experiences a common shame trigger: failure. She tries and fails, over and over, and soon she develops chronic shame in her long term memory. Another example: an adult who is a good but slow reader begins to avoid reading to curb further feelings of shame because reading "takes too long." When help is offered, the individual may avoid it because he or she is still too busy fleeing additional failure/shame experiences.

Destructive shame leads to withdrawal. A person expects that a particular task will create learning chasms and shame her. She fears even to try. She will go to great lengths to avoid whatever might lead to failure and more shame. Destructive shame, then, stifles initiative and undermines potential. This cripples intellectual pursuits.

For example, individuals who love to write, and put beautiful thoughts on paper, may lose that love after hearing too many sarcastic comments about their grammar and spelling. People with ULD learn to curtail their interests. Their intelligence takes a beating because, although they are obviously bright, they never seem to do quite well enough. When expectations are consistently dashed, shame is close behind.

Shame can also sabotage motivation. Our culture believes that hard work and adequate intelligence are a foolproof recipe for success. Individuals with ULD become confused because hard work pays off in their areas of strength. Yet, in other areas, they work and work but fail because they cannot circumvent their chasms. Their lack of achievement baffles them and those around them (Baum, Renzulli, and Herbert, 1994). Parents, teachers, and perhaps even bosses will question their motivation and accuse them of slacking. Often, people take the criticism to heart, and actually begin to consider themselves lazy. Of course, they can be hardworking and resourceful and still not able to overcome a learning disorder by force of will. This is yet another source of destructive shame.

Intellectual curiosity can also be compromised. ULD can create destructive shame by destroying one's ability to become excited about even those things that one does well. As stated previously, one of the primary affects is excitement. Like healthy shame, excitement is crucial to development because it propels learning. Children with ULD can lose some of their ability to become excited because their victories are hollow. For instance, a child with ULD can write an excellent paper, and even get a good grade, but nevertheless find herself berated by a teacher for "sloppy" spelling mistakes that would be easily avoided if she would just "be careful" or "put in the time." Ordinarily, the student would become excited about a high grade and become even more motivated to do the work. With ULD, achievement fails to become a motivating experience because initial excitement is cut off by simultaneous, unexplained failure.

Thus, children with undiagnosed learning disabilities can develop a chronic, destructive sense of shame as they perceive their growing lack of competence. The shame itself hinders learning. They find themselves in a vicious cycle: chasms lead to failure, failure leads to shame, which leads to further failure, and so on.

However, as we shall see, the people in this study, though haunted by the trauma of chasms causing of chronic shame, also possessed the ability to seek and persevere that helped them fight against the debilitating reactions to shame. Although Sparkly has massive reading problems, after being tested, she took the bull by the horns and got whatever help she could. She has managed to live with what is for her a disappointing and shameful fact: her written work will never reflect her intelligence and ability to verbalize. Even so, she has the capacity to seek by never giving up. In other words, she never stopped trying.

Somehow, over time, people can reconnect with their strengths and became resilient. How do they do that? How do people become resilient? I believe that an understanding of the seeking system: our brain's neurological capacity to explore will help us answer these questions. This seeking system explains why people with ULD can try new ways of responding to shame-induced events. This system allows people with ULD to overcome their shame through an innate driving force that creates perseverance, exploration, and the capacity to learn in new ways. In other words, the seeking system can provide a bridge between shame and becoming resilient. The following section describes the seeking system and explains how the seeking system can create a resilient response to shame.

THE SEEKING SYSTEM: THE BRIDGE BETWEEN SHAME AND RESILIENCE

"My dyslexia forced me to think for myself."

"Anticipation is the key to success."

The seeking system is one of seven biological systems consisting of genetic neurochemical networks in our brains that work to satisfy our biological fundamental urge to actively discover. All mammals have these systems because of our common evolutionary heritage.

Jaak Panksepp, the scientist who identified the seeking system, also identified other primal emotions or systems within our mammalian brains. These systems are: Seeking, rage, fear, lust, care, panic/grief, and play. Just as all mammals have the fundamental urge to play, to lust, to nurture and be nurtured, for example, we all have the urge to seek: to actively explore and discover.

This quote from Panksepp and Biven's book The Archeology of the Mind (2012, p. 103) explains so much:

> It is evident that the SEEKING-EXPECTANCY system is a general-purpose system for obtaining all kinds of resources that exist in the world, from nuts to knowledge, so to speak. In short it participates in all appetitive behaviors that precede consummation; it generates the urge to search for any and all of the "fruits" of the environment; it energizes the dy-

namic eagerness for positive experiences from tasty food to
sexual possibilities to political power; it galvanizes people
and animals to overcome dangers either by opposing them
or by escaping to safety. . . . But in the beginning, at birth, it
is just "a goad without a goal" (Panksepp, 1971) that opens
up the gateways to engagement with the world, and hence
knowledge.

So, even if we are a little nervous about exploring new situations, we are still curious about walking in woods that we've never
walked in, or we will go to a store that's just opened, or go after
that computer-game goblin in unknown territory—just because
it's there. The woods may be lovely or full of trash, the store may
be full of bargains or overpriced, or there may be an avatar death
around the next corner. But our seeking system drives us to try it.

So, clearly, if our path to learning is blocked by ULD, our
seeking system will create the urge to look for new alternatives.
Consider what scholar has to say:

SCHOLAR: Well, first of all, my dyslexia has developed analytic
    skills for me for what we might call independent thinking,
    though I don't want to use that in a clichéd sort of way. You
    know, when the old grid or patterns don't work, the mind
    has the capacity to think of new creative ways of being; and
    that's kind of nice in a way. My dyslexia interfered with these
    "normal" grids or patterns and forced me to learn to think
    for myself. I don't mean that in the jargonistic way that we
    typically say that; but rather, a lot of people solve problems by
    having people teach them to solve problems. [Because of my
    dyslexia] I couldn't be taught in the usual way and, I think,
    would go off and find my own solutions, which is exemplified
    by my scholarly work.

Let me underscore that the seeking system is not a reward system. That's a different part of our brain. This system involves the
pleasure of activity itself. It's lovely to fall in love, but the activity
in courtship can be an awful lot of fun in and of itself.

These primitive instinctual feelings instantaneously tell us when it's safe (or something is good) or when there is danger (and something is bad.) If our toddler steps into a busy intersection, we grab the child instantaneously before we even begin to think about the dangers. We just automatically act to keep the child safe.

Conversely, for many people, planning a vacation can be as much fun as taking the vacation. It's fun to explore and learn when we anticipate pleasure. This is true whether we are almost finished writing a paper, baking a cake, or getting a hole in one in the next to the last hole during a round of golf. There is great pleasure in the anticipation of success.

Clearly, the seeking system as Panksepp defines it is the bridge between shame and resilience. When we seek, we can go for:

- our strengths despite stressors
- our awareness (using emotional attention) of various specific problems
- our capacity to weigh alternative solutions to problems
- our ability to try out (risk) alternative approaches
- our drive to connect with others who can be helpful
- our sense of humor (to distill the intensity of shame)

Let's underscore the relationship between shame, seeking systems, and undiagnosed learning disabilities: Failures can clearly be due to the chasms of LD creating the emotional distress of shame. Then given our human drive to seek competency, when tools (skills) fail because of ULD, painful emotions such as hopelessness can take over and create further complications. Clearly, the key to escaping from such hopelessness is to employ our seeking system. Through the identification of learning disabilities as a problem, the seeking system can actively address methods for protecting the endangered self caused by the ULD. Therefore, by using our seeking system as a bridge between shame and resilience, resilience is reinvented over and over again.

Chapter 9

Conclusions

Growing up with ULD shapes individuals in myriad ways. It can foster an individual's determination, creativity, and unique talents. It can also make school a painful experience, block achievement, and erode self-esteem and relationships with others. The negative emotional consequences of ULD can be prevented, or at least modified. As educators, parents, psychotherapists, and concerned citizens we can work to give people with LD better opportunities to enhance their resilience.

Educators, especially, are in the position to profoundly influence young lives. Consider Sparkly's school experience:

SPARKLY: I remember coming home from school and being exhausted. I'd always have to be a step ahead of them [the teachers] so that they wouldn't ask *those* questions: "Where's your homework? Why didn't you do it?" I wouldn't know what to tell them. I didn't know why I didn't do it. I'd sit down and I wouldn't see anything. It was frustrating. I wanted the information everybody else was getting, and I wanted to get it the *way* they were getting it. And it was also more frustrating when some teachers reacted with that ignorance. I mean, as each class went on, not only didn't they care, but they were almost rude and condescending about it like, "Nice excuse. Why don't you do your work?" At that point I was ready to quit.

Since Sparkly's experience of judgmental teachers was a common one for the participants in this study, I feel obliged to comment on our educational system and the way children with ULD are taught.

Reporting about the great Leonardo da Vinci, National Public Radio once said, "Leonardo was a genius, but without the proper tools, he could have ended up finger-painting." Without necessary skills, intelligence dies on the vine. Children who grow up without skills have problems achieving, whether or not they have learning disabilities. Similarly, people who cannot read suffer, whether the reading problem is due to a constitutional deficit or environmental neglect. All citizens in this country need the skills necessary for a fulfilling life.

Academic standards, of course, cannot be compromised. Standards in skill-building must remain high, but the methods used to achieve those standards need to be flexible (Gardner, 1983). A student who is not a visual learner may be able to learn necessary skills through the sense of touch. Copying from the board is not the only way to learn to write. Some people may learn more easily if they can feel three-dimensional letters. For some students, to avoid the chasm and consequential Imprisoned Intelligence, learning computer skills may keep their intelligence mobilized. Inflexible teaching methods can contribute to Imprisoned Intelligence with all of its emotional underpinnings and aftermath.

Another serious impediment to learning is the inability of many educators to deal constructively with the chasm. Teachers must be able to identify and understand this phenomenon. The chasm is not bad. It is a pragmatic clue that another approach is necessary because the current one is not working. It is not the chasm that causes constriction of intelligence; it is the shame and withdrawal that follow. For example, if a student could say to a teacher, "I'm in the chasm," perhaps the teacher would more readily understand that motivation is not necessarily the issue. The teacher could then help the student clarify the problem and offer different teaching tools.

Emotions precede and follow learning, and teachers need to learn how to integrate emotional reactions into their lexicon of teaching strategies. It is easier to learn when one likes the teacher and is excited about the topic.

Academics and clinicians must focus their energies on this problem if substantial change is to take place. This book is based on a study of subjective experiences of adults who discovered their ULD. More studies, both subjective and empirical, must be done. It is striking that such a variety of people have had similar experiences that evolve into a similar developmental process. I hope that this book will add another dimension of diagnosis and treatment for psychotherapists and educational personnel who see people with ULD; but far more research needs to be done. There are already many dedicated professionals who are concerning themselves with this problem, and I believe that the field will continue to grow.

Imprisoned intelligence is a social problem that concerns not only educators and clinicians, but everyone. Like other previously "hidden" issues, such as sexual abuse, workplace discrimination, and homophobia, it requires public awareness to spur social change. Concerned citizens can participate in their local school boards, join LD organizations, and let the government know that they support LD programs and research. Members of the media can ensure that the issue gets adequate coverage. There are slowly evolving changes. For example, *The New York Times* reports that people with autism and Asperger's syndrome are demanding that they be accepted in our culture. They feel that they have strength and weaknesses intrinsic to their brains, not pathological problems that need to be fixed or cured (Harmon, 2004).

Many of my interviewees were able to persevere, survive, and thrive in the face of their LD, but what about those who cannot? ULD hits the economically disadvantaged especially hard: remedies such as psychotherapy, tutors, and LD testing are prohibitively expensive. It is difficult for many to get a basic LD remediation, let alone help for the emotional aftermath of LD. Change may come slowly, but it has the potential to drastically improve

the quality of life for many. When LD and its emotional consequences are understood and treated in this country, we will be
significantly closer to providing a truly public education.

I would like to end this section of the book by making a final
comment on the enormous difficulties faced on a daily basis by
those with LD. I have a sense of awe and respect for their attempts, no matter how successful, to deal with these difficulties.
No word can really capture the profound achievements of those
with LD, who most often fail to get any recognition for their la-
bors. If this book has helped even a tiny bit to encourage others
with LD, it was entirely worth the effort.

Part Two

Psychotherapeutic, Historical, and Theoretical Perspectives

Chapter 10

Psychotherapy: A Lantern for the Darkness

INTERVIEWER: So you couldn't stay in college and had to leave. OK? You came home.

BRILLIANT: Yes. My mother took me to see a therapist known for his interest in learning disabilities. He was the first person I talked to. She had no suspicion of any learning disability. She had no real definite answers as to what was going on. And, in fact, she probably thought it was her fault as a parent. So she sent me to somebody she respected, a social worker or somebody, and he brought it up.

He brought up an outside reason [the LD] for why I was having troubles in college. Before this, I just accepted that life was difficult because I had so much trouble learning and because I felt so stupid (even though I didn't always get bad grades). Sometimes I felt stupid, or didn't know what was wrong. So to think that he had an answer. . . .

The therapist recommended that Brilliant get tested for LD.

BRILLIANT: Those tests did show I had high intelligence. And I never knew that I did. I thought I was smart, that I worked hard, and that I was smart enough. But I didn't know that I was *very* smart. And in the fact that I compensated in the way I did showed that I was *very, very* smart. It validated my brain.

My head swelled [laughter]. Really, you know, I had really good feelings.

INTERVIEWER: Once you knew about the testing, did you continue in psychotherapy?

BRILLIANT: Oh yes. I would always come back to . . . I never quite believed it was true. . . . Just because it was such an un-reality. It wasn't part of my life experience or understanding of myself for . . . years. And then, suddenly, there's this new information about LD given to me. Suddenly. And it had to be integrated. I found a way to dialogue about this, and psychotherapy allowed me to process parts of my past in a new way. Memories from my past would come up about, "Oh. So this was happening because of the LD," and this gave me a new understanding of how I went about and grew. And then also to understand my emotional self. That was a whole other [thing]I had never done before.

Going to a therapist was something I might have done anyway, but doing it with this information [about the LD] was different. I had a place to talk about feeling like I had "missing parts." Now, the feeling about my having "missing parts" is a little bit better controlled. It doesn't become disintegrated. The feeling never gets so overwhelming that I really fall into a deep depression. And it probably used to all the time. I can have perspective on it. The feeling doesn't get all out of hand.

IS PSYCHOTHERAPY WORTHWHILE?

Determining how psychotherapy might be helpful to those with Imprisoned Intelligence requires an adequate definition of the word "psychotherapy." One would think that with all the books on the subject, this question would be easy to answer. It is not. Conventional definitions of psychotherapy are often limiting and misleading. *Webster's New Collegiate Dictionary* from 1981, for instance, says psychotherapy is "treatment of mental or emotional disorders or related bodily ills by psychological means." This definition is based on a medical model and focuses on pathology. Psychotherapy can, of course, be used to treat psychopathology, but it is also used by: (1) people who are in pain, for whatever reason, and (2) people who wish to understand or change their lives to a degree that they have not been able to on their own. The cultural stereotype that psychotherapy is only for the insane or hopelessly neurotic is unfortunate indeed. Rather than considering therapy as visiting a doctor for a cure, one can think of it as voluntary schooling. It is like a night class taken purely for one's own benefit. Therapy is part of a person's education, and it can enhance resilience.

Psychotherapy is difficult to describe because it can affect nearly any aspect of life: relationships, intellect, passion, creativity, sexuality, spirituality. My definition is this: psychotherapy is interactive learning about yourself and your relationships with others. This interaction involves verbal and nonverbal communication about one's emotional life with a trusted professional. It involves understanding how life's evolving patterns help and hinder daily functioning. Psychotherapy can be helpful for those with ULD because psychotherapeutic goals can include bridging strengths and weaknesses. It allows individuals to view themselves in a more realistic and hopeful light while going through the painful and difficult task of facing vulnerabilities. This process is manageable when seen in light of potential and resiliency.

Psychotherapy is not always necessary for adults with ULD. Many people have learned on their own to compensate more than adequately. Their sense of self is intact and they lead fulfilling lives. Others have found that assistance from a learning disability specialist is all that they need to proceed successfully.

But when survivors suffer from Imprisoned Intelligence, appropriate psychotherapy can indeed be beneficial. Imprisoned Intelligence leads to frustration. When frustrated, people tend to blame themselves and self-esteem plummets. Appropriate psychotherapeutic experiences, over time, can curtail this cycle and reverse damage to self.

The following questions may help the therapist decide whether a person is suffering from Imprisoned Intelligence and needs psychotherapy.

- Does a person suffer from the chasm: the seemingly endless and painful place of nonlearning?
- When one is trying to learn does the person feel roboticized or stunned?
- Is time a problem? Does it take longer to finish?
- Is the individual afraid to act on his or her initiative or be spontaneous?
- Is he or she afraid to speak up?
- Is there a perception that one's efforts are negatively judged by others?
- Is feeling lazy, dumb, or just not caring prevalent?
- Are there feelings of spaciness and/or getting lost easily?
- Does the person know the right hand from the left?
- Does the person concentrate intensely on one thing but in the process manage to neglect other critical responsibilities?
- Are stopgap measures used to avoid embarrassment?
- Does the person know they are smart but feel stupid?
- Does the person consider himself or herself an underachiever?
- Are there real differences between intelligence and achievements at school or at work?
- Even though intelligence is apparent, are faux pas often made?
- Do people unknowingly embarrass themselves in social situations and find out only when told by someone else?
- Are difficult subjects in school avoided even though intelligence tests show potential?
- Is reading or math hated?
- Do individuals automatically think about how long it will take to read a book? Is reading boring?
- Was the individual considered an underachiever in school? Was this a source of embarrassment?

- Is daydreaming a problem?
- Are job changes occurring because one's temper cannot be controlled?
- Does an obviously smart person appear not to be working up to potential?
- Does it take successful people longer than others to complete projects?
- Is one's life partitioned into segments: sometimes excelling and sometimes failing?

Many of these questions can also apply to people who suffer from problems other than ULD, but they have particular importance for uneven learners *because of the emotional residue ULD can leave*. Effective psychotherapy, then, is complicated and may touch upon myriad of aspects of the self. The following parable elaborates:

> Once upon a time there was a respected artist who created many fine pieces of tapestry that were hanging in several art galleries in town. He was considered a success. But inside, he felt frustrated. A tapestry he had envisioned for most of his creative life was eluding him.
>
> This inner picture had haunted him since childhood. It involved a hodgepodge of material with many different colors and textures: threads of silk, metal, and cotton, yarns with vastly different sizes, textures, and materials. In essence, this work represented his life.
>
> Even when he was a child this image was in his mind and as his artistic talents developed, he would play with its design and start the project over and over again. However, it never came to fruition because the knots that would maintain the structure and lock in the pattern would not hold. Obviously, critical knots were missing.

Seeing this image but being unable to create it drove him crazy. He decided to take a couple of years off just to work on this project. He tried one technique after another. Sometimes, he couldn't even get started because it wouldn't come together. At other times, he felt satisfied because the work seemed to be solid and hold its structure. But, over time, it always softened and became distorted, losing its shape and definition. Different techniques were tried over and over again. Experts were consulted. They told him to forget it, to move on to another project. But he knew this tapestry needed to be created and wouldn't give it up.

After many months, he become more and more discouraged. One day, he heard of a magical weaver in a far-off land. He decided to go to her. After arduous travel through dangerous forests and deserts, he came upon an oasis. There she was, sitting under a beautiful palm tree near a rippling brook, weaving what seemed to be a very simple fabric. Her smile created hope and peace in his heart. He respectfully approached and, through an interpreter, asked, "Please, can you help me?"

She reached for his unfinished tapestry, looked very curious, and smiled. She was obviously both puzzled and intrigued. She stared at his undefined work for many days. He painstakingly showed her how he tried to create his patterns, demonstrating all the knots he used in his attempt to lock the patterns in place. She kept asking more and more questions. He got tired of teaching and wondered if the trip had been a mistake.

Finally, she said she had learned what was wrong. The knots he knew and used to lock in colors and patterns would not work because the creation was too complicated and dense. That was why some knots, over time, began to loosen. He learned that he needed to expand his repertoire of knots.

He was very discouraged. He had spent a lifetime learning how to tie different knots. In fact, he was known as a knot expert and it was a source of pride. It was a jolt to learn that crucial knots were missing. He now understood that his knowledge, up to that point, was not enough to allow him to bring his vision to life.

The interpreter asked if he wanted to learn from her. Despite his disappointment, he nodded. After all, he came this far.

He learned that his right-handedness obstructed his capacity to create knots that would hold the patterns in place—that he needed to use both hands equally. In other words, he had to become ambidextrous. This would allow him to create new knots and give him the freedom to choose alternatives that never occurred to him before. She freed him from a right-handed bias.

He went home knowing that his work was cut out for him. It would not be easy to train his brain to depend on his left hand as easily as his right. But hope had returned. Although mastering these new techniques would be time-consuming and difficult, he knew he had reached a decisive road, tortuous as it was, that would lead him to the creation of his vision.

The lives of people with ULD are like this tapestry. The threads are the self and all that has been learned. The patterns woven and knotted from those threads are the course one's life takes. The knots are the tactics used and the choices individuals make to direct their lives.

This story suggests that psychotherapy can teach new ways to go about living a meaningful life and can keep strong hope for a better life. By attempting to understand the patterns of anxiety and depression that accompany learning failures, individuals can learn how to interfere with those patterns. This is what therapy can do for people with Imprisoned Intelligence.

Many adults who suffer from Imprisoned Intelligence could benefit from psychotherapy because they instinctively know they have vulnerable spots in their tapestries. They know that, under certain circumstances, knots can loosen and the pattern in the tapestry can lose its shape and definition. For example, a bright and creative but disorganized person can function very well under a boss who is focused on outcome, not process. In other words, the boss does not care how the employee does something as long as it gets done. No one cares if the employee makes a mess as long as the outcome is satisfactory. But if this old boss is replaced by a detail-oriented person (who expects process to be as perfect as outcome), then the employee might be in trouble. Demanding neatness from smart but disorganized people can evoke intense anxiety. Too much anxiety will keep us from thinking and performing effectively.

Psychotherapeutic knowledge is power. First of all, because of the focus on feelings, psychotherapists can help people examine their vulnerabilities in a safe, empathic environment. Anxiety can be kept within tolerable limits. Only within a trusting and respectful relationship can an individual freely express his or her true feelings; if there is worry about ridicule or a cold response, the person will not feel safe enough to start the exploration process. Safety is especially crucial for those who suffer from chronic shame, since the trauma originated in unsympathetic learning environments. However, once one finds a safe environment to explore one's weaknesses, an amazing flowering takes place. It is a great relief to talk without fear of reprisal, and a new learning process can begin.

Second, psychotherapy can help uneven learners recognize the emotional complications that cause the problems in their tapestry: For example, some necessary threads may be missing, and new skills may need to be learned. Emotional attention helps focus on what is missing. Someone who has avoided math because he cannot copy numbers accurately may have to feel and understand his anxiety about math before he can bite the bullet and learn some math. A therapist can provide necessary emotional support through this difficult time. Then, chances of learning enough math to complete a college degree are greater.

New knots, or techniques for coping with LD-related weaknesses, can be learned. In these situations, it is the learning disability itself that interferes with the unfolding of potential. For example, an uneven learner whose brain automatically reverses letters may be a superb writer who cannot get started because she will never overcome her inability to spell or master grammar. She becomes afraid to try again after so many failures. By focusing emotional attention on her fear, she will find words for it, and the verbalization in itself can diminish the effects of being afraid to try. Once the fear is validated as legitimate, a therapist who recognizes the dyslexia can more easily encourage this individual to use a computer with a spelling checker, or have a friend edit his work. The computer or editor then becomes a "bypass" that frees his intelligence by getting around the learning disability. Then it becomes easier for him to express himself and use his gifts.

Some hidden threads may need to be highlighted or clarified. Therapy can provide a platform to unearth strengths that have been invisible. Sometimes, potential can be overlooked. For example, a young gang member who dropped out of school because he could not read may assume that his keen understanding of automobiles and guns is no big deal. But if a therapist had been called in to attend to his behavior problems, picked up on the learning difficulties, and given attention to his reading problems, this young man might have become an engineer.

Many times, people deal with fear through avoidance. For example, many intelligent people avoid attempting to obtain graduate degrees because they fear research and mathematics (particularly statistics). Psychotherapy gives us the opportunity to uncover and deal with these fears and helps us figure out how to meet our goals.

One's life tapestry has to be cohesive enough to withstand outside scrutiny. For some, psychotherapy is a necessary preparation for LD testing or consultation with an LD specialist. Both of these procedures, by their very nature, focus on exposing disabilities. Being exposed in this way may be too painful for someone whose self-esteem has been damaged by years of chronic shame. A psychotherapist can help mitigate such painful feelings. Just sharing one's pain often serves to reduce it, and gaining insight into causes may help even more. Also, a therapist can offer support while one undergoes the sessions, which makes them much more bearable.

A few more words on psychotherapy and LD specialists: Interventions from LD specialists can be essential to ULD sufferers. But if shame/blame patterns have been internalized, then learning disability specialists have to deal with emotional consequences that fall outside their area of expertise. If individuals believe they are stupid, it makes the LD specialist's job much more difficult. In a nutshell, without some expectation of success, learning anything becomes difficult to impossible. An understanding psychotherapist can intervene and address this pattern of discouragement. Psychotherapists have been trained to understand and disrupt downward spirals of low self-esteem. Therefore, working with a learning disability specialist will be more effective if psychological patterns can first be understood.

In summary, going to a psychotherapist is like consulting a master weaver about a tapestry with patterns that one does not quite understand. Examining developmental and current patterns is vital, because only an understanding of the tapestry's overall design can enhance resilience by allowing an individual to alter it to properly reflect his or her ambitions and goals.

WHAT CAN BE EXPECTED FROM PSYCHOTHERAPY?

One factor found in resilient people is the need to be in control. That feels good. Psychotherapy can provide that for people. The patient needs to be in control of the treatment. The therapist must respect the patient's choice to accept or reject therapist's suggestions or intervention. The most important piece of psychotherapy for people with LD is to help them feel in control of more and more of their lives. It begins with psychotherapy.

When seeking psychotherapy, certain rights are inalienable and self-evident. Essential for everyone, but especially for people with ULD, is mutual respect between client and therapist. Uneven learners become embarrassed when their vulnerabilities are exposed by an overly critical world. They do not need therapists who perpetuate this cycle, who, for example, are sarcastic and make them cringe. Respect involves:

- *Safety.* Feeling safe enough to talk about vulnerabilities and safe enough to show deficits without feeling "pathologized" contributes to feelings of self-cohesion. For example, people who have trouble expressing themselves verbally need to find therapists who can help modulate their embarrassment.
- *The client's agenda.* People intrinsically know what troubles them. Therapists can lead individuals into other areas that might be interesting but irrelevant. For example, a therapist can ask for a life history, but if the individual has a recall problem this particular modality will not be helpful. The platform for therapy needs to focus on the person's perceptions of his or her problems. The therapist's job is to facilitate the creation of that platform. The client's input is vital. Otherwise, old school patterns can be repeated in which the agenda is set by the teacher. Therapists are not teachers. At school, it is appropriate for the teacher to set the agenda. In therapy, it is appropriate for the individual to set the agenda.
- *Timing.* Many people with ULD could achieve beautifully if only they were given enough time. Being forced to finish at school or work before one is actually done is incredibly frustrating and stress-producing. This is one reenactment that should not occur in treatment. If time constraints are a problem, the last thing needed is a therapist who pushes people to speak before they are ready. Effective psycho-

therapy can best occur within a milieu of comfort. Feeling rushed makes this impossible.

- *The client's point of view.* Therapists need to understand the client's point of view. They may, however, respectfully offer alternative perspectives that expand knowledge.
- *Therapy will not work if clients become passive and compliant. Buying what the therapist says, hook, line, and sinker, even when it really doesn't make sense, will only further repeat an unpleasant pattern from the past.* Uneven learners know all about the experience of pretending to understand when they do not, to avoid embarrassment.

Fighting against one's passivity is difficult but necessary. Compliance sabotages learning. Good therapists are aware of this problem and are trained to understand how their clients perceive life. In other words, therapy usually is not learning new things out of the blue but *adding to what is known.* To add to what is known, one must *begin* with what is known. So, if a person feels like a bug under a microscope in the therapist's office, something is wrong.

How can this problem be addressed?

- *Talk about it.* Feelings of exposure and loss of self will be a jumping-off point for further learning. If the therapist does not understand and, after several tries, cannot be educated, find someone else!
- *Putting oneself first.* Therapists are trained and paid to listen to others. That is their job. Worry about hurting the therapists' feelings should not be a priority.
- *Validating the need for connection.* One overall goal of psychotherapy is to provide a sense of connection. This does not mean that disconnections never occur. But, when one feels safe enough, then issues of anger or discouragement can be worked through. In safety, all feelings can be talked about, which allows learning. That is the beauty of psychotherapy.
- *Struggle with the chasm.* One pitfall in treatment is the re-emergence of the chasm. Rest assured, there will be times

when an individual will feel disappointed because he or she is "not getting it." The first impulse may be to suffer silently, but therapy is intended for talking about painful feelings. Getting beyond the painful feelings involves talking about them first.

It is important to underscore here that the chasm is not bad. It is a message that a new approach is needed. When the chasm hits in treatment, it can be used as a springboard to talk about how and where the disconnections occurred. Many times, therapists make some kind of leap that cannot be followed. The chasm then becomes a marker or sign that indicates that there is a gap in understanding and steps need to be filled in.

Let me give an example. If a new client comes into the office, and the therapist falls into lecturing while the client's head keeps nodding, the discussion might unfold in the following way:

THERAPIST: Am I making sense here?

CLIENT: Well, I'm not sure I understand.

THERAPIST: It must be hard to sit there trying to understand while I go rambling on.

CLIENT: [nods]

THERAPIST: Can you tell me what that feels like?

CLIENT: Well, I feel stupid.

THERAPIST: When you feel stupid, that's a signal that we've gotten off base or I'm not on the money. So, we want to respect that feeling because it helps us get back on track. Would it be possible for you to let me know when this happens in the future?

It can be difficult not to buy into a therapist's logic, because it sounds reasonable. Logic is only helpful if it resonates with good common sense. If this is not happening, the client needs to let the therapist know about this "glitch." In this way both people are creating new patterns and knots. The tapestry will be stronger in the future.

THINGS LEARNED IN THERAPY

- If one finds a therapist disappointing, it is not the end of the world. Discussing disappointment with an empathic therapist reveals valuable knowledge about how one interacts with others, and the renewed connection with the therapist will be even stronger.
- When feelings are put into words, different perspectives and alternatives can be acquired, which then promotes flexibility and the capacity to adapt.
- Learning how a person feels about learning will free the individual to learn more.
- If getting a diagnosis is important, the therapist should scout around and find empathic testers who are aware of issues with adults. In my opinion, LD specialists who only work with children are not qualified to diagnose adults. Some issues for adults are different. Appropriate tests can help people find out:
  - How to get help from others.
  - How to interact better with others.
  - How to recognize the chasm, and how to help one-selfthrough it.
  - How an individual compensates, and how to capitalize on it.
  - How to find a clearer identity. Testing should underscore astronger sense of "who you are": one's strengths, weaknesses, and goals. These issues then will no longer seem so troubling and bewildering.

Psychotherapy for some people with LD can be so beneficial. Emotional attention about pride and shame, for example, can make the shame sting less, which leaves more room to think about one's strengths as well as one's weaknesses. Self-comfort is now more possible because one realizes that endlessly attributing failure to personality flaws is incorrect and unfair. There is a new meaning added on to the memories of past failures. Invisible or impenetrable obstacles (LD, ADD, etc.), not personality flaws, created the failure in the first place. When these new meanings get incorporated into one's memory base, then feelings of self-denigration are shifted to empathy for one's memories of pain and frustration. People begin to better respect their strengths, their creative capacities for compensating for weaknesses, and above all, their resilience. This respect fuels the "driving force" which sets in motion creative compensations enhancing growth of self structure. In other words, hope is rekindled.

To summarize, this chapter shows how psychotherapy is helpful to adult survivors of ULD. Therapy can promote resilience by consolidating our emotional and intellectual lives. By unraveling the emotional consequences of ULD, people will have more options for dealing with the problem. Life takes on new meanings when the emotional consequences of our patterns of learning are understood.

Chapter 11

Treatment: A Chapter for Therapists and Other Interested People

THERAPIST: Even with all your success, do the learning disabilities still cause problems in your life?

SCHOLAR: Well, when the world gets chaotic, it gets very difficult for me. You know, simple things like when I'm involved at work, and my wife starts to talk to me on the phone, I want to kill her. When she does that my head really spins. It's enormously disorganizing. And knowing that, I can sit down and talk to her about it and we can understand that you can't do that with me [because of my inability to take in information easily through my ears] as opposed to putting blame on her or on me, like I'm so cranky, or why should I be so sensitive that I can't have her talking to me on the phone at the same time?

INTRODUCTION

This chapter is written for therapists and for interested and potential clients. Some of this material has been presented in previous chapters but is presented again from a different perspective, namely from the therapist's perspective. Looking at therapeutic issues from the therapist's perspective may prove enlightening. The attempt here is to show how psychotherapy can provide adults who are unaware, or have recently become aware, of a learning disability an opportunity to enhance resilience and improve their lives.

Furthermore, it is important to understand why the recognition and treatment of learning problems is critical. After all, people are not born cognitively equal, and each individual possesses strengths and weaknesses. The discrepancies, however, between strengths and weaknesses in bright ULD sufferers are especially pronounced. Such individuals are caught in a particular dilemma; they have not learned to expect and allow for uneven achievement. They will never achieve as well in their areas of weakness as in their areas of strength, and *ULD sufferers do not know this because their deficits are not clarified.* Therefore, no matter how successful they are, because they fail to meet their own expectations, they are left feeling incomprehensibly flawed. This "flawedness" is a secondary reaction to the primary problem of ULD and is clearly a psychotherapeutic issue.

For example, the following is an excerpt from Ann Landers, advice columnist, in the *Chicago Tribune* (Landers, 1976b).

NO CLUE WHEN IT COMES TO FACES

Dear Ann Landers:

I just finished reading your column about people who have no sense of direction. Please make your readers aware of another, even more embarrassing, glitch in some people's neurons. It is the inability to recognize people.

I have suffered from this curse ever since I was a child. When I was in college, I used to be humiliated because I could not recognize my professors on campus, just hours after I had been in one of their classes. Even today, if I were to bump into my next door neighbors while in another city, I would not recognize them until I heard their voices or saw their beat up car. Just this morning a neighbor from down the block spoke to me, and I thought he was the furnace repairman until he mentioned something about my lawn.

Since misery loves company, I was delighted when I heard others have this problem too. I was comforted when I read that novelist T.S. Stribling couldn't recognize his next door neighbors either. Soon after he won the Pulitzer Prize, he was seated next to Eleanor Roosevelt at a dinner. He had no idea who she was and kept wondering why so many people kept coming over to speak to her.

I always try to look for clues, either by listening to people's voices or letting them do most of the talking, hoping for a clue from the dialogue. I'm sure some people think I'm a snob or extremely unfriendly, but the truth is, I have this problem that is impossible to explain, so I have stopped trying. Please print my letter so people will be more understanding.

Finger Lakes, NY

~

Dear FL, NY:

Your letter illustrates yet another example of faulty cranial wiring. Your problem is probably a second cousin to dyslexia—which few people knew about until fairly recently. Children with dyslexia were thought to be stupid until research proved otherwise, and in fact, they are often brighter than average.

Thanks for a letter that is sure to make a lot of people feel better. (Permission granted by Ann Landers/Creators Syndicate.)

A letter such as this shows how cognitive endowment can have a major impact on emotional development. Without a clear conception of the problem and guidelines to address it, very bright people can be traumatized suffering from secondary painful emotional reactions such as shame.

Many uneven learners, no matter how successful they are, complain of feeling estranged or not comfortably fitting in. This feeling is the result of having to figure out creative ways around their invisible and unidentified problems. They knew they could not learn through the teaching techniques used in school. Poor handwriting does not lend itself to brilliant "board work"; it lends itself to fear of exposure. Because there were no effective teaching tools, their strategies were idiosyncratic and often stopgap. They had to rely on their own ingenuity. Independence was enhanced but so was loneliness and isolation.

How can psychotherapy help? The goal of psychotherapy for people who have suffered from this problem is to strengthen self-confidence. The following interventions can be used:

- *Explanation of the problem.* Therapists need to be alert to the possibility of ULD in clients and, if indicated, explain the emotional ramifications in an appropriate and empathic manner.
- *Integration of ULD into the client's life history.* Therapists can provide a safe, appropriate environment in which the client can learn how past experiences of both learning failures and successes affect current living. Therapists can encourage the expansion of the client's options once old cognitive and emotional patterns regarding ULD are understood.

The clinician's chief concern is establishing an empathic relationship with the individual with ULD so that his or her deficits can be understood without undue shame (Galatzer-Levy, 1993).

Therapists can help ULD adults understand and alleviate their emotional pain. This chapter is divided into three sections: Recognition: Helping People Become Aware, Integration, and Conclusions.

RECOGNITION: HELPING PEOPLE BECOME AWARE

Recognizing ULD in intelligent adults who seek treatment for other problems such as depression or anxiety can be difficult. The learning problem itself interacts and interfaces with a broader self-structure (Kohut, 1971, 1977, 1984). What makes diagnosis so difficult is: (1) the problems indeed may be psychologically based; (2) even if there is a learning disability, people may have compensated adequately and their problems may truly lie elsewhere; and (3) people may be so ashamed of their inability to achieve in their areas of weakness that an untimely discussion of the problem could cause them to drop out of treatment. Gensler (1993) reiterates this caution. He says:

> An evaluation of an adult patient specifically for a learning disability should not overemphasize the influence of learning disability on personality development. It should aim at integrating whatever is found regarding a learning disability into a more general picture of functioning. (p. 685)

When contemplating a diagnosis, respect for the client's feelings should always be the foremost consideration. Clearly the interface between constitutional and environmental factors is inextricably intertwined. Although in many cases pinpointing a learning problem is inordinately helpful, the issues are complicated because of the emotional implications.

It is important that clinicians not immediately assume that the learning disability is the only root of the problem and that diagnosis and treatment of the disability will alleviate the person's pain. Diagnosis and treatment are vital but may not help the client with concomitant emotional problems. In other words, with this population, a therapist must avoid being "a bull in a china shop" from the patient's perspective.

We will begin looking at this concept of recognition by discussing the implications and ramifications of: (1) how to recognize ULD, (2) how to introduce the concept of ULD to the client, and (3) how to introduce the concept of the chasm to the client. A judicious introduction is more important than a formal diagnosis because the problem may cause a strong emotional reaction in the client.

How to Recognize ULD

Living with an undiagnosed learning disability is not easy. People seek psychotherapy because they suffer from inexplicable emotional pain. The relationship of ULD to the presenting emotional problems may be unclear. Buchholz (1987) comments on how intangible this problem feels when first encountering a patient with ULD:

These analysands, uncertain of both their strengths and deficits, accept that help is required, but often do not know what needs fixing. At the start, neither patient nor analyst sees the learning difficulties as core material to be analyzed. (p. 432)

Early in the therapy, under most circumstances the therapist must protect and enhance whatever sense of self-worth the client can muster. People do not carry their learning disabilities on their sleeves. It is embarrassing for bright people to feel stupid.

Furthermore, as described in previous chapters, people with ULD have learned to compensate more or less, and compensations mask or camouflage deficits that could cause feelings of exposure and embarrassment. It takes time and trust to expose what is painful. Therefore, in the beginning, it is difficult or impossible to isolate the disability. Take, for example, the student comedian who hides his deficits by shifting the therapeutic focus to his clever sense of humor. This may protect him from the devastating shame of learning that "My suspicions are true, something is really wrong with me."

If ULD is so elusive, how can therapists recognize it in people who come in for other reasons? Let us begin with the obvious. It is vital to take a school history. In the patient's retelling of school experiences, clues about ULD become evident. For example, people talk of loving some classes and hating others. However, not everyone who did badly in school has a learning disability.

Another obvious sign is the therapist's observation of cognitive processing problems in the session. Because ULD is so multifaceted, it would be difficult to give a comprehensive list of all possible processing problems. The following provisional list might give a sense of what to look for. For organizational purposes, I will expand on Scheiber and Talpers's (1987) concepts of how the brain uses information. They use categories of intake, storage, retrieval, and output. Hopefully, as more is learned about the clinical issues of ULD, more comprehensive categories will evolve.

Intake

- Cannot read the therapist's face
- Vocal nuances get no reaction
- Does not seem to listen well
- Hates to talk on the phone (auditory dyslexia)
- Does not pick up on tonal inflections
- Cannot sit still and focus on the subject at hand
- Cannot look at the therapist
- Cannot comprehend what the therapist is saying
- Storage
- Easily engaged but internal processes not occurring
- Does not appear thoughtful
- The hour never gets beyond light conversation
- Client appears superficial
- Information is "interesting" but never makes an impact
- Client fears being "found out" that he or she is intellectually flawed
- Nothing seems to change

Retrieval

- Cannot remember discussions from week to week
- Cannot remember names, faces
- Remembers but it takes too long and the client loses out in conversation

- Clients constantly test themselves to see if they remember—becomes an issue
- Complains of not being able to think
- Whenever time or date of session is changed, sessions are missed
- Clumsy—bumps into things in the therapist's office

Output

- Issues of performance become highlighted
- Complains of being tongue-tied, stutters
- Handwriting will deteriorate
- Sense of animation is inhibited
- Physical constriction—body seems to freeze
- Verbal constriction—cannot talk
- Organizational problems: tardiness, poor handwriting, sloppy physical appearance

This list is fairly straightforward and while sometimes ULD can be obvious, that is rare. More often, ferreting out ULD variables in current psychotherapeutic interactions requires recognition of subtle cues. Three markers or clues point to the possibility that ULD is affecting a patient's emotional life:

1. Complaints about deprivation
2. Discrepancies between apparent abilities and achievements
3. Use of characteristic strategies to compensate for a cognitive weakness

Deprivation

Patients may complain of feeling deprived or that something is missing from their lives. They may feel their potential eludes them. They might talk about the sense of emptiness in their lives and their lack of self-esteem. They may complain about their lack of motivation, their jobs, or their unhappy relationships. Their lives seem to lack meaning or excitement. Not infrequently, they talk about a sense of boredom.

For many, this sense that something is missing reflects inhibitions that lie outside of their awareness. For example, boredom at work may be the result of being afraid to try for a more interesting job. On some level, they are afraid their deficits will be revealed. One example of such inhibition of potential is seen in the significant number of social workers I have talked with who never pursue a PhD because they are afraid of math and statistics courses. In any event, the therapist's empathic sense of the client's vulnerabilities and propensity for shame is mandatory if these inhibitions are to be overcome.

Discrepancies

Very early in the treatment (in fact many times in the first session) it becomes fairly clear that there are curious discrepancies that feel confusing to the therapist. It is common to see people who appear quite mature and "together" yet are dissatisfied with their functioning. Of course, these discrepancies may not be the result of ULD, yet they are illuminating nonetheless. Kaplan and Shachter (1991, p. 195) list the following indicators:

- Significant discrepancies between apparent intellectual ability and school and/or work performance
- Significant poverty of social judgment in intelligent adults from apparently normal families
- Cognitive distortions and distorted perceptions of life events in the face of good intelligence, reasonable rearing, and adequate reality testing
- Specific avoidance of selected tasks incongruent with apparent ability in other areas
- Hatred of reading when intelligence is adequate
- Problematic school history without evidence of poor intellectual ability or rearing
- Impulsivity, explosiveness, poor frustration tolerance, and

concentration problems in an adult with good intelligence
and reasonable rearing. This may include a pattern of fre-
quent job changes and difficulty relating to authority.

- Poor self-esteem and confused self-concept, particularly in
  school and work performance
- A pervasive sense of badness, particularly in childhood recollections, despite good intelligence and reasonable rearing
- Feelings of intellectual inferiority despite adequate educational test performance

Compensatory Strategies

In working with the recognition phase in treatment, therapists
can begin to discern strategies people use to get around areas
of shame. Compensatory strategies are the nuts and bolts of resilience. Here is where one can see how people with LD have
adapted in dealing with the inexplicable problems of ULD. One
strategy is avoidance, especially the fear of trying. Wurmser
(1987) cogently confirms such inhibitions by defining what he
calls shame anxiety. Shame anxiety creates inhibitions that keep
people from experiencing destructive shame. A case in point is
individuals who refuse to try something new for fear of experiencing the chasm. Being stuck in the chasm, the experience of
stupidity, is a humiliation that people avoid at almost any cost.
Smart people with ULD hate to look stupid. For example, bright
and capable students will avoid math or other courses for fear of
failing. In this manner, they shift the environment. One participant who could not write would engage teachers in dialogues to
learn the material and make the time pass so that the classroom
written assignments would be overlooked. Even though the outcome was not the most efficient, her capacity to creatively figure
out a way around this impossible problem enhanced her growth
and development.

Another strategy is perseverance. This self-enhancing strategy
usually promotes success. Intelligent people with ULD realize
they need to work much harder and longer. They know how and

have the fortitude to hang in there. They persevere for two reasons: (1) they have experienced the joy of learning, and (2) they are afraid of the chasm and feel that if they work hard enough they can avoid it. Psychotherapeutically, this strategy enhances the chances of successful treatment.

Last, and most important to achievement, are the creative strategies people use to get around the chasm of deficits. These strategies are idiosyncratic; people have learned to rely on their own flexibility and ingenuity. Whatever the strategies people with ULD employ, they can vary from quite successful to less than optimal. For example, when a mathematician who cannot recall information quickly is given time to process, he accesses more than enough information for the tasks at hand. If asked a question, he can compensate by saying, "I'll think about it and call you back." This gives him the time he needs but causes delays that interfere with his work. Even though his achievements are outstanding, he has always felt like a cheater because he cannot access information as other people do.

Some uneven learners find others to help them. A successful student who has trouble categorizing may request help from librarians to access information. Even though she now knows better, she still has to fight feeling as though she is cheating because she cannot do it herself. If a client is critical of his or her own learning strategies, this may indicate ULD.

How to Introduce the Concept of ULD to the Client

As noted in the section on recognition, identifying ULD markers can be difficult. Introducing ULD can also be quite tricky. In uncomplicated situations, early diagnosis may be necessary to a client's well-being. A quick referral to a competent learning- disabilities specialist can make a real difference for a failing college student or a person who is about to lose a job. The client may eagerly embrace suggestions for circumventing the problem. The emotional implications of ULD make a great deal of sense because the diagnosis provides the language necessary to move out of a confusing process and into a dialogue about feelings. As a rule of thumb, if the learning disability is interfering with daily functioning, an early formal diagnosis is indicated. Gensler (1993) states:

> An adult's decision to undergo a psychological evaluation for a learning disability is not an easy one. A patient may be more likely to accept the recommendation to seek evaluation if the learning disability is seen as interfering with activities that are vital to current income or education. (p. 685)

If the client's functioning is not significantly affected, then making ULD a topic of therapy is much more difficult. At this juncture, it is necessary to issue a caveat to clinicians. Helping clients to understand that they have ULD runs a serious risk; it is not easy for proud, independent, smart people to entertain the notion that their troubles might stem from an undiscovered learning disability. The suggestion may make them angry or devastated. Adults with ULD have worked long and hard throughout their development to compensate for their problems. Since most had to learn to compensate on their own, they are fiercely independent and understandably proud of their achievements. Their independence and pride are instrumental in maintaining their self-cohesion. Careful thought and enough time to build a relationship must precede a recommendation for testing. Consider the following quote from Levin: "Any investigation must start from what the patient finds interesting and relevant" (2003–2004).

How then does a therapist broach the topic of ULD in an appropriate, timely fashion? One way is for the clinician to be curious about the person's experiences in school. (As mentioned in the section on recognition, this is also an excellent way to detect a learning disability.) If a therapist says, "Tell me about school" and the person replies, "I hated school," further exploration might lead the client to discuss relevant constitutional deficits. For example, perhaps this person hated gym because she has motor-coordination problems. Maybe she dreaded the first class of the day because she had problems keeping track of time and was continually late to school. Creating a more empathic history for such a client is one of the goals of therapy. If the suggestion of LD makes sense to the client in this context, windows of opportunity are comfortably opened for further exploration.

The following is a brief vignette showing the interface between current functioning and personal history:

> A creative, high-functioning woman in an executive position is suffering from anxiety because she has a new boss. In the past, this woman has been respected for her capacity to make creative leaps and come up with novel solutions to seemingly impossible problems. Her secretary handled all the details. However, there was a change in administration and within a short period of time, this woman lost her secretary and got a new boss who was oriented toward detail and demanded speed in administrative duties.

> Historical inquiry about her school experiences found that this extremely intelligent woman, who was captain of her chess team, read very slowly. She always "got by" because her work was so creative and interesting that teachers were captivated by her originality and did not pay attention to the fact that the numbers of references in her papers were minimal.

> She painfully confessed that while dealing with legal aspects of her job, she did not read contracts before signing them and instead relied on her assistants, who unknowingly provided her with summaries. Her chasm was her absolute inability to meet the standards of her new boss. This left her feeling painfully anxious.

If a careful school history had not been taken, treatment might have proceeded quite differently. For example, it may have been assumed that a conflict or an unmet need caused her inability to achieve with her new boss. Her inability to read at an optimal level would never change with psychological interpretations. This line of inquiry might have led the therapist to look at underlying motivations involving her fear of her boss, which might have lead to issues involving family conflicts or an expression of self-depletion resulting from a lack of nurturing in her childhood. These factors, of course, can be important in any treatment situation, but without a proper recognition of her cognitive deficits, this woman could end up believing that her Oedipus complex or her cold mother was the principal cause of her problem. *The inability to read quickly is usually not a motivational problem and therefore will never disappear. In this case, emphasis on intent or motivation would cloud the issue and cause this woman to feel responsible for a deficit that is not her fault.*

Explaining Compliance

Another pitfall in the early stages of treatment is overlooking the possibility of compliance. Patients may "comply" with what they perceive to be the therapist's agenda and fail to bring up the issues that are important to them. They protect themselves from feeling stupid by sticking with topics that are of interest to the therapist. Unfortunately, the therapist may think everything is right on target and overlook the client's real concerns. Gensler (1993) elaborates on countertransference and compliance, quoting Poznanski (1979):

> . . . [the therapist] is likely to be threatened by his own feelings of helplessness in the situation. As a result, the interview with the patient can be distorted in several ways. One way this can happen is for the therapist, who is not in touch with his own feelings, to gloss over the degree and extent of the handicapping situation (the therapist does not clearly ascertain what the handicapped person is and is not able to do). In order to be effective, it is absolutely necessary for the therapist to recognize the environment and constraints that act upon the patient. Nonetheless, the handicapped patient often enters into a conspiracy of silence with the therapist by not volunteering practical information about the extent of the disability. . . . Rather than avoiding discussion of

the patient's disabilities, the therapist and patient may un-
consciously focus on narrow, concrete, and somewhat isolated areas of the patient's ability to function while avoiding the central issues of total adaptation. This too, serves
a defensive function for both the patient and the therapist
and helps avoid the anxiety associated with the handicap
(Gensler, 1993, p. 677).

Poznanski is writing about children with obvious handicaps.
Issues of overlooking a disability become even more complicated
when the adult patient is not even aware of the problem.

When starting psychotherapy, patients often feel as though
they are in school again and the therapist is the teacher. ("If I
do good work for my therapist, he will approve of me and I will
succeed.") Even in the best of treatments, it takes time for patients
to understand that inquiry into their emotions takes precedence
over pleasing the therapist. Moreover, talking about ULD when
one has one's feelings entirely available can prime memories that
are then seen in the context of one's current life. For example, it
is easier to look at old fears of being shamed if a person now feels
relatively safe and if she understands the interface between one's
LD and he shaming experience.

The chasm adds still another wrinkle to the early stages of
treatment. Initially, since uneven learners with ULD will do anything to avoid feeling stupid, the therapist's attempts to facilitate
learning will be undone whenever the chasm erupts. Under normal circumstances, when people cannot learn, they feel frustrated, experience some shame, and use that shame to regroup and
try another approach. When a child fails an exam, he may figure out which steps in the ladder of learning were missing. When
those steps are understood, he realizes he has to study harder or
differently so he can do better.

But when dealing with a patient with ULD who is drowning
deep in the chasm, there are no steps on the ladder to further
learning. In fact, there is no ladder! For example, a client who
has deficits in time management may be consistently late to sessions. The more the unsuspecting therapist tries to find out what
is wrong with the client's motivation (i.e., why the client is late

all the time), the more embarrassing and "chasm-like" the hour becomes. It is not that uneven learners cannot cope with "why" questions. It is that, in the past, when they were asked such questions, (for instance, "Why do you fail spelling when you are such a good reader?") they did not know. Their inability to answer evoked tremendous anxiety because they felt stupid. The therapist must be aware that "why" questions can evoke old patterns of fear of exposure. It is fear that keeps people from being able to think.

Silence can be still another pitfall. Although people need enough time to think, silence can take on a life of its own. If patients are silent for a very long time, scrambling for words, do not know what to say, or seem to be rambling, it is possible that they may be desperate to find a way out of the "hot seat" because they cannot access the information in a timely fashion. Learning then becomes impossible because clients are drowning in the chasm.

How does this "drowning process" occur? It involves the following progression: First of all, early in psychotherapy, people may feel that their attempts to investigate and learn are scrutinized and judged by the therapist. (In many cases they are correct.) Then they feel isolated and alienated, and cognition freezes. They are not able to think. Furthermore, since there is no way to remove themselves from a one-on-one therapeutic encounter, people become embarrassed and are vulnerable to a pattern of internal ridicule which lowers self-esteem. Then, since these feelings are too difficult to bear, they cut off all feelings in the therapeutic experience. They may quit treatment prematurely.

Thus, if the therapist asks questions that make an uneven learner feel stupid (such as a simple, "Why do you think you feel that way?") and the individual truly does not know, a desperate attempt at some kind of answer will ensue. Countertransference may emerge: the therapist may feel that something is missing, and this vague feeling may translate into a sense of boredom. Discussing the feeling that "something is missing" with the client can sometimes lead to a discussion about previous learning gaps, which then gives meaning to previously unrecognized problems.

This section ends as it began. It is of utmost importance that therapists see undiagnosed and diagnosed learning disabilities in the context of the client's total experience of self. ULD is one of many threads that run through the fabric of one's self-structure. To ignore this thread leaves the individual feeling that something essential is missing; to isolate the thread of ULD outside of the client's total personality is to pathologize a common deviation that needs integration, acceptance, and understanding.

INTEGRATION

In the previous section, special emphasis was placed on the recognition of ULD. This section focuses on integration; more specifically, it focuses on empathically integrating the invisible threads of ULD into the fabric of the patient's awareness. The question posed here will be: How can a therapist facilitate this integration in a way that has meaning and contributes to the client's overall emotional growth?

Essentially, integration is the use of emotional attention to enhance psychotherapeutic learning about possible learning disabilities. It is adding to or combining what is known about what it was like growing up with unrecognized learning problems. Then, people can progress from chasm-like experiences of fragmentation or feeling "in pieces" to cohesion and coherence,* in which the various aspects of the self are experienced as interrelated. Furthermore, integration entails knowledge about the difference between the causes of learning problems and consequences of emotional pain due to learning failure. This inquiry seeks to examine and question the assumptions that govern our understanding of emotional life. However, little is clear-cut.

For example, as psychodynamic psychotherapy developed, clinicians have learned to wear various theoretical hats regarding "what causes what." In the beginning Freud thought that trauma was the basis for emotional pain. He later changed his mind and

---

* See Palombo (1991) for a thoughtful discussion of these concepts.

concluded that internal conflict was the culprit. Recently, trauma has been brought back into the picture. In addition, over the years psychological theorists have added other ideas that alter our assumptions or our theoretical postures. For example, chemical imbalance is a possibility that many therapists consider; so is the quality of caregiving a client received as an infant and young child.

Though clinicians have become adept at wearing different theoretical hats, and although certain cases require unusual approaches, some of our assumptions remain constant. For example, development is an important lens through which to view the client's pain. Therapists ask: How it is that this person has come to experience so much distress? What is the history of the distress? How has it changed over time? It is not unusual to consider the possibility that development has been blocked by environmental factors. In other words, something happened, either once or habitually, that compromised an individual's development. Moreover, it also is generally assumed that when developmental needs are empathically addressed and understood, emotional growth will remobilize and potential will flower.

When treating adults with ULD, the therapist must constantly question and re-evaluate his or her stance. Certain questions must remain in the foreground. The question "What causes what?" is of central importance to ULD adults' treatment. For instance, one may assume that if the patient is a survivor of trauma or neglect, the facts will unfold naturally within a therapeutic milieu. Ordinarily, this is a fair assumption. However, because uneven learners have learned to hide their deficits by compensating, ULD seldom comes to light on its own in treatment. As explained in the previous section, how a hidden cognitive deficit is handled will massively influence the outcome of therapy. Furthermore, the cultural truism that intelligent people can always succeed if they try hard enough is rarely questioned. This oversight can mask ULD as a primary cause of emotional pain (Rothstein, 1998; Kafka, 1984). Therefore, when people suffer from Imprisoned Intelligence, the relationship of ULD to emotional pain must hover over psychotherapeutic inquiry.

One question is this: Do deficits affect relationships or do relationships affect deficits? This is very difficult to answer because the interaction or interface between LD and emotions (between constitutional and environmental factors) is complex. Yet addressing this question is crucial because, depending on what is primary, one will form different conclusions. Does Johnny not read because he gets beaten up at home, or does Johnny not read because he is dyslexic and his failure to read angers his caretakers, who then beat him up? Which comes first, his failure to perform at school or the fact that he is physically abused?

To make things still more difficult, Johnny may be an invisible dyslexic who, by compensating, has somehow learned to read. But because his father beats him up, his compensations fail, he "regresses," and he can no longer read. Diagnostic confusion reigns as the complexity of the situation manifests itself. What looks like a regression may be a re-emergence of an invisible, constitutionally based learning disability minus the individual's compensatory mechanisms.

Paradoxically, if ULD is a factor in treatment, the therapist's ability to live with a state of diagnostic confusion provides an important step toward integration. It is vital not to jump to conclusions too early. When it comes to ULD, no one theory can explain everything. I suggest that you, as the therapist, depending on the needs of the client, may need to wear different theoretical hats within each session.

Furthermore, it is important to recognize and validate the importance of shame in its subtle form. It is easier for bright people to call themselves lazy than to recognize and integrate permanent cognitive deficits. This process of highlighting and understanding reactions such as this can only occur against the backdrop of a strong therapeutic connection. The client can only expose shame and pain over being "stupid" in a trusting environment.

At this juncture, let me demonstrate how this process works in a session.

Presentation of a Case

Robert is a composite of several patients, whose details are disguised to protect privacy. He represents the kind of highly successful person who struggles with language-processing difficulties.

Robert is an engineer who successfully teaches and supervises workers who, in the past, have not been able to master necessary computer skills. Although highly respected and very well paid, he suffers from depression and self-depletion. Even with extensive help from LD consultants, if he is under stress, spelling and spontaneous speech become very difficult. Robert discovered his problem while in college and now, because he understands this problem, he compensates by carefully preparing for each presentation he makes. Because he knows what is coming, his performance is consistently outstanding. In fact, his presentations have become models for others in the company.

Robert walked into a session very angry because a good friend backed out of a planned vacation that was to have taken place within the next few days. His first impulse was to completely end the relationship.

ROBERT: He was blowing me off.

THERAPIST: That doesn't fit. Didn't you just say that he was willing to spend the week with you doing something else? He just didn't want to go to Washington.

ROBERT: Yeah, that's true.

THERAPIST: So do you have any idea why you might be feeling this way?

ROBERT: I always come back to this. This is why I have trouble with friends and dating girls. I think it's a fear of intimacy.

THERAPIST: How do you mean?

ROBERT: Well, I cut them off before they do it to me. This way I don't get hurt.

THERAPIST: It sounds like you need to protect yourself.

ROBERT: You bet. I can't stand being blown off.

THERAPIST: So you do it first. Can you tell me more? What's so hard about being blown off?

ROBERT: It's terrible. Even though I had some friends in high school, I always felt like I was one of those guys who was the person looking in from the outside at people who fit together. I was never one of the "in group." Those guys could have such a good time shooting the bull with one another. All I could do was listen because I knew if I opened my mouth they would look at me like I was out of it. They let me hang around because I was the quiet one that admired their intellect and laughed at their jokes. Now that I know how hard it is for me to talk easily, I probably was out of it.

THERAPIST: It sounds like you felt like a misfit, never fitting in.

ROBERT: [Excited] Yeah, that's it. I did feel like a misfit.

THERAPIST: It sounds like you're haunted by this.

ROBERT: [Nods. We go from his anger to his reason for the anger: feeling blown off (cognition) and feeling like a misfit (feeling).]

THERAPIST: Good Lord, what a burden. You know, it's interesting. You don't feel that way at work, do you?

ROBERT: No, I feel fine at work. I know what I'm doing and most people respect me for it. I can joke around and have a great time.

THERAPIST: That must feel great.

ROBERT: Yeah. When I'm at work, I feel like I'm all together.

THERAPIST: It's so interesting. At work, your intellect and strength have a place to go and you feel like a whole, integrated human being who can connect with your co-workers. So, I wonder, how come this stuff about feeling like a misfit comes up with other friends and with the possibility of dating?

ROBERT: Well, this old stuff just gets kicked off. I can't help it. I just start beating up on myself.

THERAPIST: What do you say to yourself?

ROBERT: "Oh, he's just blowing me off because I'm stupid, I'm boring, I'm not interesting, I'm no fun" . . . stuff like that.

THERAPIST: So you start judging yourself.

ROBERT: Well, yeah, but it's better for me to do it to myself than have other people do it to me.

THERAPIST: Really. How come?

ROBERT: Listen, I grew up never knowing when the ax was falling. I'd open my mouth and people would look at each other and then there would be silence. How do you think that felt? It was awful. I figured I was just stupid because other people didn't have this problem. Now I know better . . . [silence]. Gee, it would have been so nice if I had known that it just takes me more time for words to get from my brain to my mouth. Maybe I could have stopped beating up on myself so badly . . . if I had only known.

THERAPIST: [Softly] Yeah. That would have helped a lot. [Silence]

ROBERT: It's still terrible. The other day we had a training session. People had to go to the board. I almost didn't go because I couldn't see making a fool out of myself with spelling errors. But I thought I'd give it a try and if I got into hot water, I'd get a headache or something and leave. Well, it turned out okay. In fact [laughs] some people were much worse spellers than me. They sort of laughed about it. We all sort of laughed about it together.

THERAPIST: How lovely. You had a different conversation in your mind. So the voice you use to comfort your trainees could be used for yourself. Not bad, Robert.

ROBERT: Well, even though I'm always complaining about how much you cost, I guess I'm getting something out of this. [Laughter]

THERAPIST: You know, I think we can tease out two very important threads here. Okay?

ROBERT: Sure.

THERAPIST: Correct me if I'm wrong. If someone in the real world disappoints you, it kicks off a kind of negative internal conversation in you that causes a downward spiral. You start out feeling disappointed about something real in the world but then you believe the reason for the disappointment is that you're essentially flawed.

ROBERT: [Nods.]

THERAPIST: Then, that makes you feel worse and then you do a real job of beating up on yourself, which makes you even more discouraged and more angry.

ROBERT: Yeah, so what?

THERAPIST: Well, we have to, if you want, stop this cycle of shame by figuring out what you do to yourself versus what someone else is doing to you.

ROBERT: Well, I can't help it.

THERAPIST: Of course you can't help it. When it came to talking, growing up was a nightmare. You had no answers. There was no one to help because no one understood. So you assumed you were stupid. What other choices did you have? None! [Long silence]

THERAPIST: So how about if we try to figure out what kicks this off in you? What starts it and what stops it? Wouldn't that be nice to know?

ROBERT: Well . . . yeah. [Silence; he appears angry.]

THERAPIST: So how do you think this started? You weren't born this way.

ROBERT: Yes, I was. I've always had a problem talking.

THERAPIST: That's true. You do have a learning disability and it can take you longer to process what you hear and what you want to say. But why should you cut people off and beat up on yourself when you become sort of tongue-tied? [Long silence— he's deep in thought.]

ROBERT: When I'm working with computers, I know what I'm doing. I don't have to think about myself, and besides I don't really care how I talk because I know that I know what I'm doing. If I make mistakes I can fix them and I can help others fix theirs. That's why people like me at work.

THERAPIST: Right. So when you're in your area of strength, all the work you've done with your LD specialists kicks in. You can compensate just fine.

ROBERT: [Nods]

THERAPIST: So, we have to figure out what sabotages your ability to compensate. I've got some ideas. Do you want to hear them?

ROBERT: Yeah.

THERAPIST: Well, first of all we know you have a permanent disability when it comes to speech and that you've worked very hard to compensate for this. Most of the time your compensations work just fine. But once in a while, like in that in-service training, you get scared that your LD will be exposed and you imagine how humiliated you will feel. In the past, before you knew what the problem was, that would stop you. What's different now, because you know and have some tools, is that you can talk to yourself in a different kind of voice and hang in there.

ROBERT: Most of the time, yeah.

THERAPIST: So the first part is your disability. That's clear. The second part is more complicated. You don't beat up on yourself because of your disability. You beat up on yourself because you think you're dumb. Isn't that right?

ROBERT: Yeah, that's right. I believe I'm really stupid when I get in that place.

THERAPIST: So, beating up on yourself is the emotional consequence of living with your disability. It's not the disability itself. It's the emotional consequence. Now, Robert, we can't change your LD, but we can change the emotional consequences of your LD.

ROBERT: That's what you think. I can't stand sticking out like a sore thumb.

THERAPIST: Of course not. It's terrible to feel isolated and humiliated because you can't do what everyone else can. It makes us feel painfully ashamed and vulnerable. Nobody likes that. But, Robert, there's a big difference between being shamed by others and shaming ourselves. You and I can work on helping you cut way down on this self-shame.

This vignette captures a therapeutic process that involves helping the client differentiate between an immediate emotional reaction that is primary (a gut reaction to someone else) versus an emotional reaction that is secondary (a gut reaction to his own expectations and assumptions). Robert was truly disappointed and angry because he was looking forward to this trip. This was a clear primary reaction. However, his anger was complicated by the fact that he felt rejected. When we were able to tease out the fact that the friend was not rejecting him (because his friend wanted to spend the week with him and was even willing to take the same trip in a few months), then Robert could look inside himself and discover a secondary reaction and some bedrock assumptions: in this case, feeling humiliated and like a misfit because he felt rejected.

These bedrock assumptions develop in childhood and adolescence, when there are no other explanations for why one learns unevenly and cannot function as others do. Once people believe it to be true, they are haunted by it. They never know when the feeling of stupidity will hit. That is why these are "bedrock" assumptions.

However, once Robert and I were able to empathically discern a more accurate picture of his friend's intentions, we were able to see the difference between (1) what was going on between Robert and his friend, and (2) his internal emotional reaction that surfaced because of his negative assumptions and judgments about himself. This differentiating process involves active participation from both therapist and patient.

Each participant has a somewhat different role to play. The patient must commit to a process of learning and self-exploration. The therapist must use his or her knowledge to promote the patient's curiosity in an empathic, respectful, and sincere milieu.

Therapists might ask themselves the following questions to devise starting points for particular clients:

- Why is potential constricted in an obviously bright, functioning person?
- Is there evidence of learning disabilities?
- If so, are the disabilities the *cause* of emotional distress or the *consequence* of emotional distress?
- How did/does the disability affect the client's emotional world?
- Is the client aware of both strengths and disabilities and can he or she use strengths to compensate for these disabilities?

To work productively with these questions, the focus will be upon therapeutic interactions and interventions. The rest of this section will be divided into two broad parts: Setting the Stage: Creating the Therapeutic Environment, and Facing the Challenge: Dealing with Confusion, the Chasm, and Grief.

Setting the Stage: Creating the Therapeutic Environment

Therapists set the stage for successful treatment by providing a milieu of trust. A patient needs to feel safe, comfortable, special, and connected with the therapist in order to experience and work through the painful feelings that emerge in treatment. The following are general guidelines for creating an emotional "safety net" to help vulnerable clients feel comfortable in therapy.

Empathic Investigation

A therapist must inquire and investigate in an empathic manner. Empathy involves understanding the other person's point of view. For many uneven learners, understanding was sorely lacking in their early experiences; they were constantly bumping into others with impossible expectations and judgmental stances. Because clients are still haunted by the feeling that "no one understands," they may be prone to feeling misunderstood in therapy. Talking about these frustrating, shameful experiences is very helpful because patients will feel less alone, more understood, and more comfortable in the session. Also, when the time to do interpretive work comes, the therapist and client will have a shared knowledge base from which to work. Painful feelings will become familiar and empathically experienced by therapist and patient alike.

Differentiating Strengths and Weaknesses

Therapists differentiate patients' strengths and potential from their deficits. When people come into treatment these factors are confounded and impossible to distinguish. Careful examination allows us to begin to make sense of the confusion. First of all, therapists must be very careful not to assume that intelligence can correct deficits. For example, a bright student is verbally sophisticated but fails his tests because he cannot access his memory through handwriting. Do not say, "It's wonderful how bright you are. Too bad you can't use that to pass your tests." This kind of dialogue creates a painful re-enactment. People have heard these judgments all their lives. It only causes them to withdraw. Mirroring a patient's potential is vital to develop a positive therapeutic experience and is an important first step in the growth of resilience. Uneven learners desperately need someone to become excited about their strengths and their ambitions. Psychotherapy can provide this function for people who do not originally feel so empowered. The therapist's interest and excitement about their strengths is contagious, and eventually these feelings get incorporated into the patient's sense of self and inner world. Affirming questions such as: "What gives you pleasure?" or "What did you like to do as a child?" interfere with the sense of disconnection that goes along with Imprisoned Intelligence.

Avoiding Pitfalls

Avoiding treatment pitfalls also enhances the safety net. What are some pitfalls a therapist might stumble across during the integration phase of treatment? One involves therapists confusing their own expectations with the patient's ability. Although bright clients may appear to function extremely well, they may have hidden deficits. Clients will take expectations of their ability to perform very seriously. Encouraging high expectations for performance can boomerang if an invisible disability interferes with the therapist's recommendations. The therapist must be careful about falling into this performance trap. For example, a patient may complain about an impossible supervisor. Obvious suggestions about changing jobs or departments might backfire if, in the new situation, the same complaints appear again. Furthermore, the person may be fired because the undiagnosed learning disabilities (that the old supervisor put up with) are seriously interfering with the new job performance. To make matters worse, the patient may also feel that he or she let the therapist down. Optimally, therapy validates both strengths and weaknesses. Then patients can be free to make their own decisions.

Facing the Therapist's Feelings

Therapists need to be aware of their own feelings of helplessness and hopelessness that uneven learners can engender. These feelings can be a form of priming. Priming is a heightened awareness of a previously ignored feeling. Priming through empathic interaction enhances curiosity, and curiosity enhances resilience. For example, a patient thought he was doing okay during his probation period on his job, but in fact was not picking up the verbal and nonverbal cues of his employer. The therapist's feeling of startle and surprise when the patient appeared "out of it" helped prime the patient and therapist to become curious about this lack of awareness. Together, they discovered that this person did not get the verbal and nonverbal cues of disappointment from his supervisor.

Because people with ULD can provoke these feelings, therapists often find themselves wanting to tell the patients what to do in order to alleviate their own feelings of chaos and disequilibrium. If realistic interventions are necessary, however, it can be more helpful to suggest that the individual consult with a learning disability specialist. Such specialists know how to tell uneven learners what to do and will come up with all kinds of strategies to circumvent learning disabilities. Your job is to promote self-esteem and one vital way to do this is to provide your client with experiences of safety, validation, and partnership.

Facing the Challenge: Dealing with Confusion, Grief, and Being Stuck in the Chasm

Why is treating people with ULD such a challenge? One factor is the complicated interface between learning disabilities and emotions. Therapists must consider ULD an important factor in the totality of the patient's experience, and a possible cause of emotional pain. But flexibility is vital.

Think of ULD as a few steps in a complicated dance. Each of the steps is interesting, but the dance does not come alive until the steps are done together. Imagine dancers changing from ballet slippers to tap shoes to bare feet—all on a moment's notice, never knowing which shoes will be demanded next. Working with people with ULD can be similar to that. The shoes are like different assumptions, and the assumptions create the questions asked. If therapists believe environment is at the root of the problem they ask: What happened? Who did what to whom? How did it affect the individual's emotional growth? If LD is suspected, other questions follow, such as: How did the deficit affect relationships? How did the individual compensate for the deficit? Would the patient benefit from testing? No one pair of shoes will suffice.

Flexibility entails giving the patient empathic but evenly hovering attention, that is, listening without being too quick to reach a conclusion. This allows the patient to express what is important at the moment.

Another challenge is to help uneven learners move from a state of fragmentation to a state of cohesion in which their vitality enhances their potential. What is a cohesive self?

The self is made up of ambitions, skills, goals, and ideals, the relationships among them, and the actions that they dictate. With ULD individuals, it is precisely these components—their skills, goals, and ambitions—that become clouded, blocked, or frustrated by the hidden disability. Therefore, the self-cohesion of a ULD sufferer is constantly being jeopardized by the very nature of the disability.

How do ULD patients find and maintain a sense of cohesion in therapy? Emotional attention and verbalization contribute greatly to cohesion. To anticipate chapter 13, emotional attention increases the capacity to see things which previously have been missed. For example, a person who doesn't process how she *feels* about testing may not know what the testing really *means*. Many people get tested but really don't understand the results of the testing at all! A knowledgeable psychotherapist can help the patient connect with her emotions. When people *feel* pride about their strengths and sadness and grief over their weaknesses, they have the opportunity to enhance their resilience because the organization of the self has now changed. Testing results no longer are just a set of numbers. Putting inner feelings and thoughts into words can help people reassess and reorder their inner world and understand their ambitions, skills, goals, and ideals in a new way.

Imprisoned Intelligence and the inability to verbalize go hand in glove. Yet, for uneven learners to understand the consequences of ULD, talking is required. One of the main challenges of therapy with ULD individuals is finding ways to facilitate verbal communication. This section discusses how to create a language that makes sense to the patient and explains his or her pain. Some of the obstacles to developing a lexicon for exploring ULD are: (1) confusion, (2) the chasm, and (3) grief.

Dealing with Confusion

A therapist may start to see someone who is obviously successful and bright but seriously depressed. To make sense of the client's depression, the therapist will wonder about environmental inputs, such as a loss or a trauma, that might have contributed to it. The therapist may also wonder if a chemical imbalance contributes to the person's emotional pain. These questions will usually lead to clarification: trauma, neglect, or chemical imbalance may emerge as the primary problem. For example, if early childhood sexual abuse is discovered, this knowledge can foster the profound changes that occur in psychotherapy. Often, the client's understanding of his or her world profoundly shifts as the abuse is addressed in treatment. Although still a grueling process, a sense of cause and effect emerges.

However, if ULD is a precipitating factor in depression, confusion will increase rather than decrease. Why does this happen? It is difficult to know "what causes what" because environmental input and constitutional deficits are inextricably intertwined. There are no easy answers here.

The first rule in treating people with ULD is that the therapist and the client must form a partnership amid the diagnostic confusion.* Both must learn to respect the patient's ideas about "stupidity." Confusion in the treatment setting is vital, because prior to therapy, the individual will have suffered with inner confusion alone. The new partnership becomes a decisive intervention. If the therapist can tolerate the confusion that goes along with ULD, he or she will interfere with a re-enactment that plagues ULD sufferers. Confusion, then, is a form of memory priming. Once the confusion is empathically validated and named as such, then investigation into its historical roots provides a reframing or memory modulation that can create a very different self-organization. In the past, confusion and isolation were the order of the day. In other words, the individual's confusion is part of the material that is re-enacted in the therapist's office, but this time he or she will not have to tolerate it alone. The therapist will explore it with him or her.

Another source of confusion is the individual's disavowal or detachment from the concept of a learning disability.† While taking a school history, the therapist may find clues that an invisible learning disability affected the client's performance. However, when questioned, the client may minimize it. She might say, "Yeah, I was lousy in math, but no one is good at every subject" or "I get along just fine." Disavowal is a defense that contributes greatly to confusion.

At times, tolerating confusion can be extremely difficult for the therapist. Material presented in session can be viewed from either the perspective of a learning disability or the perspective of defective environmental input. For example, a former patient was sexually abused as a child. She sometimes wondered whether the abuse caused or significantly contributed to her ULD. Did she merely have ULD or did the abuse exacerbate a problem for

---

* Arnold Goldberg, MD, presented an interesting case that involved tolerating confusion titled "The End of Inquiry" at the meeting of the Chicago Psychoanalytic Society, September 27, 1994.

† For a comprehensive examination of disavowal I refer the reader to Michael Basch's work *Doing Psychotherapy* (1980).

which she could have compensated more easily? There is no exact answer, but a therapeutic milieu validated her struggle to find answers to such questions. The threads of ULD and environmental input will never be teased out in a clear or concise way. What is important, however, is to keep an open mind so that the person in treatment over time can consider all the pertinent points of view that have meaning. In other words, the confusion needs validation.

What further muddies the water is that whatever you look for in the patient you will probably find (Goldberg, 1990). If you ask an environmental question, you will probably get an environmental answer, and that answer will carry some truth:

THERAPIST: Why didn't you like school?

JOHN: No one liked me.

THERAPIST: Why not?

JOHN: Everyone picked on me because I was poor and my clothes didn't fit.

THERAPIST: That must have been so difficult.

If the therapist has her or his environmental cap on, this answer will suffice. It certainly makes sense. When kids look and feel different, problems with peers can certainly arise. Furthermore, as this story is being told, it is important to validate what the person is feeling.

The same question can have a ULD slant:

THERAPIST: Why didn't you like school?

JOHN: No one liked me.

THERAPIST: Why not?

JOHN: Everyone picked on me because I was poor and my clothes didn't fit.

THERAPIST: Were there other kids who were poor and looked it?

JOHN: Yes.

THERAPIST: So why you?

JOHN: Well, they weren't stupid.

THERAPIST: You felt stupid? How come?

Again, what is most important is staying empathically attuned. When treating someone, it is usually beneficial to make his or her agenda center-stage. If the patient is curious about "stupidity," it could be helpful to keep a ULD hat on and continue the exploration. If the patient is absorbed in alienation and embarrassment, exploration might only heighten the pain because he or she feels like a specimen.

Separating a patient's ULD from environmental influences is a process that never stops. The treatment goal becomes not merely understanding what happened (although this is a vital component), but also to teach uneven learners how to take responsibility for the complex sorting-out process. One caveat: clients cannot blame their parents for invisible learning disabilities, although they may well be responsible for not addressing the problem. Most often, the parents were also in the dark.

The Chasm

As described earlier, the chasm is a chronic hyperawareness of a futile attempt to learn that is coupled with shame. It is a traumatic reaction to disappointed expectations with far-reaching emotional consequences. Individuals experience the chasm as enduringly shameful, and as a place over which they have virtually no control. It occurs when, no matter how hard they try, they cannot fulfill the standards or expectations set by their inner or outer world.

It is very important to underscore here that in the chasm, it is not the LD itself but the dashed expectations that causes traumatic shaming. It is also crucial to remember that the chasm, in itself, is not bad. Essentially, it is healthy. Shame is a disconnection from others because current tactics are not working and it is necessary to regroup. Nevertheless, if, instead of being an occasional painful feeling, the chasm occurs too often without apparent rhyme or reason, it can become toxic and fixed within our repertoire of painful feelings.

Why does the repetition of the chasm become traumatic? First of all, one is unable to predict when it will occur, and this uncertainty increases learning failures because fear of cognitive freezing makes people afraid to try. No one likes to feel embarrassed by failing to "keep up with the class"; furthermore, if people fear they will look stupid in the near future, this contaminates initiative. Without initiative learning dies a painful death.

Second, people with recurrent chasm-shame experiences feel judged. Patients report that the chasm becomes fixed when they feel judged too often, and when they have no way to remedy the situation. Others' disapproval can be a subtle but potent force. Disapproval can be conveyed through: outright verbal expressions; tone of voice (irritated, patronizing, sarcastic, full of contempt, etc.); gaze (rolling one's eyes, closing one's eyes in despair, looking away with impatience, etc.); or body language (tapping one's feet or hands in an impatient way). Patients may misperceive the body language, tone of voice, and so on of the therapist because they have come to expect it. When this happens, clarification of the therapist's intent is mandatory. If patients feel silently judged, they will withdraw.*

Third, the chasm becomes traumatically fixed when one cannot meet the demands of the clock. In our culture the concept "slow" is nearly always equated with being "dull . . . mentally dull; stupid; naturally inert or sluggish; lacking in readiness" (*Webster's New Collegiate Dictionary,* 1981). In contrast, "quick" is equated with intelligence. A teacher who says a child is quick is, in essence, imputing something about that child's intelligence.

---

* If you're interested in the psychological ramifications of nonverbal communication, see Chapter 5 of Levin (1991).

Learning involves first being able to tolerate not knowing. Most people without learning disabilities find that not knowing leads to knowing. People with ULD find that, in their areas of deficits, not knowing leads to more not knowing. Uneven learners know how to work hard. But mere hard work is not enough if their intelligence is imprisoned by ULD. As not knowing becomes more and more associated with humiliation and exposure, people become afraid to try. Giving up may then affect other areas of learning not obviously related to the area of concern. For example, the inability to spell correctly or copy from the board in a timely fashion can impede learning how to write. In many cases, therapists may have to slow down to accommodate their sense of timing to the patient. Some patients need a great deal of time to think and respond. Others respond very quickly. Sometimes, in fact, some patients become irritated when the therapist is slow to respond. This too becomes a therapeutic issue for further discussion.

How does the chasm manifest itself within a psychotherapy session? How does the therapist know the chasm is being reenacted in the hour? What is helpful? Here are some indications that the client may be entering into a chasm state:

- There may be bodily changes: flushing, an avoidant shift, looking away, a painful silence that lasts too long, a vacant stare, a rigid stance. Meaningful interactions deteriorate; the patient seems to be grasping at straws. At this point it is crucial to restore emotional contact and to avoid actions that interfere with connection.
- Some people defend themselves from the pain of the chasm by a subtle withdrawal, which is quickly replaced by a secondary defense such as anger or disavowal.
- Patients attack their own motivations. Perpetual self-denigration may permeate the therapeutic hour. People often refer to themselves as stupid or lazy. Many uneven learners have long histories of being called lazy, thoughtless, uninvested, careless, or worse. After hearing insults often enough, an individual internalizes them. Reciting this lita-

ny of alleged faults can indicate that the client is sliding into the chasm.

- The therapist may feel a sense of "running into a wall," a feeling of abrupt confusion coupled with a sense that all connection with the patient has been lost. Something should be said to clarify the situation, but there is absolutely nothing to say. The therapist may begin to feel bodily discomfort, such as a creepy feeling on his or her skin (Bollas, 1983).
- Patients who seem "all together" at one session may inexplicably "fall apart" at the next. Intelligent uneven learners are extraordinarily resilient; however, when under sufficient stress, their compensatory capacities unravel because compensations rapidly ebb and flow. It is difficult for clinicians to know whether people look "regressed" because they are defending against painful emotional material or whether the regression reflects a temporary loss of compensatory strategies. For example, one dyslexic patient knows that when she is fatigued and stressed, her handwriting deteriorates. She jokes, "It's not a good time to write a check." Another who normally is quite verbal will suddenly become tongue-tied.

Assuming that the clinician has a good idea when the client is in the chasm, what should he or she expect next? The chasm is not an enemy to be fought, but a potential therapeutic tool. If the chasm can be understood in a way that is meaningful to patients, they will be much closer to calmly experiencing their problems. Then the learning process can begin.

If a chasm experience is incorrectly labeled as defensive and motivationally based, rather than secondary to loss of adaptive capacities and strategies, then the cycle of blaming motivations is re-enacted. Telling patients that they are regressing or defensive is akin to telling them that they are not learning because they do not try hard enough. This is a crucial distinction that clinicians need to think about.

Another subtle but important distinction must be made: the therapist needs to differentiate between the chasm itself (as primary) and the feelings that protect against the chasm (but are secondary). There is a big difference between the primary gut-wrenching response of the chasm and the secondary protective emotional reactions that people use to protect themselves from the chasm.

Again, the issue of theoretical "hats" and how assumptions affect the course of treatment is vital. More specifically, are the patient's problems and pain a reflection of the following:

- Underlying environmental trauma such as abuse?
- Underlying developmental delays such as self-depletion?
- Cognitive, constitutional deficits such as ULD?
- A secondary defensive reaction that protects against the chasm?
- A secondary defensive reaction that protects against overwhelming recollections of abuse?
- A secondary defensive reaction that protects against fragmentation?
- An indication of the unraveling of usually firm (or fragile) capacities to compensate?

At this point, the therapist may think: How am I to determine whether symptoms are the result of psychological pain that needs further exploration or the result of cognitive deficits that are permanent, need validation, and require compensatory strategies?

Struggling with symptomatology that could be either motivationally based or constitutionally based is indeed difficult. Furthermore, if the problem is ULD based, the client's ability to compensate will vary, often to extremes:

THERAPIST: [gently] Why did you cut class today?

TEENAGER: I don't know, I just didn't want to get up.

THERAPIST: Something must have been bothering you.

TEENAGER: [annoyed and feeling stupid] No, I just didn't want to go. [The chasm hits because he doesn't know how to answer. Silence.]

THERAPIST: You're so quiet. Maybe you're quiet because you're afraid to talk or maybe something is making you mad. [This interpretation assumes an emotionally based problem.]

TEENAGER: Yeah, I'm mad because I'm so stupid. [The patient stops talking and starts looking at the clock, then bolts out of the room as soon as the hour is up.]

How can one approach the treatment of this client? First of all, if this client had known about the chasm, he might have been able to identify and talk about his isolation, embarrassment, humiliation, and exposure. The silent chasm-shame cycle might have been interrupted earlier. *In other words, a discussion of the chasm as both phenomenon and experience becomes a decisive therapeutic intervention.* Identifying the chasm as a signal (as opposed to just feeling the mind freeze) enhances resilience. Now the source of what precipitated the chasm can be brought to light and alternative approaches to the problem can be considered.

Of course, it is paramount that any investigation of the chasm be done empathically so that the client's feelings of isolation can be managed. Within a safe milieu, a different understanding of past and present functioning can evolve. As a consequence, the individual will no longer feel as alone. Then there may also be less vulnerability to internal and external ridicule.

Living with confusion is the name of the game for therapist and client. The chasm (which is the epitome of nothingness) gradually becomes more defined once it is identified. Awareness of this nonlearning, frozen, empty place is useful as a marker. To put this in the patient's language, the question becomes: "Am I shamefully frozen because I can't learn or am I shamefully frozen because I'm afraid to look at something?"

Irrespective of the cause, the therapist works with the patient until the patient has the resources to discern the source of discomfort. It is the patient who, over time, can determine whether the chasm points to innate deficits that require careful strategy building and remediation or to psychological deficits that require psychological investigation and interpretations.

Thus the awareness and understanding of obstacles becomes the window of opportunity for therapeutic interventions. The chasm is not easy to see in vivo because it is too shameful and is quickly replaced by some protective device. Nevertheless, the therapist can recognize the chasm when it manifests in treatment. As noted above, the chasm can be seen as a signal that withdrawal is occurring. Withdrawal followed by consideration of new or different strategies becomes crucial in helping the client reestablish conditions that allow learning.

How does the therapist help the patient identify and reconstruct this problem? Feeling cognitively frozen, stupid, and exposed is a nonverbal experience that needs to be put into words. When this happens, the chasm gains a context, and can be recognized by the patient. The sharing lessens the client's sense of isolated exposure.

Once a shameful cognitive freeze is identified and dealt with, expectations begin to change. It becomes all right to feel stupid because this feeling is merely a tip-off to important information. Linking curiosity to the feeling of "not getting it" becomes a decisive tool for further therapeutic growth. Moreover, it is easier to figure out appropriate strategies to circumvent the chasm-shame cycle in the future when shame is no longer a major obstacle. To enhance the possibility of sharing material such as the chasm, certain ground rules are helpful:

1. The patient sets the agenda (not the therapist).
2. Early on, the therapist must explain that feeling stupid is to be expected in therapy. Prior to therapy, not knowing makes people with ULD feel defective. This experience will probably be re-enacted in the session involving the explanation of such ground rules, but this explanation creates a bridge for further understanding.
3. Because the chasm is a reaction to disappointed expecta-

tions, therapists assume that they inadvertently have been or will be the cause of clients' shame. They should explain this to clients. Then, hopefully, clients can be less inhibited in sharing what caused them to feel stupid. Then, client and therapist together can trace how the chasm evolved in any particular session. The burden of shame shifts from the patient to the therapist. Almost always, if one observes empathically, there is a viewpoint from which the patient is right. In other words, there is an advantage in at least temporarily assuming that in some way or other, the therapist made a judgment that evoked the chasm.

When the chasm manifests itself in treatment, the goal is to modulate its intensity. Figuring out how to soothe someone who is drowning in the chasm can be very difficult, particularly in the beginning of treatment. Whatever is said may exacerbate the feelings of exposure; on the other hand, silence can be golden, but can also make people feel further trapped in the chasm.

In the beginning of treatment, ascribing motivational causes to the chasm can be disastrous because people are feeling raw and exposed. *Any comment that makes individuals feel minutely observed by the therapist will generally not help because the feelings of exposure are so pronounced.* One patient started to blush and turn his eyes away from the therapist, who said, "You look so embarrassed. What's up?" He walked out of the room. Later, he said he could not talk and the assumption that he should say something when he could not gave him no choice but to leave.

There are times when metaphors can be extremely helpful, because this form of communication allows the patient to withdraw from the chasm by focusing elsewhere (Levin, 1991). "When *people* are interested in what they are experiencing their primary cortical areas for speech, vision and touch activate simultaneously" (Levin 2003–2004, p. 17). Here's an example of how a metaphor might contribute. When working with someone who is trying to integrate their LD into their lives but who can only feel good about their strengths or conversely ashamed of their weaknesses, I suggest they imagine a child's teeter-totter—with one end being their strength and the other their weakness—and ask them to stand in the middle to help balance out both. As people imagine themselves balancing themselves on that teeter-totter, *they can bridge both their strengths and weaknesses at the same time.* However, there is a caveat: "The potential to learn is not actualized, however, if the analyst does not observe the following rule: he or she must start any investigation from what the patient finds interesting since then the patient will be building new knowledge from a bases inside their zone of working memory activation" (Levin 2003–2004, p. 17n).

Sharing a personal experience with the client may also alleviate the intensity of the chasm. At other times, simply the sound of the therapist's voice is more soothing than the words spoken. Patients may leave favorite books with the therapist, and at times it is helpful to read them a pertinent section. Within the confines of appropriate boundaries, sharing affection for the patient can be helpful. Occasionally, the therapist may hum favorite tunes. One client would draw the way she felt. Another started to write. What is important to remember is that when the chasm hits, verbalization leaves. Furthermore, if people know that once or twice a week they can be with a therapist who understands the shame they experience, they will be able to better endure painful experiences and learn how to soothe themselves. In time, this process can be explained to the client as a developmental necessity. The clients will learn to respect rather than attack their frustrated feelings and wishes. Being stuck in the chasm is a boot camp for resilience. The pain of helplessness, humiliation, and shame forces people to figure out ways to avoid this experience. Adapting and finding compensations to keep out of the chasm is a sort of training for people—as they plug into their own fortitude, they gain the flexibility that allows them to figure out work-arounds.

When treating uneven learners with ULD, one goal is to engage in the mutual process of struggle: to pull out the clues that facilitate a better understanding of how cognition and emotions connect. When this happens, the person in treatment begins to consider new learning options and eventually creates a sturdier sense of self.

Grief

Uneven learners mourn when they discover their ULD. Feelings of loss and deprivation manifest themselves when people begin to realize either that no one understood the problem, that no one was interested or cared, or that their shame over unexplained failures stifled their curiosity and desire to learn.

It is a psychotherapeutic challenge to allow these experiences to unfold in a timely way. The duration and intensity of a patient's grief will depend on circumstances. College students who struggle with their deficits daily may be dramatically confronted with their feelings. Those who are understanding how ULD has contributed to depression will grieve more sporadically but just as intensely.

This process is not unlike the mourning process described in psychoanalytic literature (Freud, 1917; Kaplan and Sadock, 1991; Pollock, 1961; Moore and Fine, 1990; Krystal, 1988). This grief is a watershed that allows people to come to grips with their deficits. Surely, it is easier to think of oneself as competent but lazy than to accept that one is *not* lazy, but disabled.

Deaf people also go through this mourning process. Although they know they are deaf, in therapy they mourn for a hearing world they will never know (Stein, Mindel, Jaboley, 1981; Levin, 1981). The same process holds true for ULD sufferers. Over time, the grieving process allows them to reintegrate what they have learned about themselves and what they must give up.

The losses such clients experience have three different components. They grieve for what might have been; for what will never be; and for what they have to face.

Grief for what might have been. These days, parents with ULD are gratified to see that their learning disabled children receive help in school. However, it is painful for them to think about what might have been had their caregivers only known about their

ULD. They think about the educational opportunities that are forever closed to them. Choices about ambitions, colleges, vocations, and even friends might have been very different. Furthermore, when adults with ULD acquire new learning strategies, they become painfully aware of what was missing during their school years. If the problem had been diagnosed earlier, and if appropriate supportive assistance had been available, much of the emotional pain could have been avoided. The example of intelligence tests is instructive. Deficits and strengths can cancel each other out so that people end up looking average. That may have meant average classes, average colleges, average friends. There is much to grieve for.

Grief for what will never be. Living with ULD makes people ingenious. They learn to get around their disabilities in one way or another. This evokes a sense of pride. True Grit in Chapter 1 is an example of this. However, when newly diagnosed individuals have to rely on others and learn new ways of compensating, their independence and ingenuity are challenged.

Self-esteem temporarily plummets as they realize they can no longer live by the creed: "I can do anything I want if I work hard enough." Psychotherapy provides a milieu in which their feelings of loss can be explained as part of the mourning process.

This leads to another loss: the loss of self-pride.* Many adults with ULD have very high standards and goals for their own achievement. They expect themselves to do very well, and in areas of strength, they do. When testing forces them to reassess their goals as untenable, they may feel great loss. Their internal self-structure is temporarily challenged. In the past, when they did not enjoy the success they expected, they could criticize themselves for not trying hard enough and continue to believe in their own perfectibility. When they learn of their ULD, they are forced to realize they can never achieve certain goals, no matter how hard they work. They also compare themselves to others who achieve quickly and easily in their areas of weakness. These

---

* Shane's (1984) explanation of primitive grandiosity in children with learning disabilities is applicable here.

comparisons highlight their loss and, until other compensatory structures develop, they struggle with a sense of despair. People have to change their "internal picture" of themselves as highly intelligent but "not working hard enough" to highly intelligent but unintelligent in certain areas. This is a jolt. Mourning creates a bridge for connecting the intelligent and unintelligent parts of the mind. Psychotherapy validates grief and validates the individual's strengths and weaknesses. This validation modulates the grieving process so that, over time, one can integrate both strengths and weaknesses into a cohesive sense of self.

Grief for what must be faced. Learning how to compensate for a learning disability may be the hardest job individuals ever face. If they hope to make any progress, they must think about and carry out tasks that they may have avoided for years. For instance, a dyslexic sociologist who hates math may have to: (1) realize that he has avoided math completely, and (2) decide that he will never achieve his goals (say, to carry out a sociological study with statistical significance) unless he both learns as much math as he can and asks for help from his colleagues. This individual now has to confess his weakness and spend hours poring over elementary statistics, at which he is painfully slow and inaccurate. As he studies, the chasm will probably reappear. He may wonder if he should go back to doing small, qualitative studies that do not reflect the scope and significance of his ideas. Fortunately, it will get easier. Especially with the help of a good psychotherapist, he can adapt to a new reality. He can alter his self-structure to include his disability, and he can begin to feel pride in his newfound compensations. When he finally completes his study (and knows that he can do more in the future), he will feel a peace and satisfaction that eluded him in the past.

Clearly, psychotherapy can help people through the necessary experiences of grief and mourning, interfering with the disappointment and hopelessness that accompany diagnosis. It is imperative that the therapist maintain empathy in the face of possible unreasonable assaults that might occur defensively when a client tries to avoid facing these issues. Learning how to help patients modulate their massive disappointments without shaming them is one of the more difficult "basic problems" of psychotherapy.

Treatment also includes helping people adapt by encouraging the growth of compensatory structures. The therapist helps the patient discover effective ways around the learning gaps. This is where the fields of learning disabilities and psychotherapy intersect. Each field contributes to a knowledge base that can help people who struggle with Imprisoned Intelligence.

The resilience and courage people show when they struggle with newly discovered seemingly insurmountable problems is to be admired. Their fortitude promotes independence and their flexibility enhances their capacity to adapt. In other words, they have a flexible sense of independence. They know how to keep going when the going gets rough. They do not give up.

Some Final Comments

This discussion of integration will conclude by reiterating that the chasm/shame/exposure experience is the end result of years of unattended cognitive deficits. This chasm, the cognitive freeze, the frozen inability to think or perform, all lead to emotional pain and contribute to the constriction of learning. It evolves in the following manner:

1. Learning frustration (when one wishes to learn and cannot figure out how to do so) leads to feeling lost and exposed.
2. Tragedy occurs in the form of a learning failure. People blame themselves and their motivations because no explanations are forthcoming (at least, none that protect the self). Erroneous assumptions about not trying hard enough cause people to despair and denigrate themselves, with long-term effects. Even after people know about the chasm, it still takes a long time in therapy to rid themselves of self-abasing thoughts and feelings.
3. Shame over not knowing, without the possibility of feeling

reconnected to others and oneself, causes trauma. Because there is no help and no hope of help, feelings of aloneness lead to the realization that one is more or less permanently isolated. Then hope is lost. Consequently, when a person discovers Imprisoned Intelligence, it feels like a revelation.

4. Many people develop, on their own, incredible resilience in figuring out strategies to get around their cognitive problems. These strategies can range from extremely effective to ineffective. Unfortunately, the way around the problem often involves avoiding areas of weakness rather than finding ways to learn in spite of the weakness.

The material presented on the chasm is confusing because it will not be clear when to employ which steps. For example, some clients find it helpful to learn how shame and withdrawal from shame work. Others do not. Unfortunately, there are few straightforward suggestions. For this reason, it is helpful to identify the chasm and appreciate its emotional consequences. Armed with this, the therapist can begin to pick and choose what might be helpful to individuals who struggle with Imprisoned Intelligence.

CONCLUSIONS

A very high-functioning professional man had a word recall problem. Normally, this did not interfere with sessions. The therapist could usually supply the word he was struggling to find and the hour would flow. One day, however, his need for silence was misinterpreted. The clinician thought he needed time to think, but he fell into the chasm. He was furious. He felt the therapist was demeaning him by "putting him on the spot." Rage erupted, but the therapist vigorously denied any intent to shame him. Over a period of several sessions, he was able to talk about the shame and humiliation of not being able to think and verbalize in a timely fashion. Then the therapist could empathize with his sense of excruciating exposure. Because he was extremely bright and in other areas of his life performed in an outstanding manner, his pride could not endure the disappointment and shame of feeling so stupid. In treatment he learned that he did not have to suffer these massive disappointments alone. In time, as his rage diminished, he began to appreciate that his sense of shame was understandable and that it reappeared because of old interactive patterns that erupted when he felt stupid.

Because the relationship had stood the test of time, he could use his shame to reconnect and the therapist could again validate his interest and excitement in his areas of strength. Eventually he learned to use his intelligence to protect his disability. He would say to people, "I need time to think about this" or "Can you help me? I can't think of the word I need." If he encountered people who shamed him, he would protect himself by withdrawing his trust and looking for more appropriate people who could understand that a very bright man might still have a "glitch."

Clearly, helping people adapt to learning deficits is not easy. It is difficult to live with cognitive inconsistencies because people base their self-esteem on their intellectual competence. So, ULD can create enormous frustrations that have implications for treatment. Psychotherapy provides a setting wherein these frustrations can be clarified. Then treatment can provide a sense of connection because now the client feels someone else can understand the critical dimensions of the problem. Because this population is intrinsically intelligent and motivated toward success, creativity and self-motivation are enhanced.

Therefore, when Imprisoned Intelligence causes psychological pain, therapists are needed. Sensitive therapists with clinical multidisciplinary expertise are vital for the proper analysis of the combined cognitive and emotional factors in ULD—for example, to help identify previous emotional pain or help people face their cognitive deficits.*

To help adults who have suffered from ULD, a bridge needs to be created between learning disability specialists (who are not trained psychotherapeutically) and psychotherapists (who are not

---

* The findings in this study corroborate Fred Levin's (1991) work regarding the need for interdisciplinary research.

trained in learning disabilities) in areas of theory and practice. The goals of the two disciplines are different, but to treat this population, an interface is vital. Although LD specialists help with recognition of LD, skill-building, and ways around the problem, they are not trained to help people with the emotional ramifications of LD. Unless their emotional problems are addressed, people may be too embarrassed and ashamed to benefit from LD specialists.

Throughout the course of psychotherapy, people come to understand that wrestling with these invisible deficits is an unfolding process that never ends. People learn that they need to learn *how* to learn differently—that there is more than one way to skin a cat. Confusion is replaced with a (not necessarily easy to live by) sense of order *and* a different sense of self-organization.

People change their outlook, their expectations of themselves, and their capacities to use others in fruitful ways. They develop a new sense of cohesion and coherence. Personal histories are reinterpreted. For example, there can be a new understanding about how, in order to learn, one may have "manipulated" other people. Also, blame of parents and teachers can shift because the individual now realizes that no one knew about ULD. Conflicts about individual responsibility in specific learning situations can be reexamined and understood. For example, the individual can now ask, "Can I not learn or do I not want to learn?" People can be uncomfortably jealous because others who do not suffer from this problem can intellectually perform so flawlessly and easily.

In essence, psychotherapy allows the following process to unfold:

- Learning about ULD brings relief and validation.
- People understand that they have suffered silently due to confusion, lack of knowledge, and unwarranted attacks on their motivation.
- The deficit plus the chasm affects self-esteem.
- The inability to learn as others do in areas of weakness causes grief.

- A different personal definition of learning evolves over time.
- People learn to modify perfectionistic goals through the interaction with appropriate mentors.
- People must adopt different learning techniques, which can be extremely painful.
- There is a feeling of connection with others who have similar problems.
- Through this process, people gain a new understanding of themselves; for instance, they may see themselves as survivors of an era when understanding of cognitive deficits was poor.

As people work through their grief, their emotional attention helps them adapt to their new self-knowledge. There is a sense of coming to terms with oneself. Self-organization changes and memories get modulated. Individuals learn to compensate differently. For example, some people in this study are very proud of their ability to understand the ramifications of ULD and create successful learning strategies for themselves both at school and at work. They no longer need their previous compensations to avoid embarrassment. The pain does not disappear, but the problem is seen within a greater context of self.

To summarize, psychotherapy enhances resilience by nurturing fortitude and flexibility. The process encourages people to plug into their own potential and not give up, while at the same time, to be flexible enough to attempt learning new perspectives in order to achieve and enhance their potential. Psychotherapy, in essence, provides a setting where emotional attention to problems can occur, which then allows for alternative ways of perceiving problems. The modulation of painful current and past memories makes all the difference! The therapist in effect encourages the release of innate potential and thus provides the environmental nurturance that allows for new growth and development.

Chapter 12

Neurocognitive Foundations of Learning Disorders and the Chasm Experience

by Jay Einhorn, Ph.D.

The chasm experience occurs when a person who knows herself (or himself) to be a fundamentally competent person suddenly and inexplicably finds herself unable to function in a cognitive domain in which other "ordinary" people seem to be quite proficient, and in which she is expected by other people to be able to function effectively. The injury to the individual's self-concept is exacerbated when she is treated by others not as if she has suddenly discovered a cognitive inadequacy but as if she is deliberately creating it—because she is "lazy," "isn't trying," "doesn't want to," or even "is oppositional to authority."

Let's consider the example of a dyslexic child who comes into basic literacy instruction, usually in kindergarten or first grade, who has been "normal" in every way until then. That is, he's learned how to walk, speak, and understand speech, toilet train, and behave socially to a certain level. He is more or less just like his peers. He may have been better than others in, say, sports, teamwork, leadership, vocabulary, speech fluency, singing, mechanical skill, perceptiveness and empathy toward the feelings of others, or mechanical or social problem solving. He may have thrived in the social and preacademic opportunities of preschool and kindergarten. Now, suddenly and unexpectedly, the teacher is teaching something that everyone else gets but him. She is writing signs on the board that are supposed to be sounds and words, and the other kids can say them along with her, but the signs make no sense to him, no matter how hard he tries. As time goes by, the other kids learn more and more, and he falls further and further behind.

What's happening? It has to be a mystery to the child. Perhaps she feels humiliated that she isn't keeping up with others. Perhaps she asks for help and is told to try harder and pay attention. Perhaps she doesn't worry about it and focuses on the things that she can do well, which might be drawing, socializing, or playing.

The situation becomes more complicated for our dyslexic child as people begin to react to the fact that he's not learning. His teacher says he isn't trying hard enough and tells him to try harder. He is trying as hard as he can, but it's not working. He gets bored and anxious during lessons when he doesn't get it, and his attention strays off the lesson; maybe he draws or builds with blocks or talks with other children. His teacher says that he isn't paying attention and admonishes him to pay attention. He finds that paying attention doesn't help. Bored with a lesson he can't get and feeling guilty and inadequate, he may become a class clown, cracking the other kids up, to the teacher's increasing chagrin; now he's becoming oppositional. Or he may become a bully, bolstering his injured self-esteem by physically intimidating and dominating others. His teacher tells his parents that he isn't learning because he isn't trying and isn't paying attention, so now they're on his case.

Eventually, the teacher may recognize that he is trying, and conclude that he is just stupid, not a very bright light. The child may pick up the teacher's attitude; "It's hopeless, I just can't learn." If his teacher is better trained, she may realize that he is dyslexic and refer him for special education services. This necessary intervention might add to the child's feeling that there's something wrong with him. A high-school student described the experience of walking out of her classroom and down the hall to the special education room, throughout elementary and junior high corridors, as "the walk of shame."

Special education remediation (the process of teaching children with learning disorders to use compensatory strategies to acquire skills, such as decoding written language that they can't learn normally) is more effective for some children than others. Success depends on the complexity of their learning disorders and the skills of their learning resource (special education) teachers.

As a result, there are two broad neurocognitive domains contributing to the chasm experience. The first is the neurocognitive processing underlying the performance insufficiency itself; in this case, learning to read. The second domain is the neurocognitive processing underlying the self as it responds both to that performance insufficiency and also to how others treat one about it. The experience, put into words, is something like: "I can't do this. I'm no good. I hate this." Perhaps, sooner or later, it will extend to, "I hate myself," or "I hate them."

Let's consider the two domains more specifically. They are the cognitive domains of learning and learning disorders, and of the experience of self.

NEUROCOGNITIVE FOUNDATIONS OF LEARNING DISORDERS

The foundational discovery in the field of learning disabilities is that neurocognitive processing disorders are responsible for specific learning disorders in children of otherwise normal intelligence. The field of learning disabilities began when neurologists, psychologists, and others discovered that some children who had been given up as unteachable or retarded seemed to resemble adults who'd been of normal intelligence until they sustained a brain injury. After being injured these adults needed special forms of instruction utilizing the concept of compensatory teaching, that is, making use the cognitive abilities that remained intact after the injury to compensate for the ones that had been damaged. Some of the "unteachable" children could learn to read, it was discovered, through "multisensory" methods, such as feeling raised letters on blocks or writing them in sand, or by learning

special methods (such as intensive phonics and related instruction) for systematically decoding the letters and words that most
children learn to recognize through ordinary instruction and
repetition (known as the "whole language" method in education).

These discoveries led to the creation of the field of Learning
Disabilities. The name, "Learning Disabilities," decided upon
at a seminal conference in Chicago in 1963, was suggested by
the pioneering educator Samuel Kirk (Lerner, 2003). It replaced
other terms such as "organic brain damage" and "minimal brain
damage" in use at the time. Today, the terms "learning disabilities" and "learning disorders" are used interchangeably, and we
speak of a spectrum of "attention disorders."

Before looking at the specific types of learning and attention
disorders, we should consider whether they are all, in fact, disorders.

Are All Learning and Attention Disorders Really Disorders?

There is a controversy among researchers, educators, and
therapists about whether all of the learning and attention styles
diagnosed as "disorders" in modern psychoeducational, psychological, and psychiatric practice are, in fact, disorders. There is
a compelling evolutionary argument that many children who either don't learn to read normally, or whose attention style is not
well suited to academic learning in classrooms, actually have no
neurocognitive dysfunction at all. What they really suffer from,
from this point of view, are the assumptions in academic and scientific folklore that all normal children can be taught to read and
to learn by the same methods. Because of these fallacious assumptions, the contention goes, we misdiagnose normal children as
abnormal.

Joseph Bogen is the neurosurgeon who conducted the initial
"split brain" surgeries, which cut the corpus callosum (the huge
bundle of nerve fibers that connects the two hemispheres of the
brain) of patients with severe and intractable epilepsy. Bogen's
studies of perceptual changes in his patients after surgery place

him in the first rank of modern students of brain function (Bogen, 1969). At a conference that I attended in the late 1970s, Bogen observed, in response to a question about whether dyslexia was due to brain damage, that it is a mistake to assume that all biologically normal children will be able to learn to read. He pointed out that all biologically normal children accomplish a set of basic competencies for survival by the time they are five years old; they walk, speak and understand speech, and have learned basic social behavior. These fundamental competencies have been selected through evolution over countless centuries in which they were necessary for survival, and are shown by 100 percent of normal children; they are not, Bogen, emphasized, described by the normal curve. The ability to read, on the other hand, has only been expected of children very recently in evolutionary terms—for merely a century or so, depending on where one wants to begin counting, and then only in cultures that deliberately aim at universal literacy. It should not be expected, therefore, that reading ability characterizes all people. Instead, it is distributed along a normal curve (Bogen, 197X).

Another physician who raises substantial questions about the appropriateness of traditional concepts of intelligence is pediatrician Mel Levine. In a series of books including *A Mind at a Time,* Levine advocates a multifunctional view of intelligence in which social skills are as important as analytical ones, and social deficits are as potentially debilitating as the kind that show up on the academic report card (Levine, 2002). Psychologists such as Robert Sternberg and Howard Gardner have also raised fundamental questions about the appropriateness of traditional concepts of intelligence. Gardner pioneered the "Multiple Intelligences" concept, in which literacy and academic analytic skills are only two among a group of intelligences (Gardner, 1983). Sternberg developed a tripartite model of intelligence—analytic, creative, and practical (Sternberg and Grigorenko, 1999). Such models of intelligence challenge the appropriateness and comprehensiveness of the traditional model which implicitly assumes that success in a Western classroom is the most appropriate expression of brainpower. (It's an interesting reflection on the way cultures cling to their folklore that the myth of academic brilliance necessarily being associated with perceptive capacity in life persists despite all the evidence to the contrary.)

Socioeconomic Viability

I have proposed the concept of "socioeconomic viability" as the most important criterion for evaluating success in adulthood, both for adults as individuals and for the academic and other preparatory institutions which produce them (Einhorn, 2004). This refers to the ability of the adult to be successful socially and economically in life after school. By this criterion, many children with learning or attention disorders in school do quite well in life after school, and many who do quite well in school have disorders in life after school, because they are not able to be successful socially or economically. The Western way of education, based on universal literacy and years of classroom learning, is itself, in historical context, a cultural experiment that has yet to be comprehensively assessed. Throughout most of human history, children have learned from watching their parents and other adults actually do things and by helping out by doing actual tasks, in the process of which they learned skills of increasing complexity and responsibility. This is learning by watching and doing, formalized in apprenticeship.

Limitations of the Traditional Educational Paradigm

There have always been educators who advocate for a more multifunctional vision of learning and practice of teaching, but they have always been a small minority and very much swimming against the deeply established current of educational institutions and institutionalized thought. The reigning educational paradigm assumes that there is one way, or one best way, for children to learn, and that it is organized around learning verbal information in classrooms. Thus, to the paradigmatic assumption that all normal children come to school with neurocognitive readiness to learn to read, write, and calculate, we must add the related assumption that they will be able to learn to do so through whatever mode of instruction is favored in the academic institutions of the place and time. In our time, this means mainly learning by rote.

It's probably the case, however, that some children who are diagnosed with learning and attention disorders in modern American classrooms would be perfectly normal in preliterate cultures, while others would be abnormal in any culture. The goal of education should be to prepare children for adulthood by finding out how each child learns and teaching her—not to treat children as if they are more or less identical widgets on an assembly line. But education is still mainly mechanistic rather than psychological in its understanding of what learning and teaching are. And the prevailing psychology of education has itself been quite mechanistic until relatively recently, when new knowledge about the structure and function of the brain replaced the simple reward-and-punishment paradigm of behaviorism.

It is not only teachers, therapists, students, and parents who are concerned about learning disabilities who have noticed these limitations in mainstream education's practices and view of human nature. The main complaint that leaders in business, government, and the military express about newly recruited personnel—that they lack practical problem-solving, collaboration, and leadership skills—appears to reflect a pervasive discrepancy between the achievements of formal education and success in life in the world after school (Raven, 1984). So, it's probably the case that educational institutions will someday recognize many different kinds of intelligence, and many different ways of educating students, within the context of a much broader appreciation of what normal neurocognitive function is.

NEUROCOGNITIVE BASIS FOR LEARNING AND ATTENTION DISORDERS

Having said that, within the American socioeducational framework and elsewhere, the diagnostic criteria for learning and attention disorders specifically include impairment in schoolwork (American Psychiatric Association, 1994). This leads to the question of whether there are specific aspects of brain function that underlie the spectrum of learning disabilities and attention disorders.

Researchers are beginning to discover some of the kinds of neurocognitive processing associated with inability to learn to read through ordinary instruction. Three findings of much interest are:

1. Some children's auditory language processing confuses the sounds of similar sounding phonemes (the basic sounds of any language). The sounds associated with the letters "d" and "b," for example, are not distinguishable to some children. Auditory brain wave studies show that their brains do not detect these subtle differences in sounds. Of course, this impairs their ability to learn to read when these letter-sounds are involved. This can be helped with special training, for example, slowing down the sounds to below normal speaking speed so that children can learn to detect the difference (International Dyslexia Association, 2005; citing work by Paula Tallal).

2. Some children have subtle visual processing disorders which cause them to confuse the sight of similarly shaped letters. The visual shape of letters is called their "orthography," and these children have orthographic decoding problems. The shape of the letters "d" and "b," written in the lower case, appear to be the same to some children. Brain imaging studies show that they do not recognize letters with quite the same parts of their brains or in quite the same way as children who can read normally. This, too, can be helped with special training, for example, helping children to learn how letters feel, as in writing in sand or holding wooden block letters while learning to recognize them on the page.

3. Some adults known to be dyslexic were discovered, on autopsy, to have abnormally symmetrical brains. Most adult human brains have a slight bulge in the left temporal lobe (at the side of the head, approximately by the ear). Presumably, this developed because the left hemisphere, in most adults, does most of the lan-

guage decoding and processing. These dyslexic adults had left hemispheres that were symmetric with their right hemispheres in the temporal areas; that is, their left hemispheres had no bulge (International Dyslexia Association, 2005; citing work by Galaburda).

Common Types of Learning Disorder

Dyslexia, in the sense of being unable to learn to read, to decode written language, is only one of a range of learning disorders that a clinician in the field of learning disabilities will encounter quite often. They include:

1. Reading decoding: deficiencies in sounding out the letters and/or words.
2. Reading comprehension: deficiencies in understanding what one has read.
3. Mathematics calculation: deficiencies in adding, subtracting, multiplying, or dividing, even when the problem is set up on the page.
4. Mathematics comprehension: deficiencies in understanding mathematical operations (addition, subtraction, multiplication, and/or division), and in understanding what word problems mean in terms of the relationships between quantities they express.
5. Auditory language processing: deficiencies in understanding spoken language (especially a problem in lecture classes and similar situations).
6. Expressive spoken language: deficiencies in being able to identify, sequence, and deliver speech, even though the speaker does know what he or she means to say.
7. Written expression for content: deficiencies in being able to produce written content, for example, answers to questions, especially when more than a very few words are called for.
8. Written expression for structure: deficiencies in being able to learn and use the structures of written language, such as

spelling, punctuation, capitalization, and grammar.

9. Social learning disorders: deficiencies in understanding social behavior, including such nonverbal behaviors as body communication (facial expression and body movement), tone of voice, and proxemics (interpersonal use of space); deficiencies in empathic understanding of others; deficiencies in understanding the unspoken subtext or implications of speech.

10. Executive function disorders: deficiencies in attention (including hyperactivity and/or distractibility to the extent that learning is substantially impaired), deficiencies in organizing, integrating, or sequencing of information; deficiencies in learning to develop new behaviors and habits in adaptation to environmental changes, including new learning, being in new situations, or responding to changes in one's environment; deficiencies in being able to prioritize and to maintain focus in accordance with one's priorities, including deficiencies in focusing attention and maintaining attention without distraction; deficiencies in being able to monitor the response of the environment to the self and the self to the environment; and make adaptations as required to fulfill one's priorities and goals.

A Brain-Based Neurocognitive View of Learning Disorders

Everything we can say about the brain is oversimplified, but there is an emerging consensus among scientists and professionals who work at the intersection of the study of brain structure and function, on the one hand, and the study of learning and learning disorders, on the other. I hope my colleagues will allow me to generalize in order help readers understand learning disorders in the context of brain structure and function, and invite correction to, and extension of, this consideration. Please keep in mind that this model of functional distribution applies to most, but not all, adults, that some people are "wired" differently, that children's hemispheric function isn't fully lateralized until adolescence, and that everyone is unique.

The brain structures whose activities underlie learning and learning disorders mainly involve three major brain systems—the left cerebral hemisphere, the right cerebral hemisphere, and the frontal lobes. The frontal lobes actually are part of the left and right cerebral hemisphere—they are just the parts at the front—but, because they are responsible for so much of what we call "executive function," they can be understood as a separate brain system (Goldberg, 2001).

The left cerebral hemisphere is a sequential processor, and its one-step-at-a-time activity underlies much of our language processing. If I want to spell the word "pat," for example, I have to use the letters "p," "a," and "t" in exactly that sequence and no other. If I use the same letters in a different sequence—"apt," or "tap"—they don't mean the same thing at all. Only the sequence "p-a-t," in that order, means "pat." Similarly, words that are similar to "pat" but not quite the same—"bat," for example, or "pad"—although including almost identical elements, don't mean the same thing, or even anything like it. A teacher might say, to Pat, who is tapping his desk during a lesson, "It isn't apt to tap, Pat," and this makes perfect sense (although it may be hard to say, and might present a real processing problem to a student with an auditory language processing deficit). The same elements in a different sequence—"Apt tap isn't it Pat?"—are nonsense in that situation; although they could conceivably be used in this sequence to comment on, say, a successful bunt in a baseball game, or a good putt in golf. These are examples of how the left hemisphere works. Since much of our language processing involves sequences—letters in just a certain sequence to form words, words in just a certain sequence to form sentences, and so on—the left hemisphere is very much involved in the basics of encoding and constructing language. That's probably why that bulge evolved on the left temporal lobe. (Incidentally, a sudden unexpected shift from mainly left- to mainly right-hemisphere language processing might well underlie the humor in puns, or in the language-play of such writers as Dr. Seuss. The reader or hearer is suddenly shifted from literal content to a completely unexpected perception of some relationship which may have little or nothing to do with the apparent literal content.)

It makes sense to suppose that the left hemisphere is even more involved in literacy—in reading and writing—than in spoken language. Children learn spoken words as sounds with meanings—"da (dad), ma (mom), my (mine), na (no)." The left hemisphere is involved in stringing the phonemes along to make a whole word, combining phonemes into words of more than one syllable ("daddy" replaces "da"), and combining words into statements: "No, Daddy! Mine!" But the meaning of the words—in this example, what belongs to whom, and the subtext which involves the relationship between the speaker and the person to whom he is speaking—primarily depends on the characteristic processing of the right hemisphere. So it makes sense to expect that both hemispheres are probably working in a fairly balanced way in the acquisition of early auditory (heard and understood) and spoken (expressive speech) language.

Written language, even for children who can learn it through the normal method of demonstration and drill, is a much more sequentially loaded process, in which the signs (the written letters and words) and sounds (phonemes, syllables, and words) are separated from semantics (meaning). It's interesting to speculate that the widespread adoption of reading and writing—literacy—as a more or less universal goal of education may have resulted in a change in human brain function, expressed physically as changes in the left hemisphere and left-right balance in childhood, and experientially as the ability to detach temporarily from meaning in order to conduct a sequential process which will eventually become meaningful. (There's a potential research direction here, for you scientists or graduate students, in imaging the brains of children learning spoken versus written language, then imaging them again a few years later to compare patterns of task-related brain activation, and perhaps comparing children from literate and nonliterate cultures on various kinds of linguistic tasks.)

The right hemisphere is a relational perceiver that integrates simultaneous inputs into gestalts, or patterns. Recognizing faces and orienting geographically are examples of right-hemisphere functioning. The right hemisphere's language functioning operates similarly. The understanding of the meaning of the phrase "The early bird gets the worm" takes place mainly in the right hemisphere, even though the left hemisphere processes the sounds and words in sequence. This is an example of analogy. Patients with injuries to the front part of the right brain may lose some or all of their ability to understand analogies. Such people might understand this phrase to mean, "The bird got the worm," or, "Too bad for the worm" (Ornstein, 1997).

An even more advanced form of right-hemisphere language processing is metaphor. When they were young, I told my children the story of the lion who had never seen his reflection. When he came to a pool in which he saw his reflection, he thought it was another lion and was afraid to take a drink until a little butterfly told him he could (Shah, 1998). It's a lovely children's story (the Hoopoe Press book presents it delightfully) but it has inner meanings that can be important for adults. For example, I once told that story to a social worker who had been encouraged to apply for a department director's position, but was reluctant. It helped her to clarify which of her reservations about the position involved the realities of the job, and which were her own projections.

Now, the words to the story are decoded mainly in the left hemisphere, but it is the right hemisphere which perceives the gestalt, pattern, or meaning of them, and which can apply them to other situations, and recognize it when someone else makes the connection. Thus, problems with decoding written language— learning to sound out the letters, then the words—are probably mainly due to left-hemisphere glitches in making associations between the way words sound (phonemic structure) and/or look (orthographic structure). However, problems with understanding what written language means—reading comprehension—if decoding is functional, are probably more due to right-hemisphere glitches in understanding the gestalt or pattern of the language.

The more that comprehension of a passage of written language requires a perception of "subtext," reading "between the lines," or gleaning implications, the more dependent it is on the perceptual aptitude of the right hemisphere. Some children learn to read normally, in the sense of decoding, but their ability to understand the implications of what they read lags behind. These children often are also unaware of social cues, and may have difficulty sustaining relationships outside of highly structured situations, such as academic, religious, or athletic activities, or even within them. In mathematics, they may tend to make mistakes because they miss the meaning of the operational signs, adding when they should be subtracting or multiplying. The operational signs tell what the relationship between the numbers is, for example, 2 + 2 expresses a different relationship between 2 and 2 than 2 − 2 does, and that difference in relationship makes all the difference to the answer.

Subtle glitches or deficits in left- and/or right-hemisphere processing, or in their interconnection (since the two hemispheres work together to carry out most of the cognitive operations we do), seem to underlie, and be responsible for, learning disorders. We've looked particularly at reading decoding and reading comprehension, so now let's consider other learning disorders that are commonly encountered.

1. *Dis-sequential speaking.* Some children learn to speak well enough to convey what they mean, but they may often not speak in sentences, and they may use words in unusual or incorrect ways. Their spoken language may not read correctly if written down, but people usually understand what they mean. Some of our highest political leaders speak in this way, so it isn't necessarily an insurmountable barrier.

2. *Auditory language-processing deficits.* Some children's language processing, that is, their ability to understand what people say when they are being spoken to, may be impaired, even though their hearing is fine. They pass hearing tests with flying colors,

but make mistakes on easy tests of listening to what is being said to them. This is a very subtle disorder, because it isn't easy to identify unless you look for it with special tests. Audiologists specializing in diagnosing language-processing deficits diagnose central auditory-processing disorder (CAPD) in some children, where the language processing is presumed to somehow be degraded in the neural circuitry between the inner ear and the cerebral cortex, so that the signal that the cortex receives to interpret is degraded. Other children may have language-decoding issues at the cortical level, where sounds are simply misinterpreted.

3. *Mathematical calculation deficits.* We've already considered the problem of understanding what mathematical signs mean, but some children seem to have sequential problems in calculation even when they understand the sign and when the numbers are written down in front of them. A reasonable guess is that left-hemisphere-sequencing disorders underlie such deficits.

4. *Mathematical concept deficits.* Some children have difficulty understanding what word problems mean. They can calculate problems when the numbers are set up in front of them, for example, 10 / 2 = 5, but they can't solve problems like, "A long distance runner ran ten miles in two hours. What was his speed in miles per hour?"

5. *Written expression deficits.* Some children, including children who have normal spoken and auditory language processing, have deficiencies in writing. These deficiencies can affect handwriting (forming letters), the structures of written language (spelling, grammar, punctuation, capitalization), or the content of written language—just getting your thoughts translated into writing—or any combination of these. Since these problems can show up separately—that is, some children have dreadful problems shaping letters but can spell, punctuate, and generate content, while others can form letters but not spell or punctuate, and still others can shape letters and spell but not generate content—it makes sense to

assume that different parts or combinations of parts of the brain are involved in these different aspects of written language.

6. *Social learning deficits.* Social behavior has its own codes, analogous to language and, as with language, some children are cognitively better equipped to learn them than others. Body language, including the subtleties of movement and facial expression (Ekman, 2003), voice tone, the use of words to give unspoken hints of intention or interest (or lack of it), recognizing when people in groups are or are not open to being joined, all require the ability to perceive the signals which convey the meaning and content of behavior. The right hemisphere seems to underlie much of this processing. Nonverbal learning disabilities (NVLD) are being more frequently diagnosed as a source of social deficits.

7. *Executive function disorders.* The executive functions, mainly located in the frontal lobes of the left and right cerebral hemispheres, are likened to the conductor of an orchestra, or the chief executive officer of an organization by Elkhonen Goldberg (Goldberg, 2001). They organize, prioritize, maintain focus, inhibit distraction, monitor feedback from inside the self and from the environment, and adapt based on the interplay between priorities, needs, and opportunities. Attention deficit disorders seem largely to involve the frontal lobes (although other brain structures are implicated, and there seem to be several different kinds, probably an entire spectrum, of attention disorders).

Avoiding Overlocalization

The study of the neurocognitive basis of learning and learning disorders has come a long way. It is unlikely that I could hear again such a statement as I overheard fifteen years ago at a conference on learning disabilities and education, when one participant said to another, "Just because he has a processing disorder doesn't mean he has a brain disorder." I wanted to ask her where she thought the processing was taking place. Fortunately, there is no need to ask the question now. Clearly, the processing is taking place in the brain, and this is just about universally acknowledged.

Having said that, we need to avoid the pitfall of overlocalizing processing disorders in the brain. Reading, for example, involves many discrete functions that have to be coordinated. Letters, words, and sentences need to be visually recognized and integrated. Punctuation marks also need to be recognized, decoded, and combined with the letters, words, and sentences, into syntactical and grammatical language that has semantic meaning. Various parts of the brain are involved in these processes, and have to be coordinated and integrated into what, for most older children and adults, is experienced as the seamless act of reading.

Social relationships have complexities which involve different parts of the brain. Recognizing a friend, knowing what our relationship with him is, recognizing how he's feeling at the moment, and what his availability for relationship or needs from us are, involve many different parts of the brain working together simultaneously, the left hemisphere as well as the right.

Executive functions, although mostly mediated by the frontal lobes, extend beyond them. There are different kinds of memory, for example, which executive functions call upon for different tasks. The memory for how to ski or play a song on the guitar is different from the memory of what someone's face looked like, and both are different from the memory of what her voice sounded like or what she smelled like. All these are different from the memory of times we shared together, different from the memory of what she meant to us at the time, and different from the memory of what we decided she meant to us after she moved away and we lost touch. Without access to memory, executive functions can't do their work.

Executive functions also rely on being able to turn newly learned tasks into more routine and habitual ones. The cerebellum, at the lower rear of the brain, is very much involved in routinizing learning, making some action or process that we have to learn, initially gradually and step-by-step, become automatic and habitual. If the cerebellum is damaged, or if the connections between the frontal lobes and the cerebellum are not working properly, new learning can't become automatic and habitual at the rate that is necessary for successful learning and adaptation in most situations.

So, although it's true that we are learning more and more about how different parts of the brain are responsible for different forms of cognitive (or information) processing, it's also true that we're learning that different parts of the brain are involved in most of what we do. If we could see the brain as it looks on a computer-enhanced image, we would see different parts lighting up with different colors to represent different intensities of engagement. As the individual did any specific task, the colors would stretch from front to back, from side to side, and from top of the brain to deep within it, and they would change, and change, and change.

NEUROCOGNITIVE FOUNDATIONS OF SELF

We know much more about the neurocognitive foundations of learning than we do about the neurocognitive foundations of the experience of self. We do know that different parts of the brain have different contributions to the experience of self. What we feel as "I" is the product of a kind of neurobiological net of functioning involving many different cognitive processes, changing all the time to reflect changes in these processes and their relationships. It may be the case that the experience of an individual which extends backward in time as a durable entity is itself something of an illusion, created by our neurobiological self-net in the present, which is itself always changing. If so, this would tend to confirm the teachings of mystics that the self is, in fact, an illusion, and lead to some interesting questions which I can only mention here, like, What kind of perception might underlie or supersede the illusory sense of self? What is the goal of the spiritual quest, and How does brain activity adapt and organize to support that?

The sense of self is experienced in different ways at different times, depending on our motivations and our orientation. Some people derive their sense of self largely from their relationships with others, while some keep score by counting, for example, money earned, home runs, mountain peaks climbed. Some organize themselves in time, by appointments in the calendar, while others do so by projects. Some people define themselves in terms of skill sets and competencies. Our sense of self may depend, to a greater or lesser extent, on where we live and how we dress. Our sense of self depends partly on how others treat us; it's always interesting for me to see how people treat me differently if I am introduced as "Dr. Einhorn" or simply as "Jay." How we experience ourselves in relationship to other people, too, depends on what we want or need from them, as well as what we can perceive of them.

All these ways of experiencing the self can be misleading. Memory, for example, is constructed rather than actually recalled as we usually understand it to be, and can vary from time to time, and even be fundamentally changed by suggestion. This includes the memory of events that happened to us, of when they happened, what they were, and what they meant (Engel, 1999).

We experience self in creative ways; we surprise ourselves, sometimes, by the things that we think, say, or make. An artist once told me that she loved to paint because through her work she discovered who she was. Perhaps at the most fundamental level, we experience self as the observer which cannot itself be observed; even when observing other aspects of self. Arthur Deikman refers to this as the "observing self" (Deikman, 1982).

Many of the same parts of the brain that contribute to learning abilities and disabilities also contribute to the sense of self. The frontal lobes, the seat of the executive functions, profoundly affect our sense of self. The awareness and monitoring of internal states, as well as the perception and interpretation of our relationships with others, are mainly the functions of the right frontal lobe, which has a bulge, in most people, that the left frontal lobe doesn't have. The asymmetric bulge in this area seems to be similar to the bulge which most people have in the left temporal lobe, which plays a major role in language processing. It is the right hemisphere, and especially the right frontal lobe, that has major responsibility for recognizing and interpreting other people's feelings expressed nonverbally (in facial expressions, body language, and voice tones) and interpreting the meaning of those emotions for our relationships with those people. It makes evolutionary sense to suppose that the brain has adapted to add tissue to the parts most heavily involved in language and social processing.

The emotional centers lie deep in the middle of the brain. The hippocampus is involved in memory and the amygdala in emotion. Memory and emotion together account for a great deal of how we react to events. It is, after all, the combination of memory and emotion that distinguishes mammals from reptiles, and allows mammals to learn from experience as instinctively hardwired reptiles cannot. In human beings, the interpretation of events, mediated by the frontal lobes, connects cognitive attribution with emotional reaction. How we react to others' behavior, for example, often depends on how we interpret it. If a colleague is rude, for instance, we may react differently if we interpret this as a deliberate insult, or as merely due to a lack of training, a recent career disappointment, a bad day in divorce court, or a brain injury. Most of our emotional reactions reflect our attribution of what an event means.

But some emotional reactions are more immediate and less mediated by the frontal lobes. There is a "fast track" (LeDoux, 1996) directly to the hippocampus and amygdala for events which seem to pose an immediate threat. This fast-track system enables us to react quickly in order to save ourselves, but is also responsible for some terrible mistakes. Malcolm Gladwell, in Blink, notes that many police departments in recent years have banned high-speed chases, not only from a concern about hitting an innocent bystander during the chase, but because of what happens after the chase, when police officers in a dangerously high state of arousal may make critical mistakes in rapid perception and judgment (Gladwell, 2005).

So, what we experience as "self," at any given time, is profoundly affected by the ongoing processes, the functioning and interaction, of various structures within the brain that change in their ratios and priorities depending on many variables in what happens to, around, and within us. How we experience "self" also varies with our changing states of appetite and need. At one time, for example, we may be willing to risk a great deal for a sexual experience with a certain person, while at others we would never consider it.

All of which brings us back to the chasm. The astonishment that one is unable to learn something or do something, when one is able to learn and do so many others, and the shame that one is disappointing oneself and others, are often compounded by how a child with a learning disability is often treated; scolded, blamed, teased, or excoriated for "not caring" or "not trying hard enough." These experiences are both created in the self and between self and others. Because, if one of the mysteries of the self is that it is more than the sum of the parts of the brain, another mystery is that it is itself created as an interaction between the individual and the significant others in his or her life. Paradoxically, the self, which can be seen as the most intimate and personal part of an individual, is supraindividual; created and maintained, to a large extent, through interactions with others.

Neurocognition of the "Chasm"

The "chasm" experience is an experience of the self as suddenly, inexplicably, incoherently incompetent. The shame that it brings with it is an expression of our perception of inferiority in relationship with others. The panic that it brings is an expression of our helplessness and disorientation, and these can lead to other responses, such as rage, or hopelessness, and depression, or the need to restore a sense of competence through manipulation of others, or seizing mastery where one can, or seeking instant assuaging of the state of self through the use of intoxicants.

The little intimate and personal self is even larger than we have thus far considered. If conscious awareness of self, the "I am," is a sum that is more than the parts of the brain that contribute to it, and if it is also a sum of the interaction of that individual with all the other selves who have touched it, then the other selves who have touched it include uncounted individuals throughout history and into the present who have had some form of contribution to the culture within which that individual has emerged and evolved. The chasm experience, then, is a sort of dislocation of the self in its context of relatedness to these uncounted others in the cultural milieu, as well as an experience that results from many parts of the brain—involving perception, emotion, memory, attention, emotional self-regulation, executive function—working in disharmony, and in a manner that paralyzes the self and degrades the functioning of the brain in which the experience is produced.

At best, the "chasm" experience challenges the self to respond to the situation in which it finds itself helpless by finding a way to be empowered and effective, to regain control. But such responses can be ultimately self-destructive—as in addiction or illegal activities—as well as productive and self-confirming; some of our highest achievers and greatest social contributors are persons with learning or attention disorders. Many adults with learning disabilities and attention disorders whom I have known, for example, have achieved highly in life—especially after school—partly because they were driven to never again feel the helplessness of the chasm experience.

Even such success, however, may be won at a steep price. The single-minded determination to use whatever abilities one has to overcome obstacles and succeed can drive a person to accomplish great goals in life, while also narrowing his focus so intently on that achievement, that existential survival as a viable self rather than a hopelessly ineffective one, as to diminish much of life that isn't involved in that challenge and accomplishment by banishing it into the imperceptible background. And that, too, results in a certain diminishment, a certain disorder, a certain degrading, of the self, even in people who have achieved highly.

Chapter 13

A Neuropsychological Look at Learning to Be Resilient

By Myrna Orenstein
and
Fred Levin

Dear Readers: We wish to warn you that in what follows, there will be some comments here and there in another language, namely, that of neuroscience, so you may wish to take a pass on it and that's fine! But if you stay the course, you may also find yourself learning some interesting, even exciting, new information and ways of looking at LD. In this chapter we shed some interdisciplinary light upon a most complex subject. After reading it, you may find it easier in the future to follow developments in the neuroscience of LD as they are published or reported in the media. And, you'll have a new appreciation of what's happening "under the hood," as it were.

—Myrna Orenstein and Fred Levin

"It always amazes me," I said to Hawk, "how some kids
can grow out of the trash heap they started in."
—Back Story, 2003 (Robert Parker)

How do smart people with LD become so resilient? We believe the best way to answer this question is to understand the nature and growth of resilience by examining the interface between neuroscience, cognitive psychology, and psychoanalysis. Or if you prefer, between emotions and learning. But this attempt is complicated because, from a multidisciplinary perspective, the study of resilience is rooted in biology as well as psychology. The study of biology is based on observation, and yet psychology involves thoughts and feelings which cannot be observed directly. So, looking at resilience from both perspectives is indeed a challenge. At this point we would like nothing more than to be able to define resilience in terms of both neuroscience *and* psychology but scientific knowledge is still evolving. Clearly, the science we are trying to explore here is a work in process.

This chapter will look at how resilience in people with LD evolves and grows from an inside-out, psychoanalytic and neurocognitive perspective. This perspective allows us to concentrate on subjective emotional experiences of resilient individuals with learning disabilities, while simultaneously maintaining our curiosity about the scientific basis for the resilience in the first place. So if you would be patient with us, by the end of this chapter on resilience, you will have significantly new knowledge of how neuroscience and psychology enhance our understanding of the interface between learning and LD.

Generally, people think of resiliency as the ability to bounce back. This represents a focus on outcomes, reflecting the favorable results that resilience can provide. But resilience is also something we "do," not just something we "think about." In a way, it's like our having the right anatomy. We just take our resiliency for granted. For example, if our thumbs are working fine we really don't think too much about them. However, if we injure them, and then try to write something, we become suddenly aware of what we are missing. Resiliency falls into the same camp. We take it for granted because it includes an automatic component of being able to seek, to respond "no matter what." A good example of resilience in everyday life can be seen in J.A. Jance's mystery *Until Proven Guilty*. Two detectives working on a homicide case of a five-year-old girl find that someone higher up in the department has been leaking very detrimental information to the press and complicating their efforts to find the killer. The story goes like this:

"Do we let him get away with that?" Peters exploded when I finally let him talk.

"We don't have a whole hell of a lot of choice."

"It's" ... Peters stopped, totally at a loss for words.

"It's the way it is," I finished for him, "and nothing you or I do is going to change it. We just have to work around it, that's all."

Obviously, these resilient detectives expect success because they know how to work around problems; and this is one key benefit of the seeking system at work.

LEARNING, EMOTIONAL ATTENTION, AND RESILIENCE

"The idea here is that what you believe in, what interests or excites you, and what you desire, also invites you to learn more about it, and ultimately changes your brain permanently in the direction of generally facilitating further learning" (Levin, 2003–2004, p. 22)

We begin this section with the assumption that certain emotions facilitate learning and learning facilitates resilience. But why is this so? Well, it seems logical that in order to be resilient one must be able to learn alternatives when there are obstacles. Recognition of obstacles can involve unpleasant feelings of fear over potential failure. We call this recognition of what we feel "emotional attention." We find that smart people with learning disabilities who pay emotional attention to feelings involved with failure or the specter of failure know how to reinvent learning styles when they need to. In this way they can then make accommodations to deal with difficult academic demands and get pleasure and profit from their own insights and creativity!

If we are failing, instead of avoiding what we feel by escaping, for example, into drugs, alcohol, or video games, we can recognize our embarrassment and helplessness about failing and have the fortitude and flexibility to face the problem. (There is more information about fortitude and flexibility in the next chapter.) Emotional attention, then, is a cognitive awareness of what we are feeling that can have profound impact on our learning. Our feelings can then propel us to look for help or study different alternatives, simply to avoid the unpleasant feeling of being stuck.

The study of emotional expression as a discipline is relatively new. But observations on this subject go back at least to Aristotle, 2,500 years ago. Darwin (1859), Tomkins (1987), Nathanson (1987), Basch (1988) and Ekman (2002) have all contributed to the understanding of how feelings are reflected in universal facial and nonverbal expressions. Tomkins is one of the premier systematizers in the area of emotion studies. In particular, he underscores the importance of affects (basic feelings) as they influence our development. For example, on the positive side, Tomkins refers to interest, excitement, enjoyment, and joy. (More about Tomkins's work can be found in chapter 8.) We see these positive feelings reflected in our caregiver's face, posture, and voice, which then enhance our resilience. For example, when a child is just starting to walk, the caregiver will stand in front of the child with his or her arms out and encourage the child to take his or her first steps. The child sees the interest and excitement which gives him the confidence to try. As confidence grows, he or she walks more and more until the child is running!

As stated earlier, basically, such feelings of accomplishment are experienced as validation. The overall experience then becomes encoded into new long-term memories and integrated into our evolving organization of self. The pleasure of these experiences further propels us to try again to find a means of expression for our strengths, and hopefully, our efforts are eventually rewarded. Surely, emotions are very powerful forces that determine and facilitate what we learn. "You go girl!" is an expression of our emotional need to seek to achieve.

There is important evidence (Levin, 2003a; 2003b) that successful solutions to different problems hinge on the role of our affects, or feelings, to selectively activate specific neurochemical transcription factors. Transcription factors are proteins which can turn on the genes for creating the new long-term memories that record these new insights and growth in us. Usually, we learn best what is interesting to us and tend to forget the rest. How many of us have learned the material to pass an exam and then forgotten it as soon as the exam is over? But how great it is for us to recognize that our capacity to learn can grow throughout one's lifespan and take us into very new and very sweet territory.

So let's consider a definition of learning:

> Learning is the incorporation of new facts, perceptions, [feelings] and ideas. It is also the mastery of new processes, styles, and formats of thinking and interacting, . . . An essential aspect of learning is the addition of something new to an existing structure, producing a necessary change in that structure. The structure that is modified is both the body of knowledge already held by the learner and his [or her] self system. What is learned changes what was preexisting. (Fuqua 1993, p. 14)

By this definition, learning changes pre-existing knowledge, which surely enhances resilience. The biology of learning is too complex to condense into a short paragraph or two, but clarification of one core element dealing with the emotions in resilience may help the reader begin to understand how learning occurs and intelligence is released. When we are comfortably learning, our brain chemistry changes in specific areas in our brains. This can happen because our emotional attention initiates the complex series of biological brain-related changes that include (1) the formation of new synapses, (2) our capacity to seek, and (3) ultimately the capturing of new knowledge in the form of novel neural networks (Levin, 2003). The next few pages identify parts of the brain that are involved with feelings and cognition. Knowledge of these structures is important because of the neurochemical interface between them. We need to underscore that the systems of mind/brain that involve feelings and cognition are not as clearly separated as we once believed them to be. What a relief!

1. The *thalamus and brain stem* principally receive sensory input. The brainstem deals with the basal ganglia which are important regulators of physical and emotional "balance" and complex coordinations between brain systems. Essentially, these two components are critical for affect

reception and transmittal, and the use and retention of this information by and for the self.

2. The *hypothalamus* deals with what used to be called "drives" or basic needs (as well as with emotional memory and experience): for food, temperature regulation, oxygen, sex, etc. The lateral part of the hypothalamus is a critical element in the seeking system (Panksepp, 1997). Dopamine is one of its major neurotransmitters.

3. The *anterior cingulated cortex* (ACC) is a leading part of the executive control network (ECN), described by Posner et. al. (see Levin, 2003). Its functions go beyond selective attention, and its ventral portion is especially focused on feeling-related experience. The ACC can change rapidly (on the order of milliseconds), as is true of many cortical areas. The ACC also tries to anticipate events and thus generally protect our safety and relationships.

4. The *amygdala* is critical for fear conditioning. It watches for environmental dangers, and can be toned down by feedback from the orbital frontal cortex ("it's not a snake, just a stick!"). Its overactivity can result in panic or phobia, and is associated with posttraumatic stress disorder (PTSD). Oxytocin and vasopressin are neurotransmitter/hormones that regulate the functional core of the amygdala.

5. The *pariacqueductal gray* (PAG) is a critical deep structure for feelings, for matching emotional needs with the hypothalamus system (for appropriate action plans). Its complexity is great. Its changes occur over extended time periods (hours, days) in contrast to the cortex and ACC, which fluctuate moment to moment. Ultimately, it helps us match feelings with appropriate responses, and avoid creating danger for ourselves and others.

6. The *cerebellum* is important for movements (actions), anticipation, and learning. It first coordinates the movement of our limbs and later it takes over the coordination of

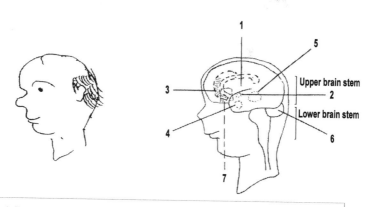

1. The thalamus (T) and brain stem (BS)
2. The hypothalamus (H)
3. The anterior cingulated cortex (ACC)
4. The amygdala (A)
5. The periaqueductal gray (PAG)
6. The cerebellum (CB)
7. Selective prefrontal cortex, especially the ventromedial frontal lobe (VMFL)

Figure 1. Brain structures involved in learning.

our ideas, as well. Much work on this has been done by Masao Ito (see Chapters 9 and 10 in Levin, 2003). There is no question that our cerebellum is capable of profound insights that can help us change how we see our world, see others, how others see us!

7. The *selective prefrontal cortex*, especially the *ventromedial frontal lobe* is important for decision making and emotional judgment. If the ventromedial frontal lobe is damaged, dreaming stops. Dreaming is deeply meaningful mentation that helps us consolidate memories, create new knowledge, and avoid costly mistakes. This creation of new knowledge involves creating data bases in our brains that are much more creative than in any time in our life history, and which can dramatically improve our relationships with others and with our self as well.

But this list is not all! Each of these structures in the diagram participates in a learning system in which feelings in relation to critical needs are linked to a larger network of cognitive and intellectual functions involving judgment, psychological insight, empathy, etc. These enlarged networks (especially in the cerebellum, though not limited to it) can then perform mental and cognitive tasks that were not possible before! Transcription factors working on brain cells (neurons) are also critical, since they turn genes on (or off) to create new synapses that enable new long-term memories to form (Levin, 2003). This formation of new long-term memories helps us properly understand and learn from our experiences. By these means, long-term memories help us respond to new experiences in appropriate ways that improve our sense of competence and connection with others.

We end this section by underscoring that emotional attention involves new emotional arousal which can propel learning which greatly enhances resilience and a sense of self-confidence.

SEEKING: THE DRIVING FORCE IN RESILIENCE

In Chapters 2 and 8, we introduced and elaborated upon the concept of the seeking system. Here we explore in greater depth the insights of Jaak Panksepp's research on the seeking system in order to show how his research contributes to the stories of the resilience of individuals presented earlier in this book. Our attempt is to present this information in a way that can be understood by laypeople. We apologize for what might be missing, as well as what might seem too simplified for those with neuroscience backgrounds.

What is the seeking system? As discussed briefly in Chapter 8, Panksepp has done extensive research into the networks of emotion. These networks consist of neurons and neurochemicals that are activated when instinctual, conscious nonverbal feelings arise. In his research, Panksepp focused on a core set of fundamental neurological urges, including the urge to seek. The seeking system in particular is the set of neurons and neurochemicals that are engaged when one feels and carries out the urge to try out new ideas or actions. This seeking system helps create a "persistent exploratory inquisitiveness" (Panksepp and Biven, 2013, p. 34) and helps excite us about learning and discovery. The seeking system propels us to be fearlessly curious about new roads of inquiry. It's the opposite of boredom.

For example, one of the participants in this study had an auditory processing problem that kept him from taking in information through his ears, causing him to flunk his French class. This did not stop him. The next year he studied Latin and aced the course because Latin is a written language. In this way, his superb visual skills were put to good use while his compromised auditory capacities were not as vital. His capacity to "seek" helped him find a way around his inability to learn from hearing.

Clearly, the concept of resilience is complex. One's resiliency in responding to a challenging situation depends on multiple factors that involve genetics, temperament, and environmental input, coupled with the developmental unfolding of cognitive, behavioral, and emotional factors. These complex elements combine in various ways to create a driving force for *seeking* to learn new ways of coping with seemingly insurmountable obstacles. Surely, people cannot adapt to problems without first learning something new.

So how do people with LD become resilient despite such seemingly insurmountable obstacles, such as their struggle with reading?* As mentioned earlier in this book, it is now known that all mammals have an inherent genetic predisposition to "Seek;" in the sense of going after what one wants (Panksepp and Bivan, 2012). This exploratory urge, and the parts of the brain we call "the seeking system," play a key role in fostering resilience.

In order to understand the implication of these systems (and particularly the seeking system), we need to understand how Panksepp and his colleagues conducted their research. Let's be-

---

* We will intersperse quotes spoken by the participants in Orenstein's study that are used in other parts of this book for different explanatory purposes. In this section, the quotes are used to show how their resilience is experienced.

gin by asking, Who is Jaak Panksepp, what did he discover, and how did he discover it? Dr. Panksepp is a neuropsychological animal researcher who came from Latvia to get his doctorate in the United States. In order to support himself while going to school, he worked in an inpatient psychiatric hospital where the emotional lives of patients were clearly in the forefront of his experience. This interest propelled his curiosity about the nature of feelings (Weintraub 2012).

Panksepp has a bio-evolutionary perspective. That is, he assumes that the animal brains that he uses in his research are ancestral versions of our own brains. Panksepp's view is that our brains developed and evolved for millions of years (Navarez, 2013). He cites MacClean's work which shows that the brain evolved to form three discreet sections: primary, secondary, and tertiary. This evolution or growth started with the base of our brains (the bottom which sits atop our spinal cord) which Panksepp calls "primary," continued to produce the "secondary" section (which is in the middle of our modern brains), and finally led to the "tertiary" section (the outer portion of our brains).

The primary, most primitive section lies right above our spinal cord in exactly the same place in mice as in men and helps govern these seven, basic affects or feelings:

1. nurturance (the need to care for our young),
2. play (intense physical engagement
3. seeking (the need to explore and learn)
4. lust
5. panic/grief (feelings of pain due to separation from nurturers, a pain that promotes social bonding)
6. fear (the wish to escape),
7. rage (the capacity to fight).

Panksepp's research suggests further that, just as mice and humans have certain parts of their brains in similar locations, mice and humans appear to experience similar primal urges. If this is indeed so, than one can imagine these seven feelings or urges being experienced by cave people before words evolved.

This evolutionary growth eventually produced the second section of the brain that experiences empathy, shame, trust, blame, pride, and guilt. (These more complicated feelings involve the area of the brain near the amygdala and basal ganglia.)

Finally the last third of our brains evolved, the outer portion that gives us our logic and intellectual capacity to verbalize, to create icons, to evaluate and measure. (For those readers who might be interested, there is a cartoon in *The Archeology of the Mind* that nicely depicts these divisions in our brains [Panksepp and Biven, 2013, p. 35].)

This outer layer, called the neocortex, is heavily influenced by primal feelings. In the past, and still today, many philosophers and scientists generally assume that our neocortex, the part of our brain that deals with words, math, reasoning, and so forth, controls our raw emotions. Panksepp says no. In fact, Panksepp found just the opposite. He has shown that it's these seven affects in the primal primitive parts of our brain that heavily influence our logical thinking.

This view, that our primitive emotions influence how we think, is revolutionary and certainly not accepted by the entire scientific community (Panksepp, 2012, p. 12). But for our purposes, this knowledge about the seeking system beautifully explains the motivation and resilience described in this book.

The previous section discussed Panksepp's evolutionary perspective on the brain. Now we present his neuropsychological perspective. Let's start again with a definition: An *emotional brain system* is a set of genetically encoded neurochemical and electrical networks or patterns in our brains that transfer some particular type of information from one neuron to the next. These patterns are anatomically located in similar brain regions in all mammals whether they be mice, dogs, or humans. "They are ancestral tools for living—evolutionary memories of such importance that they were coded into the genome" (Panksepp and Watt, 2011). Imagine a pattern of fireworks where one flare sets off another which then sets off another, and so on. They say we have more neurons in our brains than stars in the sky. So these neurons connect with each other to form a vast multitude of patterns. Can you imagine all the electrical-chemical patterns that fire in our brains? What a phenomenal instrument we all have within us.

Millions of these patterns fire off in our brains all the time. It's incredible. Panksepp and his colleagues have isolated patterns in animals that correspond to certain behaviors or actions that is found in humans (Panksepp, 2010). Panksepp says that while he finds particular neurochemical patterns to occur with behaviors, the association of these neurochemical patterns with affects or feelings has not as yet been scientifically proven (Panksepp and Biven, 2013). Clearly, he is making a hypothesis here. But science starts with hypotheses to be proven or disproven. The hypothesis is a beginning and it's not too great a leap to start with the assumption that we all want to be nurtured, to seek, to play, and to seek.

Panksepp's scientific approach was to plant electrodes into the brains of mice. Then, by looking at their behavior and listening to their vocalizations, he could map the neurochemical patterns associated with the basic feelings, affects, and needs that the mice experienced. More generally, from numerous experiments, Panksepp found that when animals engage in specific behavior involving pleasure and unpleasure, specific networks in the brains would always be active. Furthermore, he learned that in addition to the innate pleasure in rewards, *there is an additional, innate biological pleasure in seeking that is independent of the reward system.*

Here is an example: In one experiment, mice with electrodes inserted into their brains experienced either (1) seeking or (2) food rewards without seeking. The electrodes allowed the researcher to see what neurons would fire and what patterns of neurochemical activity would arise when an animal exhibited certain behaviors. He would drop a mouse into a box with two levers: one that would allow the mouse to engage in seeking behavior and a second that would offer an immediate reward of food Without any environmental input, the animals were free to press either lever.

Panksepp's experiments produced several fascinating findings. From his experiment with the box with two levers, Panksepp found that, unless the animals were starving, the mice would consistently choose seeking over food (See Weintraub, 2012). Panksepp elaborates on the function of this neurochemical brain system.

> It is evident that the SEEKING-EXPECTANCY system is a general-purpose system for obtaining all kinds of resources that exist in the world, from nuts to knowledge, so to speak. In short, it participates in all appetitive behaviors that precede consummation: it generates the urge to search for any and all of the "fruits" of the environment; it energizes the dynamic eagerness for positive experiences from tasty food to sexual possibilities to political power; it galvanizes people and animals to overcome dangers either by opposing them or by escaping to safety; it invigorates humans and prompts us to engage in the grand task of creating civilizations. But in the beginning, at birth, it is just "a goad without a goal" that opens up the gateways to engagement with the world, and hence knowledge." (Panksepp and Biven, 2012, p. 103)

Panksepp lists six criteria for defining fundamental emotional urges (Panksepp, 2010). The urge to seek satisfies these criteria:

1. The urge to seek instinctively causes exploratory actions
2. The urge to seek prompts exploratory actions in many different circumstances
3. The urge to seek lasts longer than the circumstances that prompt the seeking
4. The urge to seek can cause a person to notice things they did not notice before
5. The urge to seek can cause a person to learn by different means and to think about things differently.
6. The urge to seek changes as we continue to develop and learn.

Given how fundamental is the urge to seek, it is not a surprise that it drives people to pursue resilient responses to challenging situations. One's inborn urge to seek creates a curiosity to try alternate approaches. When the alternative approach works we would call it a resilient response to a challenging situation.

Reading problems interfered with Sparkly's wish to learn, but she overcame them by asking questions. Scholar's desire to write beautifully crafted scientific papers were not thwarted by his organizational problems because he hired a secretary to organize himself. One woman who so badly wanted to conquer math went back to school in her forties and massively struggled until her dyslexia was discovered. Logic would have told these people to give up. They did not and kept seeking.

In conclusion, we want to emphasize what we now hope is obvious to you, the reader: First, emotionally connecting with others who can help us learn is vital. Second, that seeking (unless we are in a panic and need to flee) is a pleasureful experience that is experienced consciously. It can indeed be gratifying and is a pleasure in and of itself to anticipate a reward and actively look for ways around obstacles. Clearly, the capacity to connect with others and to "seek" makes life more resilient.

Chapter 14

Learning to Be Resilient: What's Needed When We Have LD

By Myrna Orenstein
and
Fred Levin

BACKGROUND ON RESILIENCE

Historically, resilience has been studied extensively from a risk-resilience model. Resilience is a psychological concept that evolved from development psychology and came about through the study of psychopathology and stress. Researchers looked at crime, housing, trauma, and emotional and physical deprivation, and created a model which looked at the level of risk (Haggerty, et al., 1994; Wang and Gordon, 1994). Developmental psychologists like Werner and Smith (1992) and Felsman and Vallaint (1987) followed people over decades in studies of highly stressful communities. When they followed up on these large populations of individuals who had been subjected to high risk, the psychologists expected to find outcomes of psychopathology. But interestingly enough, not all such individuals exhibited psychological problems. In fact, a significant number of subjects ended up healthy! Even a subgroup of delinquents, for example, ended up off drugs and settled in solid marriages. No matter how much risk and trauma in their development, they married, had jobs, children, became tax-paying citizens, and so forth. In other words, they were able to adapt and generally override the dangerous risks in their lives.

Heartened by these results, educational psychologists began to investigate why some children in school with very troublesome backgrounds can develop such resilience (Wang, Haertel, and Walberg, 1994). Researchers began looking at concepts of stress, risk, development, and coping. More specifically, from profiles of attributes in resilient children, concepts emerged such as locus of control, self-esteem, self-efficacy, and autonomy. Lack of passivity, the capacity to interact with others, and high inner expectations were seen as positive markers.

NEUROPSYCHOLOGICAL FACTORS IN LEARNING RESILIENCY

It should be obvious to most serious students of resilience that no one completely understands yet how resilience can be reliably enhanced, although the literature is full of many useful ideas. Our intuition suggests that it is only through our attempt at better understanding the thoughts and feelings of people who have experienced and successfully navigated the struggle with LD that we will develop significantly improved methods for helping those whose struggle with LD has been less successful. So we will now present four different major concepts that help us understand how we can learn to be resilient. These four concepts are (I) fortitude (II) flexibility (III) seeking, and (IV) competence.

I. Fortitude and Resilience: Hanging in There

Fortitude is an inner strength in the face of adversity that provides a staying power even when circumstances are challenging or painful. We all have the urge to achieve and to overcome hurdles, but fortitude allows us to keep going when our efforts to explore are delayed and when the going gets tough. We all celebrate acts of physical courage, like when a fireman goes into a burning building to save a child. In this book, we celebrate acts of emotional courage. Fortitude is the willingness to "hang in there when going gets tough." For example, we celebrate when someone with LD shows the courage to explore different approaches to learning and is willing to risk the disappointment of an alternative approach not working but being brave enough to keep looking for successful alternatives. When a person has the fortitude to keep on trying, even when the results of the initial tries might be disappointing, we call it resilience.

The origins of fortitude, which are often influenced by the personalities of the people involved, is beyond the scope of this book. Nevertheless, it is important here to note the interrelationship between fortitude and the inner propulsion to explore and to achieve. A person who has a strong urge to explore and to achieve is more likely to say, "I'll give this another try." In other words, a person with a strong and encouraging seeking system is more likely to experience the persistence of fortitude.

Resilience also involves being stubborn. There is an unwillingness to fail that is fueled by our inborn seeking system in our brains. This genetic hard wired system in our brains carries us forward to continue to look for alternative options to seemingly impossible problems. An example would be the amazing ability of the wheel chair runners who compete in marathons. These are people who are not stopped by adversity, but who instead are driven to keep "pushing forward." Here, one can easily see how the seeking system and thus, more generally, resilience, involves our "hanging in there" while in the act of striving towards success and the avoidance of failure.

It is tempting to think of fortitude as a personality trait, that you either have it or you don't. This view overlooks people's capacity to learn fortitude, for example when people learn that a few tries that don't quite work can put them on a path to finding a successful alternative. In addition, this view does not take account of our inborn drive to explore and to try out new alternatives.

II. Flexibility and Resilience: The Ability to Work at Being Self-Organized

Flexibility is nimbleness of mind. It involves the capacity to spontaneously depart from one's usual patterns, to think novel thoughts, or have novel behaviors in order to meet the demands of one's world. This capacity is one hallmark of resilience. The concept of flexibility is complicated because there are so many difficult-to-define variables that influence our incredible neuropsychological capacity to adapt. A further complication is that flexibility arises from a developmental process that begins in infancy (in the form of our built-in potentials) and can grow if we nurture it. Resiliency includes the ability to adapt to environmental stressors by cognitively sizing up problems, emotionally determining how serious they are; and finally finding ways around them. Being flexible in our thinking and feeling allows greater choice for problem work-arounds and underscores what resilience is all about.

Because of the complexity of this concept, we are dividing the subchapter to discuss three concepts that influence resilience: emotional attention, the ability to self-organize, and the capacity for working memory and modulation.

We want to underscore that Fajardo's (1991) conclusions about organization beginning in infancy reflects the important notion that resilience can grow (Smaller, 2012; Tolpin, 2002). Self-organizing is a spontaneous process in which one orders concepts, ideas, thoughts, and feelings. This process is a meaning-making process within us that allows us to arrange internal and external information. Self-organizing is inherent in resiliency. Throughout life we take in new information about the world and about ourselves in it, integrating new thoughts, behaviors, and feelings. This self-organizing involves all kinds of environmental input, which either enhances or detracts from resiliency. So when caregivers can provide the necessary input of physical and emotional nurturance, people can more freely self-organize and thus reorganize themselves and learn. This persistent self-reorganizing is reflected in all growth and development. It is *the* hallmark of our capacity for flexibility and resilience. We change to accommodate the demands of our environment while simultaneously achieving important goals for ourselves as they come into mind.

Let's begin at the beginning, with Orenstein's (2000) definition of "self." The self is the internal image or set of beliefs about who we are. When Shakespeare wrote "To be or not to be," he surely was talking about a self-experience. The self is the organizing receptacle through which everything in our inner and outer world flows. The self takes in all pertinent information, metabolizes it, and causes us to think, feel, and behave as we do. Some people describe the self as "the totality of one's experience" (p. 187). When we look up to a teacher and the teacher compliments us, our sense of self or our self-esteem is enhanced. This gives us the impetus to continue to seek and to learn. And, of course, that is what resiliency is all about.

What does self-organization mean? We suggest that self-organization is the collective being that our self-organizing efforts create, based on our efforts to organize our thoughts, feelings, and behavior in a cohesive way that makes the most sense to us (Modell, 1993; Gedo, 1984; Kohut, 1971). The resulting self-organization includes both our inner or private self and our interactive or social self. For example, if we are worried about our aging parent, or we need to study for school, or we have to shine our shoes, or we need to shop for food because we are hungry, our self-organization brings order to our lives and helps us decide what to attend to and what to put off or prioritize differently. Self-organization is influenced by both nature and nurture. The self-organizing process integrates feelings with what we learn in order to make the critical decisions in our life.

How does self-organization influence resiliency in people with learning disabilities? Students with inherent self-organization problems can have a hard time in school because their minds cannot stay focused on what's most important in a given moment. For example, although they do their homework, they may lose it or forget to bring it to school. It can be most frustrating! But in cases like this, resilient students who know they have organizational problems learn how to use others to support them. They have or can find nurturing people who can help them organize themselves. Then, the organizational problems can be diminished so learning can continue and benefits will be obtained!

THE GROWTH OF RESILIENCE: THE NEED FOR WORKING MEMORY AND MEMORY MODULATION

Working memory is a system in our brain that holds and manipulates many aspects of current information for a short period of time. Computers have a comparable feature called RAM (an acronym for "random access memory"), which holds our document for editing or processing before it is saved back into long-term storage. Working memory is similar. The brain brings to mind previously saved information. We can then work with it. Any changes we make, such as modifying views of past events, can then be stored in permanent form. This kind of working memory enables us to learn how to manipulate what is in the forefront of our mind and store away what we are learning as new long-term memories! And these memories foster our resilience because they can become permanent guides for more intelligent decision-making in our future!

Here's an example of how new perceptions can change working memory and the meanings of old memories. Consider how we look at our parents as we age. We may dislike our parents as teenagers yet find that our feelings change as we become parents ourselves and learn much more about the difficulties of parenthood. We then understand our parents in a new light. So what has changed in us? Not just our memories, but their associated meanings and feelings, and with this our self-organization itself. "Now that I'm a parent myself and have a teenage child, I can see how I put my parents through the wringer." This capacity to change our working memory fosters our assumption that we can do it again. This is resiliency in the making.

The changing of memory allows for continual shifts in our self-conceptual framework over time. Here's an example: A college student was angry at her professor for demanding a work assignment the next day. She did the assignment, but along the way realized the professor reminded her of her own mother. Before arriving at school, her mother had talked about the student's LD in the presence of her siblings. The student became profoundly embarrassed. But now, with the professor's help, she realized that he (and her mother) had been right! Without pressure, she would have blown off the assignment. But the homework brought some new learning together in important ways. This episode ultimately led her to feel much better about her mother's concern and affection for her! She began to think about her mother's actions differently and, in that way, her memory about her mother's actions were reconstituted. This memory shift not only fostered a new perspective on her mother but also fostered the capacity to enhance resilience by this integration of a new way of seeing life.

Such shifts in memory appear in the psychoanalytic literature as the German word *Nachträglichkeit* or the French term *après coup*. *Nachträglichkeit* translates literally as "afterwardness," and *après coup* as "after action." These terms refer to significant shifts in how one recalls specific events: memory shifts that can occur long after the events originally occurred.

Animal research is providing increasing understanding of the process by which traumatic memories can be modulated by subsequent pleasurable emotional experiences. At MIT, scientists demonstrated this effect in mice:

The scientists trigger negative memories in mice by giving them mild shocks on their feet.

The scientists were able to identify specific neuron patterns in the brains of the mice that registered these negative memories.

Then, the scientists activated these neurons at the same time as they created a pleasurable setting, by putting female mice in with the male mice in the experiment.

The result, the scientists found, was that creating a positive environment while the negative memories were being triggered caused the negative memories to become less intense.

The scientists also found the converse result, that triggering a positive memory while the mice experienced a negative environment caused the positive memory to lose strength as well (*Nature*, August 27, 2014). We can infer from this experiment that the emotional contents of our memories change when we have new experiences that put the memories in a new light.

Freud's psychoanalytical concept of *Nachträglichkeit* is at work in the MIT scientists' experiment. This concept describes how shifting emotions and learning influence the interaction of past and present memories and, conversely, how past and present memories influence emotions and learning. In a sense, they capture how our mental capacity for increasing flexibility and thus resilience works. For example, if a current emotional experience gives us new insight, we will likely change the meaning assigned to the memories of similar experiences in the past. As one participant said "I can look back with some sense of hindsight." "I mean, it really was like, you know, having my life as a jigsaw puzzle with two-thirds of it missing." By the same token, if we better understand a past experience, it can change and expand our understanding of the meanings associated with similar *current* experiences as in: "My dyslexia [experience] forced me to learn to think for myself." So new insights effect changes in old experience and vice versa. In complex ways, our flexibility to continuously reshuffle the mental deck promotes learning to be resilient.

SEEKING: THE DRIVING FORCE IN LEARNING TO BE RESILIENT

The driving force is an inner propulsion that pushes us to keep striving for success. We do not have a choice here. As discussed earlier, Jaak Panksepp has shown that we all have a primal urge to seek, an urge to explore that pushes us to try new options, and that this urge is brought forth by the seeking system in our brains. Thus, the seeking system is the neurological component that creates a "driving force" to try alternatives that we might otherwise be afraid to try. Even if we're worried that another try will just result in more disappointment, the seeking system gives us the motivation to give it another try anyway.

A. Seeking Knowledge

All of us are hard-wired to learn. An example is a child learning to walk. A child's capacity to learn to walk and talk are hard-wired, biologically based abilities as is an individual's capacity to look for preferred methods to meet our need to accomplish tasks. Scholar's switch from French to Latin is a great example.

It seems that this driving force has at least two probable sources: (1) it comes from inside, from our seeking system which propels our "inner driving force," and (2) it is facilitated by others who mentor or encourage us. In the latter case, it appears that inborn-biological capacities to seek are "released" by this nurturing involvement from others. We see this "inner driving force" as an outcome of the seeking system: *the* spark that begins each developmental step. And it reflects the activity of a brain that feels positively connected to critically needed other brains that feel positively about who we are and what our potentials are for success.

In *Exceeding Expectations*, Reiff, Gerber, and Ginsberg (1997) suggest that successful outcomes in people with LD begin with the feeling of desire. They talk about people having "a fire in their belly" (p. 135) which could be seen by some as a stubborn persistence. Because this drive is so intense, some might even label it obsessive/compulsive (i.e., pathological). We disagree because this stubborn persistence can be seen as a component in our capacity to seek, which surely promotes resiliency.

From our perspective, there is often something intense about how creative, intelligent individuals with LD go about the process of learning. Importantly, this intensity is *not* pathological; rather, it is part of a healthy seeking which arises from the primal urge to seek. This intensity is required to carry out what we see as a biologically based, hard-wired program in one's brain that needs a platform for expression. Let us elaborate. Neuroscientifically, the driving force first activates something we would call emotional attention (Levin 2003, p. 15). Emotional attention in turn activates the transcription factors (described in Chapter 13) that have the capacity to turn various genes on or off, for example, the genes that cause new synapse formation. (In other words, genes are critical for the learning process to proceed.) Once these new synapses form, they can capture new long-term memories. The net effect is to facilitate learning by supporting the formation of new memories on emotional demand.

This "driving force," this inner compulsion to learn or achieve, overlaps with desire, motivation, and initiative. But is significantly different because it's not just an inner feeling. The driving force influences the interface between our constitution and environment. Under good enough circumstances, our built-in "driving force" meets human support and then together the two create a spark that fuels a comfortable process of learning. We believe this "driving force" or seeking is an explanation for why some resilient individuals with LD are able to be successful in spite of previous histories of great difficulty. Basically, people who have access to their "driving force" capitalize on their strengths because they never give up. "I just knew that I could do whatever I wanted to do. It just took a lot longer time to do it in." "I never stopped trying." "I would simply refuse to give up." Shifting to areas of fortitude probably works by multiple means, including helping one tap his or her flexibility, which enhances resiliency because the driving force to master also enables us to take more risks.

Consider the people who had trouble in school but are successful in business. When no longer confronted with their previous frustrations in learning, their resiliency leaps to the forefront. Now, no longer routinely confronted by the chasm caused by impossible educational demands, they find that focusing on their strengths is a pleasure. It's like being able to run because shackles or weights have been removed from one's ankles. In the LD world, one attribute that helps people achieve in the face of possible failure is intensity and persistence. This driving force is biologically rooted to propel people to continue seeking; to "slog through the drudge" of learning disabilities. It is a fundamental component in one's capacity to adapt and compensate, which leads to increased or enhanced resilience.

B. Seeking Nurturance

We have created the concept of "environmental releasers" (ER) to describe resilient nurturers in our world who can facilitate within us the feeling of hope in our capacity for growth. These are trusted mentors (such as parents, grandparents, teachers, coaches, etc.) who give vital help to one's growth and development. These nurturing mentors assist the adaptive changes in our self-organization which is so important to the overall process of learning (see Friedman, 2014).

One key to learning is that our emotional attention initiates the complex series of biological brain-related changes that include (1) the formation of new synapses, (2) our capacity to seek, and (3) ultimately the capturing of new knowledge in the form of novel neural networks (Levin, 2003). Surely, learning enhances resilience.

These trusted people we admire facilitate our inner capacity for positive self-respect. In other words, when we see that others believe that we are valuable and that our potential is worthwhile, we can feel good about ourselves. They support our self-respect and release our capacity for resilient action. It's important to underscore that when we are interacting with an important caregiver during a critical time in our development, the input from the other person (the environmental releaser) has the potential of activating inner programs in our genes that facilitate feelings of self-worth. This can occur when, for example, a child comes home pleased and excited about good grades. When the child eagerly shows his or her grades to the caregiver, and the caregiver is pleased and excited as well, the child sees that enjoyment and feels a pleasureful sense of competence which promotes his urge to do it again in the future—hence, resiliency grows.

We will focus more now on the specific impact of these interactions with trusted loved ones. The process has three basic elements. First, there is the individual, the self, with its inactivated programs or potential in the brain for the growth of important learning functions. Second, there is the caretaker's action or behavior, such as a smile or an excited voice, which is validation of the individual's potential and achievement. Third, because the individual feels safely supported by this caregiving validation, there is the release of an innate potential based upon the self-caretaker interaction. The overall impact includes physiological and neurochemical/neuroanatomical changes in our brain, the effect of which is to make these inactive programs or potentials active.

For example, if the timing is correct developmentally, a stellar review at work or receiving an A from a revered professor releases or activates a psycho-biologically built-in pattern in our mind/brain that allows for feelings of enhancement and pride in our capacity to learn and achieve which feeds our "driving force." "If I'm heard, I can switch to another way of learning." "Since the normal ways didn't work, I felt like she and I were working together to figure out creative ways to free my intelligence."

Although mastery can occur when we are working alone, when we get stuck we benefit greatly from the wise and gentle assistance of others. Mentors and other important people in our life can change the actual physical makeup of our mind/brain by influencing how we think, feel, and act. They encourage our inner driving force. Conversely, the lack of a response, or a negative response, can throw cold water on our fledgling initiative.

In this way, environmental input becomes as important as genetic factors. It is our contention that biological changes in our brains caused by well-timed environmental input facilitate learning resiliency. Sometimes this appears as literal "aha" or an "oh, I get it" reaction. The ever-growing capacity for initiative and resilience enlarges as it goes because excitement is contagious. Our initiative is fueled from the genuine interest in us from important others. The sensation that our excitement is shared helps us get excited by our ideas! Sharing how good it feels to have achievements in learning can then tip the scale in favor of improving our confidence, our drive to accomplish, and even our capacity for empathy. Therefore, engaging and empathizing with the feelings of other people allows us to reach out more easily to get the help we need.

It certainly helps to be lucky enough to find someone who has faith in us and faith in our ability to succeed in our areas of strength. This point is illustrated in the movie *Million Dollar Baby*. A key moment in this movie is when Clint Eastwood's character accepts his new student of boxing (in his role as her coach) because he sees her potential. Then she, herself, begins to appreciate her own potential. It's not surprising that admiring looks from a mentor can plug into earlier positive memories of a trusted caregiver having faith and hope in our potential. These self-enhancing memories from our past ("My grandmother always believed in me") can fuel current feelings of positive self-regard that can lead to invigoration and learning. Furthermore, memories of positive experience can support us in finding means of expression for our strengths, even in the face of profound frustration. These memories give us hope and fuel our sense of purpose in life. It's much easier to look for alternative ways to adapt to problems when we feel all right about ourselves. As True Grit said, "My dyslexia forced me to learn to think for myself." "I can choose the necessary tools to help me learn another way."

We believe that hope plays a decisive role in our inner "driving force" in improving sense of competency and self-esteem. Educators, then, can facilitate resilience in their students by encouraging them to live up to their potential and meet their goals. Such teachers *are not wasting their time.* On the contrary, it's crucial that they learn how to teach resilience or (at a minimum), how not to kill latent resilience in their students.

We end this subsection by listing some of the feelings in mentors who are environmental releasers that facilitate development in their mentees, children and adults alike. Again, these people can be parents, grandparents, or other relatives, teachers, coaches, scout leaders, librarians, and so on.

1. Quiet pleasure in the person's strengths.
2. A sense of awe in the person's strengths.
3. Interest and excitement in the person's strengths.
4. Humor and delight seeing the person's potential.
5. An expectation and belief in the person's strengths.
6. A validating smile and/or touch.

Successful caregivers are those who evoke a sense of awe and respect in the people they are caring for. We often idealize our caregivers, viewing them as having greater protective powers, which helps us feel more safe. Most people remember school experiences where an idealized and loved teacher made learning so much fun. Idealization creates the capacity to feel safe when interacting with someone you respect and admire. In a child's development, the child needs to idealize the parent and feel safe to continue to seek and explore her means of creative expression. Just look at a child's face when he sees the pleasureful excitement in his or her caregiver's face as he or she takes that first step. And, when exploration leads to new learning, quiet inner pride over our fortitude and flexibility surely enhances our capacity for resiliency.

COMPETENCE: THE OUTCOME OF LEARNING TO BE RESILIENT

What is competence? It's complicated. Most definitions involve some level of achievement. Webster's unabridged dictionary (1979) describes competence as "having ability or capacity." The Microsoft WORD dictionary says that competence is "the ability to do something well or to a required standard." In essence, competence has a close relationship to our self-control, achievement, and the pleasure of personal self-expression.

Michael Basch, a psychoanalyst, says that

> "In the behavioral sphere, . . .[competence] takes the form of exercising control over external events. In respect to brain functioning and the neurophysiological substrate of behavior, competence is achieved as a result of the brain's capacity to establish [comfortable] order. On the level of introspection and reflection, competence is experienced as self-esteem. In the sociological universe of discourse, competence consists of healthy adaptation; and in the world of art and esthetics, competence is akin to harmony."* (1988, p. 24)

---

* We will be looking at competence from an integral in-depth psychological perspective. For the reader who is interested in the sociological perspective, there is a vast literature out there involving resilience and education, Please see our literature review for more information.

Competence in the world of learning disabilities is not uncommon because people with LD (by necessity because of learning deficits) get good at seeking alternatives; this can be a source of pride. Clearly, when we have used our strengths and our capacity to compensate for our weakness to successfully meet the demands of one's world, successful seeking has been at work. Competence occurs when we have the fortitude to face challenges, the flexibility to pursue better approaches, the necessary self-organization to expand memories, adequate emotional attention to what needs fixing, and hopefully finding important nurtures who will to support our quest for successful approaches.

When we master something, it feels good, and we feel competent because *we have also learned that we can learn*. This insight promotes resilience. For example, Adelman and Vogel (1990) suggest that insight about how one's learning disabilities work can enhance compensations and successfully enable people to assume more responsibility on the job. As one participant in the study said, "You know, when the [methods] don't work, the mind has the capacity to think of new creative ways of being; and that's kind of nice in a way." Furthermore, when we have deficits, the push for the pleasure of mastery is more intense because there are obstacles to overcome. Clearly this push to master and learn despite deficits enhances resilience. People keep trying until they find a way. Here is where persistence pays off. "My dyslexia interfered with these "normal" [methods] and forced me to learn to think for myself" (p. 87).

Competence begins in infancy, where one can see the seeking system at work. Studies of infants corroborate the biological underpinnings of this need to search one's world which complements an urge to pursue mastery and control (Lichtenberg, 1988). For example, in one experiment, infants learned to turn their heads to the left when a bell was sounded and to the right when a buzzer rang. Much to everyone's surprise, the initial reward, milk, became uninteresting to the infants. The reward for these infants really involved seeking or looking for "some internal demand to respond correctly or solve a problem" (Basch, 1988, quoting Papousik, p. 26). So, even in infancy, seeking, along with our driving force to pursue mastery, is surely an contributor to resiliency.

Hopefully, over time, we mature enough to exploit our "driving force" to recognize that some activities are more critical for success than others. We know we cannot perpetually avoid learning important but difficult-to-learn skills. "I do it [compensate], but I hate doing it." "I need to research every damn thing that comes up . . . nothing stays in my head." "I resent having to work so hard."

The quiet pride and pleasure that comes from the capacity to persevere and achieve despite learning obstacles is one hallmark of resilience (Person 2002) and surely enhances our driving force. "I just knew that I could do whatever I wanted to do." "I figured out how to get by myself." "I've always stood on my own two feet." "I loved getting good grades, and after a while, I demanded that of myself. . . . Nothing short of perfection would do." Finally, a pattern of reliable competence (influenced by earlier memories of achievement and mastery) emerges and itself contributes to the habit of learning. "I would simply refuse to give up." During World War II, when things didn't look so great, one popular song was "We did it before, and we can do it again"; the "it" refers to winning a world war. In this way hope builds on itself and makes growth and learning not just possible but probable.

However, emotional reactions to deficits can create serious internal demons of self-doubt, and self-esteem is easily undermined when the LD sufferer experiences major doubt about his or her overall value. "Blaming myself is like a habit I can't break." And doubt about one's capacities can be a constant companion in bright people with LD who are forced to confront their disabilities on a day-to-day basis. "I still think the conventional way— that I should be able to pick up a book and read it." "I can get it, but I feel humiliated because it took me too long." Furthermore, it's surprising to learn that there are very successful people with LD who harbor a secret fear that they will be "found out" to be a phony and stupid. "If I did well, I figured it was a lucky guess." "I never really knew when I wrote a paper whether it would be an A or an F, but somewhere, I trusted that it was okay."

However, competence through the knowledge and enhancement of one's strengths is a resiliency enhancer because it can override the feelings of doubt about one's effectiveness in areas of weakness. People can "hang in there when the going gets tough" even though they must work harder than others. Their self-esteem and driving force that keeps them seeking demand this of them. True Grit, from chapter 1, was continually forced to confront his difficulty in reading at school but nonetheless drove himself to achieve. When he lost his job, his driving force enabled him to struggle with "being stuck in the chasm" while propelling himself to outstanding success in the area of his strengths. "I got back up on the horse and went out and, you know, pursued my own business." "I'm not a whole, perfect person, and I've got some missing parts, so that feels bad. And then I say, but you've got all these other talents and skills, and a lot of people have missing parts. . . . I say to myself, you know, you're not going to ruin your life over this. You just can't."

It helps us to know that other people with LD have all repeatedly experienced failure, otherwise they would not have been diagnosed with LD in the first place. Something had to be wrong with their approach to specific learning areas that was not their fault. Once people know there is a problem—once the problem gets their attention—they figure out ways to adapt to that problem. "Being stuck in the chasm" forces people to be more flexible and look for alternative ways of succeeding. "My brain works in slow motion, but I know that two hours from now something will kick in." "I just kept on fighting." "I did not take the advice I was receiving from the rest of the world, and I'm glad I didn't because I'd be sitting in a mental institution if I had done that."

Memories can now be seen in a new light. In other words, we can experience *Nachträglichkeit*, the retranscription or revision of meanings assigned to the memories and feelings about past failures, which can alter our judgments of self from critical to compassionate. Our new, more positive feelings about our capacity to successfully struggle with our LD is a resilience promoter. Now we are actually proud of ourselves for overcoming a difficulty that we were not responsible for. "I was always an ambitious and driven kid. And when I was in junior high, I had a headmaster who was fully convinced that I wasn't very smart and that I was an overachiever [laughter]. Unfortunately he passed away, because I always wanted to go back and tell him about myself."

When one finally masters something, memories of past failures makes the current mastery all the sweeter. People realize they can indeed compete. But conversely, there is a down side as well. When people receive their diagnosis and learn about many important compensations, they become frustrated and angry over their past unnecessary failures and begin a process of emotionally "working through" the past. Interestingly, this anger fuels their competitive spirits. Even though they may have to work harder, people enjoy competing with others now that they can. Competition, if one is proud of one's strengths, can become fun even if one loses. But one cannot compete unless there is some self-assurance that sufficient inner strength is there, waiting to be unleashed.

Competence in people with LD is further enhanced when they find their niche in life. They find a world where their strengths are enhanced and validated by the people in their chosen world. "This is no longer school, school is way in the background now [and] no one even cares about that." The highly intelligent accountant working in the business world does not have to worry about writing poetry or learning languages (as he once did in school). Others in his field will respect his accomplishments.

CONCLUSION

In closing, we want to underscore that learning disabilities interfere with our capacity to seek and make it challenging to acquire the necessary tools for learning. But, under optimal circumstances, including having a proper and timely diagnosis, the resilient individual with LD can plug into their seeking system and *can* have the fortitude to hang in there to achieve his or her goals and also can have the flexibility to keep trying different methods of learning until these goals are achieved. Over time, those with LD will likely increase their flexibility, fortitude, and potential for changing their self-organization. When we are more empathic with our past circumstances, we can protect our self-esteem and learn not be so hard on ourselves regarding past frustrations and/ or failures that would have been problematic even for Einstein! The old adage "If you don't succeed, try and try again" needs to be modified. More to the point would be: "If you don't succeed, try and try again *differently* until you find the right path to success." The people described in this book deserve our respect for their incredible resilience. They have managed to deal with the risks of LD. In fact, in some cases, the LD actually enhanced their resilience because, even under adverse circumstances, they activated their seeking system and became driven to adapt, persevere, and learn how to overcome their learning gaps.

Epilogue

We thank you, the reader, for having the perseverance to finish this book. Parts of it were not easy.

You have read the third edition of this book. The first edition focused on the shame and the self- esteem assault that people experienced when for no known reason (for no diagnosed reason) unbridgeable chasms in learning created disappointment in one's capacity to achieve. In effect, the first edition was about how people dealt with the psychological challenges caused by undiagnosed learning disabilities.

The second edition added discussion about resilience, which is the flexibility and drive to find alternative paths to success when the normal path is blocked. In effect, the theme of this added discussion is that the challenges that people with undiagnosed learning disabilities face can be addressed by looking for alternative approaches to learning.

This third edition describes recent research identifying our fundamental urge to seek and explore. When we feel shame from failing to fulfill expectations, our urge to seek and explore can help give us the drive to look for alternative approaches. In this sense, the urge to seek helps provide a path or bridge from shame to resilience. Seeking stops people from being stuck. Seeking is a catalyst that helps free imprisoned intelligence from frozen shame and gets people moving again. Understanding this force for resilience helps us understand why so many people with undiagnosed learning disabilities can persevere in their search for ways to learn what they are expected to learn.

I hope you share my vast regard for the resilient people who were stuck in the chasm, who had the ingenuity to seek alternative possibilities, and to find a niche for themselves that allowed them to flower.

It's a good step forward that more and more children are lucky enough to be diagnosed earlier, so interventions can be incorporated as they develop. But there are so many traumatized smart people who, no matter how smart and successful, feel secretly flawed.

We hope this book has helped them to be free of their secret shame and imprisoned intelligence.

~

Addendum 1

Self Psychology and Imprisoned Intelligence

A common theoretical approach to many issues in psychology is called "self psychology." This approach provides a useful perspective on the issues described in this book. For example, self psychology provides useful insights into how the shame experienced by those with ULD can lead them to be wary of even trying to learn, which can lead to what we call "Imprisoned Intelligence." The goal of this addendum, then, is to provide the reader with a bridge linking self psychology, shame, and Imprisoned Intelligence. This addendum will also use affect theory's concept of shame (explained in Chapter 2) to theorize about Imprisoned Intelligence. The integration of these two theories will help to explain the painful emotional experiences associated with Imprisoned Intelligence.

Self psychology is a developmental theory conceived by Heinz Kohut (1971) that explains both growth and constriction of the self. Self psychology helps us understand the consequences of living with ULD. It also offers a lexicon that seems especially appropriate for discussing the emotional consequences of ULD.

Although they do not explicitly address ULD, self psychology and affect theory's concept of shame help explain the suffering of persons with this problem. Sporadic learning failures threaten self-cohesion, and repeated learning failures can create a cycle of shame, despair, and self-denigration. As low self-esteem becomes entrenched, it becomes increasingly difficult to break learning blocks. The painful subjective experiences described by the participants described in Chapters 3 through 6 strongly correspond to self-psychological descriptions of injury to the self.

LEARNING AND IMPRISONED INTELLIGENCE

To understand the impact of ULD on the self, it is imperative to understand that learning and mental health are very closely entwined. Learning is enhanced when the student is interested and excited. Learning is a precondition to leading a full life, to enhancing one's potential, and even to survival. Because learning and learning disabilities are so closely intertwined, I will repeat Fuqua's definition of learning.

> Learning is something we do in school, something we do in therapy, and something we do day to day. It is integral to the very act of living. Without learning we would not adapt or grow, we would become stagnant and rigid . . . we must learn in order to survive and thrive. The process of learning goes beyond structured education settings to the very fabric of our existence. (1993, p. 13)

However, humans are not learning machines who constantly gobble up new information whenever they happen upon it. Learning is best done in a timely fashion so that new knowledge can be integrated with what is already familiar. Fuqua's (1993) comments illuminate this process:

> Yet with all we have to recommend the activity, we still find ourselves resisting the process [of learning] at times. Even as you are reading now with the hope that you will hear something new and enlightening, you must be looking simultaneously for the familiar landmarks of ideas already mastered, signposts pointing toward familiar ground. Too much newness all at once is overwhelming to us, and even when we seek out new knowledge, we find ourselves avoiding the process while simultaneously feeling the urge to pursue it. (p. 14)

Appropriate timing is vital to learning. Furthermore, learning involves flexible use of new information to create a different order in one's brain. Here again is Fuqua's (1993) definition of learning:

> Learning is the incorporation of new facts, perceptions, and ideas. It is also the mastery of new processes, styles, and formats of thinking and interacting, both with each other and with the environment. . . . An essential aspect of learning is the addition of something new to an existing structure, producing a necessary change in that structure. The structure that is modified is both the body of knowledge already held by the learner and his self system. What is learned changes what was preexisting. (p. 14)

Learning is a singular internal experience that involves the brain's capacity to change what one knows. Levin (1991) states: "Learning seems to involve some process in which the various learning subsystems of the brain are able to exchange data" (p. 43). Of course, circumstances and encouragement from others also contribute to the learning process. But eventually one's own brain needs to do the work if learning is to occur.

LD creates obstacles that obscure and obstruct the learning process. As one study participant explained, "Learning is like climbing a ladder one step at a time, and for me, there were too many rungs missing." If one wishes to learn but obstacles prevent learning, over time, frustration looms larger and interest shrinks. Without interest, the learning process falters. Interest propels learning and shame prevents it.* Interest and shame are powerful forces that act upon the self. To clarify these relationships, self psychological concepts will now be applied to the experience of Imprisoned Intelligence. I will discuss and describe self-states, selfobjects, development, cohesion versus fragmentation, deficits, compensatory structures, and disavowal.

---

* As underscored in chapters eight and twelve, the "seeking system" can drive us forward toward learning even when the prospect of shame inhibits us.

THE IMPACT OF IMPRISONED
INTELLIGENCE ON THE SELF AND SELFOBJECTS

In uneven learners, Imprisoned Intelligence is a blow to their sense of self. In areas of strength they perform very well, and they expect themselves to perform just as well in areas of weakness. When learning failure occurs, they experience a shameful cognitive freeze and withdrawal that impacts massively on self-esteem. After their initial bewilderment, such individuals report that they soon learn not to count on others for help with their learning problems. They then become discouraged, their interest in learning wanes, and the lonely struggle with defeat causes them to shamefully withdraw. They assume that the problem is their fault, and they attack themselves. For these individuals, the absence of empathic others results in profound loss of self-esteem.

Self psychological theory offers a powerful explanation of what is taking place here. According to self psychology, the developing self needs certain empathic responses from others to remain healthy and intact. If all goes well with the developing self, the adult can appropriately use others to maintain a sense of well-being, cohesion, self-enhancement, and sustenance.

Empathy is crucial to the developing self (Kohut, 1984). It is the capacity to think and feel oneself into the inner world of another person—even when someone else's feelings they do not match one's own. For example, I may hate to fly but might get excited when others tell me about *their* excitement when flying; I may not be interested in art, but, to propel the development of my child's self-esteem, he needs me to understand his excitement about the pictures he paints.

The self of the very young child relies almost exclusively on the parent's ability to be empathically nurturing and responsive. When this happens, the child's self is reinforced, and he feels "all together." Kohut calls this a feeling of cohesion (Kohut, 1977). When a child's needs are empathically fulfilled, caregivers are providing what Kohut calls "selfobject" functions.

THE IMPACT OF IMPRISONED INTELLIGENCE ON DEVELOPMENT

The development of the self involves three evolving transferences to selfobjects: idealization, mirroring, and twinship. These transferences create a world of self/selfobject experiences in which ambitions and ideals can grow and flourish (Baker, 1987; Lieb, 1990). Often ambitions and ideals are contradictory, and this creates tensions in the self. Kohut (1977) described contradictions between ambitions and ideals as producing a "tension arc." A tension arc is: ". . . the abiding flow of actual psychological activity that establishes itself between the two poles of the self; i.e., a person's basic pursuits toward which he is 'driven' by his ambitions and 'led' by his ideals" (p. 180). The cohesive self uses ideals to direct ambitions. The goals set by one's ambitions and ideals are accomplished by use of one's talents and skills (Kohut, 1984). Resilience involves the capacity to use one's talents and skills when dealing with stressful situations. In this sense, resilience is the flexibility to address this tension arc in a way that resolves the contradictions between ambitions and ideals. People use their talents and skills to figure out ways around problems that may interfere with their potential (ambitions and ideals). From this perspective, resilience allows us to circumnavigate our vulnerabilities, to act such that our vulnerabilities cause no shame. Resilience, then, is the outcome of our capacity to protect the enthusiasm for our goals from disillusionment, despair, and defeat.

Skills must be learned and talents must be developed. Therefore, if an undiagnosed learning disability interferes with the flowering of talents and the learning of skills, the cohesive self is compromised. For example, a college student who has good ideas but writes very slowly may become terribly frustrated and do poorly during an in-class essay test. Taken alone, this incident is not devastating, but when students have similar experiences throughout their entire academic career, they may suffer considerably. When talents and skills are blocked, emotional growth and fulfillment are also blocked. Palombo (1979) describes the psychological state of a child whose learning and achievement has been repeatedly blocked:

> Such a child [with learning disabilities] would begin to feel baffled recognizing that something is very wrong with him. He may feel narcissistically injured and withdraw from those around him or may compensate for the inadequacy and vulnerability by symptomatic behavior such as unmodified grandiosity or omnipotence. He may immure himself within a wall of narcissistic self-investment which isolates him even further from the environment. (p. 37)

The child becomes ashamed, withdraws his or her interest in the world, and ends up investing in only unmodified grandiosity.

Self psychology's focus on three developmental lines can help us understand how ULD prevents the blossoming of potential. In the following sections on idealizing, mirroring, and twinship transferences, you will see how undiagnosed learning disabilities compromise development in intelligent people.

Idealization

The idealizing transference involves relating to a selfobject that one admires and perceives to be flawless and all-powerful. From basking in the selfobject's perfection and power, the individual feels protected. In adulthood, the transformed idealizing transference no longer demands that the selfobject appear perfect and all-powerful; rather, it describes a relationship with an admired other, such as a mentor. However, in childhood, the selfobject is literally perceived as ideal, perfect, and unconquerable. When the selfobject cannot live up to this impossible standard and makes a mistake that is not too severe, this is an opportunity for optimal frustration and transmuting internalization. It is a "good enough disappointment," which allows the child to develop self-soothing capacities and a more realistic view of the world.

To learn, children need the feelings of security and safety provided by the idealizable selfobject (Baker, 1987). When teachers and parents (selfobjects) fail to understand their learning problems, children feel uncomfortable and unsafe both at school and at home. Instead of an "optimal frustration," this constitutes a major selfobject failure: the selfobject's perfection, power, and ability to protect is, in the child's eyes, absolutely denied. The selfobject can no longer be trusted as protector. Rather than allowing transmuting internalization and growth, these selfobject failures occasion withdrawal, shame, and repression of the transference need.

Because the selfobject (the teacher or parent) does not know about the ULD, the child cannot count on the selfobject to maintain his or her sense of self-worth in the face of school failure. The child no longer feels safe and constantly fears being labeled "stupid." Over time, the child abandons all hope of receiving help. The tragedy is that parents and teachers with good intentions are not aware that the child's needs are not being met.

Furthermore, it is difficult to learn in an antagonistic setting. Not surprisingly, students learn more easily from teachers whom they respect and idealize. In turn, parents and teachers feel pride when children learn. Genuine pride in the child's capabilities is difficult to maintain when the child appears to be working below capacity. Parents and teachers also blame themselves for the child's failures.

The following scenario is common: A teacher works with a ULD child who appears to learn nothing. The teacher becomes frustrated. Because the child's problem is not identified, the teacher feels helpless, and her pride in her teaching abilities is wounded. The teacher feels ashamed and withdraws. The child becomes aware that the teacher is disappointed in him. In the face of the teacher's impotence, the child is forced to see that his teacher cannot help or protect him. The idealization process that promotes learning is then curtailed.

Mirroring

Mirroring is the experience of having one's value and worth reflected in the eyes of a caregiver (selfobject). Appropriate mirroring of early grandiosity evokes the child's self-confidence and interest, which propel achievement and learning. Conversely, when appropriate mirroring is not available, the child's grandiose self is repressed and stagnates at a primitive level. Then the grandiose self cannot be modulated by input from the world (Shane, 1984). Children with Imprisoned Intelligence often lack appropriate mirroring because their caregivers cannot mirror good traits that they do not see.

Almost all uneven learners know they are intelligent, but feel that exposing their intelligence to new learning is too risky. The saying "pride goeth before a fall" is pertinent here. Good enough disappointments (optimal frustrations) encourage flexibility and creativity. For example, a child who fails his spelling test because he did not memorize the words that week can, with some encouragement from his parents or teacher, get an A the following week. However, if the child has a memory-recall problem, he will not only dread spelling but become reluctant to write papers that would further expose his inability to spell. In many cases, he will refuse to do work or will do it in a haphazard manner. Then he can always tell himself, "I could have done better if I tried." In cases like this, ambitions remain primitive and grandiosity is unneutralized.

In usual circumstances, if selfobjects modulate the perception of omniscience in young children through appropriate and tolerable experiences of disappointment (optimal frustrations), the demands of the grandiose self are lessened, ambitions become realistic, and children learn how to regulate themselves (Kohut and Wolfe, 1978). Tolerable disappointments do not cut off interest, but allow children to learn from failure.

When children suffer from ULD, both parents and child know that the child is not pleasing the parent, and appropriate mirroring fails to occur. For example, a father who has an interest in Little League may not mirror a child with perceptual motor problems that prevent him from catching a ball.

No learner can know it all, but what would be considered minor failures by other children may trigger fragmentation in a student who has unmodulated, impossible expectations—an outcome of a primitive grandiose self—because the student has never learned to handle small disappointments.

After diagnosis, those with previously undiagnosed LD must confront their overblown expectations of easy learning and perfection when they face their areas of weakness. It is not easy to face deficiencies previously disavowed to protect grandiose expectations. However, the process of confronting and treating LD allows persons to remobilize development, modulate unrealistic expectations, and eventually enjoy a firm self-esteem based on genuine understanding of their gifts and deficits.

Twinship

Children have a powerful need to feel a part of their class. They want to fit in. This need is a manifestation of the twinship transference. When children suffer from ULD, they experience themselves as "different" without knowing why. They may have trouble finding friends in class. When they do not feel like valued members of the class, children may become more afraid to expose their learning difficulties. They become fearful and afraid to try. Other children may notice their weakness and single them out for teasing.

Of course, ULD children are not alone in feeling left out, friendless, or persecuted at school. Schoolchildren can be inordinately cruel, and the objects of cruelty are not only those who seem to be stupid, but also smart kids, ugly kids, poor kids, shy kids, kids who are bigger or smaller than the norm, or kids who are vulnerable in any way. Any child who is habitually teased or excluded is likely not only to have trouble learning, but to feel depressed, anxious, and miserable.

Children with ULD may be quite successful at avoiding teasing. Often these children are so practiced at concealing and compensating for their deficits that they appear to fit in perfectly with the class. However, despite their appearance of normality, they know themselves to be different, and may feel even more anguished about having to pretend. Whether they give the appearance of fitting in or not, they feel isolated. They may withdraw and become subject to chasm experiences. As with the other transference needs, when children's need for twinship is not met, their pain snowballs. Their feelings of isolation and exclusion interfere with learning, and their failure to learn increases their hopelessness and isolation.

As one might imagine, development is often arrested along all three lines simultaneously. For instance, a child will not look up to a teacher who cannot help him, so the teacher offers little mirroring and the child does not feel like a valued member of the class. Alternately, the child may be popular with his peers (meeting his twinship needs), but exasperate the teacher, frustrating his needs for mirroring and for an idealizable selfobject. A child who has some needs met is in a better position to develop a core of vitality and hopefulness that will allow him to compensate for deficits. The child whose needs are frustrated across the board is less able to maintain adequate self-esteem, develop creative compensations, or withstand fragmentation.

IMPRISONED INTELLIGENCE AND DEFICITS

When ULD sufferers cannot learn something that they think they should be able to learn, they experience the failure as a deficit or lack: something is missing. This feeling resembles the depletion states described in self-psychological literature. The term *depletion* describes the state of "something being missing" in one's psychological makeup. It is an awareness of an emptiness or a deadness inside one's self and a yearning for others who might facilitate feeling alive again (Palombo, 1985b).

While self psychology emphasizes emotional deficits, the field of learning disabilities emphasizes cognitive deficits. Both deal with "lacks": the former presumes a lack of responsiveness from selfobjects; the latter presumes a lack of endowment. Although some self-psychological literature addresses cognitive deficits (Kohut, 1971, 1977; Tolpin, 1980), the psychoanalytic assumption is that lack of appropriate nurturing and resultant self-deficits are the primary problem (Palombo, 1979).

To understand the psychological world of the ULD sufferer, both kinds of deficits are crucial considerations. A typical scenario might be: a cognitive deficit causes a child to fail to meet the caregiver's expectations, perhaps by receiving poor grades. As a result, the caregiver is angry, frustrated, or disappointed and can no longer nurture the child adequately, which makes the child's Imprisoned Intelligence even more pronounced. A cognitive deficit is almost always accompanied by a lack of support and nurturing.

Deficit leads to deficit. Fortunately, the pattern does not continue indefinitely. Participants reported that a new pattern is set in motion by testing. The process looks something like this: (1) The cognitive deficit results in Imprisoned Intelligence. Adverse emotional reactions follow, including shame and withdrawal. Aspects of development are constricted. (2) Development is remobilized after testing and diagnosis. Suddenly, there are new possibilities for dealing with learning problems. The tendency to withdraw diminishes because the deficits are now identified and there is hope for remediation.

Innate cognitive deficits may not be preventable, but emotional deficits are. Early testing and diagnosis seem to offer strong protection against developing later, ULD-related emotional problems. Individuals who are tested and diagnosed at a young age do not exhibit low self-esteem (Kosarych-Coy, 1984); they develop effective compensations and function at an age-appropriate level. Their success is partly due to the fact that they have a vocabulary with which to understand their deficits. Language allows the experience to be put into a context in which solutions become possible. One successful man in this study who grew up with a verbal learning disorder explained why a lexicon is important to him:

> I didn't have a mechanism for dealing with the teachers who wanted to see me as stupid, who found me frustrating, who reacted very negatively to my inability to spell and to write well. . . . and to be honest, I think there are an awful lot of anal-compulsive people out there who see it as their

job as to get Johnny to spell it right and don't have a particular model to have a mind, to help [them] to learn to think.
So it would have been very useful for me and my parents to
have this rhetoric to deal with the teachers.

IMPRISONED INTELLIGENCE, SHAME, AND FRAGMENTATION: THE CHASM

There are striking similarities between (1) fragmentation, (2) shame, and (3) the experiences of the chasm. The three terms describe a single experience that is the result of insufficient compensations and defenses in combination with a fragile self. Fragmentation can occur in individuals who have not developed self-soothing capacities and are therefore vulnerable and dependent upon selfobjects to perform selfobject functions (mirroring, idealization, twinship). When the selfobject fails to perform its function, the individual is massively disappointed and subject to fragmentation states.

People with undiagnosed learning disabilities may have a greater propensity for severe fragmentation. Because they are unable to understand their LD, compensatory structures fail them more often. When compensatory structures fail, fragmentation and low self-esteem seem to whirl out of control. Fragmentation, then, is very similar to the chasm. Compare a description of fragmentation on the left to a participant's description of the chasm on the right.

FRAGMENTATION	CHASM
Patients describe this [fragmentation] in a variety of ways. Some feel that they are falling apart; some that they are lost in space without any supply of oxygen; others that they are treading water in the middle of the ocean with nothing solid to touch, no one nearby, and ever-present danger of sharks; still others feel dead. (Baker and Baker, 1987)	I had a chasm of no knowledge, just this place inside of me that, you know. . . . It was an emptiness. You know, like, if you were to draw a picture of my body, that there was this great space that other people had filled up, that I didn't.

To avoid the chasm, the individual may avoid situations that have triggered feelings of fragmentation in the past. For instance, a ULD student who receives an A with negative comments about spelling or neatness may feel no accomplishment, but experience only the crush of defeat as earlier school traumas are revisited. Fuqua (1993) elaborates:

> A person with a sense of self-cohesion feels lively, effectual, and confident. A person who is fragmented complains of listlessness, disorganization, inability to concentrate or think straight, feelings of depletion, and difficulty following through on things. Sometimes, she also feels enraged. The universal urge in the psyche is to try to reinstate a sense of cohesion whenever it is disrupted. (p. 15)

A perpetual feeling of insecurity is associated with fragmentation/chasm. Because wildly fluctuating self-experiences are triggered by environmental demands, sufferers can never depend on feeling good or stable for any given period of time. Their self-states may vacillate between cohesion and fragmentation on a daily basis. For example, a slow reader may feel cohesive before a test because she has prepared and knows the answers. Her self-esteem plummets during and after the test because she did not have enough time to show her knowledge. Therefore, her suffering is twofold: not only does she have to withstand the chasm itself, but she remains in a state of fearful apprehension. She never knows when something will come along to threaten her cohesion. Unlike a cohesive self, she does not have "the sense of continuity of the self in time" (Kohut, 1984, p. 65). The pain of this state may be hard to grasp for those who have not experienced it, but it is a problem of ontological scope: one's very existence feels tenuous and uncertain.

Self-cohesion is a necessary precondition for learning. When people have cohesive selves, they are invested in themselves and interested in their world. When people are fragmented, thought processes freeze and interest withers away (Nathanson, 1987). The chasm then is the nucleus around which pain and low-esteem coalesce. It affects many areas of experience and can seriously inhibit learning.

Even after testing, persons have to repeatedly face the chasm to make headway against their learning problems. Sometimes they also endure or fear ridicule from the world. Despite these struggles, most persons with ULD are able to progress in their careers and lives without a catastrophic loss of self-esteem. Perhaps their success is due to strong compensatory structures, or the self-regard they gain by mastering discouragement and hardship (Gerber and Reiff, 1991). Additional research is necessary to determine when and why the chasm is experienced, as well as how it is laid to rest.

IMPRISONED INTELLIGENCE AND EMOTIONAL DISTANCING: DISAVOWAL

Most people cannot tolerate swinging from cohesion to fragmentation that seems to occur without rhyme or reason. To protect themselves, they learn to distance themselves from their pain. One way to achieve the desired distance from emotions is through disavowal. Disavowal is knowing a painful fact but feeling nothing. The fact itself is not repressed, but the emotions surrounding it are. As Basch (1998) describes it, Disavowal

> blocks the formation of a bond between perception and affect. . . . [It] is directed toward danger from the external world. Disavowal, by preventing the formation of an affective link between a potentially traumatic experience and the affect it would ordinarily be expected to arouse, minimizes that experience's importance for the self system, for, though acknowledged, *what is not affectively charged* can be disregarded. (pp. 124–125, emphasis mine)

Take, for example, a civil service worker who reads slowly but needs to pass an exam to get a promotion. After each attempt the exam is returned with a failing grade. Because the stakes are high, when the worker sees the grade, he feels nothing but emptiness and adopts an "I-don't-care" attitude. Only later do the shame and disappointment hit.

Imprisoned Intelligence is often accompanied by disavowal. Many people accept the fact that they are different, but until the diagnosis, they have no emotional reaction. Because they are vulnerable, they organize their world by rationalizing their differences as simply a way of life. In other words, disavowal is a step beyond frustration: when frustration can no longer be tolerated, it is replaced by a feeling of nothingness.

The Testing: Interrupting Disavowal

Diagnostic testing interferes with the disavowal associated with ULD by facilitating: (1) attempts to change and confront inadequate ways of compensating, (2) the process of working through grief, and (3) enhanced communication within the self and with others.

Confronting Previous Compensations

One area that is challenged is individuals' pride in their independence—previously a compensation that allowed them to maintain self-esteem in the face of unsupportive teachers and parents. As discussed before, in the past, because no one was there to help, survivors learned to figure things out for themselves and created ingenious compensations for their ULD. For years, an independent stance may have served them well. Now, pride and self-sufficiency may no longer be adequate solutions; testing indicates a disability, best handled not by independent effort, but by consulting professionals and allowing them to help. One person reported:

> I learned that I operate in some areas on a third-grade level. I did go for tutoring for a while, but I quit because it was much easier to be a doctoral student than it was to be working with phonics. It was too hard. I couldn't do it. It was easier, you know, back on campus, being a doctoral student.

This brilliant person found it too difficult to live (even temporarily) in a world where she felt so stupid.*

---

* Here is an example that shows where self psychology diverges from my findings. Kohut's description of compensatory structures suggests that once the structures become integrated, they

Confronting pride in one's independence with the need to be dependent to learn in areas of difficulty corresponds with Kohut's concept of archaic grandiosity. The feeling that "there's nothing wrong with me and I can do whatever I want if I only try hard enough" is challenged by the testing. People learn that some things cannot be done at all, and some things will take a great deal of effort. Testing, although illuminating, also constitutes a narcissistic injury.

For example, when people with LD first learn to deal with their deficits, their weakness becomes painfully clear. At first, learning is awkward, painfully slow, and difficult. This insults their pride in their intelligence, because learning in their areas of strength is so easy, and that is what they expect of themselves in every arena. When expectations of easy learning are confronted by reality, the chasm can follow. One young woman with dyslexia said that before her diagnosis, she compensated for her extremely slow reading by asking lots of questions in class. When she got to college, however, this method of learning annoyed the professor. After her diagnosis, she had to focus on keeping quiet and taking notes. Needless to say, it was very difficult. Not only did she have to endure the chasm until new skills were in place, but she had to give up a comfortable solution.

The contrast between attitudes before and after testing exemplifies how, to protect oneself from further painful exposure, one's pride goes underground. Grandiose expectations are split off and unavailable for selfobject modulation.

Ironically, before diagnosis, it is this unmodified grandiosity that propels people to compensate creatively for their Imprisoned Intelligence. After diagnosis, primitive grandiosity was neutralized. Interestingly, this was not accomplished gradually through transmuting internalizations, but by facing a disappointment immediately and all at once.

---

continue to provide a valuable source of self-enhancement. This is not necessarily the case for ULD sufferers. The compensatory structures they relied on before diagnosis are not always appropriate for continued use. They may need to be examined, re-evaluated, and sometimes discarded after diagnosis.

Grief

As discussed in the chapter on treatment, grieving occurs when grandiose expectations are denied by reality. It is truly difficult to understand that, no matter how smart you are, areas of learning that seem easy to others can be difficult to impossible. But over time, as people learn new strategies, they learn to modify their grandiose expectations. One aspect of reconciliation is understanding that learning takes time.

Those who have silently suffered with Imprisoned Intelligence move from naiveté to maturity; even in the face of the difficult transitions described above, they did not lose hope. After the diagnosis, things change: words and feelings begin to come together and make sense. The problem does not go away but becomes integrated into one's concept of self.

Enhanced Communication with Self and Others

Almost everyone interviewed felt relieved to be able to label what they knew but could not verbalize until the diagnosis. When empathic failures occur due to others' misunderstanding of ULD, there is now a vocabulary with which to explain the failure. Verbalization also interferes with disavowal by creating a link between cognition and affect where there was none before. Until the diagnosis of a learning disability, there are no words with which to examine this disavowed state; after diagnosis there is a lexicon of words to describe ULD experiences.

Disavowal can be seen on a broader scale as well. For example, prior to diagnosis, the world ignores a person's cognitive problems and the associated psychological ramifications. After diagnosis, if allowed an opportunity to communicate their feelings to a sympathetic ear, people can then move away from a defensive fragmenting position toward compensatory strategies. This is the maturation process that I have called reconciliation.

Also, armed with new information, individuals can reinterpret their personal history. Mentors, when available, are able to rekindle idealization when the mentor is aware of both the individual's strengths and disabilities. Parents who did not have the knowledge to help their child with the ULD can now offer support to their adult offspring struggling to live with the disability. Intellectual strengths and disabilities can be seen as a whole. Hope, therefore, is rekindled.

Learning about narcissistic deficits and the psychological treatment of ULD will be beneficial to this population. This research only begins to answer questions about how defensive structures are replaced by compensatory structures. In psychoanalytic terms, how does structuralization occur? Is it always an unconscious process? Also, is there a difference between high and low achievers in compensatory structure formation? Why do some people with serious disabilities achieve while others do not? Perhaps Kohut's concept of vigor (1977, p. 100) provides a clue. Levin's (1991, p. 43) ideas about interhemispheric connections may offer another explanation. Other environmental variables may come into play as well, such as parental judgment of academic success and failure. Perhaps the type of compensatory structure determines success. So much remains to be learned about this new field of inquiry. But Kohut's concepts help to bridge the fields of learning disabilities and psychology. We each have talents and skills that help us formulate our ambitions in the context of our ideals, and attention to those talents and skills plays a decisive role in self-development. When we are attentive to our talents and skills, we can use them well to navigate the contradictions (the "tension arc") between our ambitions and our ideals, and we are likely to feel good about ourselves. When our talents are not enhanced and our skills are not developed, psychological problems can arise. Although deficits can be filled in with compensatory structures, this process will not occur easily when undiagnosed learning disabilities lead to empathic breaks (within oneself and with others) that cause shame and intellectual constriction. People become afraid to try because they cannot tolerate unexplained failures. This is Imprisoned Intelligence.

CONCLUSIONS

One of Kohut's crucial achievements was to introduce and promote understanding of concepts such as fragmentation, grandiosity, and compensation. He also created a view of development based upon an empathic understanding of transference needs. Perhaps more important, he created a lexicon with which to discuss the phenomena that he observed. Clinicians may agree or disagree with his ideas, but with his words, they can carry on a discourse which would not otherwise be possible. Imprisoned Intelligence also creates a lexicon, and it is my hope that the new language can be used by others to create a dialogue. There is so much to be learned about this new field of inquiry, and a real need exists to bridge the disciplines of learning disabilities and psychology. Kohut's concepts give us tools that enhance the building of these bridges.

Self psychology, with its emphasis on deficits and self-esteem, provides an appropriate context in which to study Imprisoned Intelligence because (1) Kohut's concept of cohesion is a necessary component in learning; (2) fragmentation, of which shame is a component, makes it very difficult or impossible to learn; and (3) learning involves optimal frustration—the capacity to tolerate, over long periods of time, small, progressive disappointments.

Clearly, the emotional consequences of ULD become psychotherapeutic issues. The detailed personal accounts of the subjective stories of adults with ULD have produced my concept of Imprisoned Intelligence. Though many learning problems are environmentally based, many are innate, and the two call for different treatment strategies. My clinical experience suggests that a psychodynamic psychotherapy, informed by knowledge about learning disabilities, can be successful with this population. Here, self psychology is an especially useful psychodynamic model, since many of these individuals seem to suffer from "self problems": low self-esteem, repressed archaic grandiosity, empty depression, and tendency to extreme shame states and fragmentation states.

Furthermore, adults with ULD feel that their psychological development has been compromised by the lack of awareness of their disabilities. Baker (1987) concurs that a needless tragedy of Imprisoned Intelligence can occur:

> With exceptional responsiveness, they [children with learning disabilities] can learn well and do not develop secondary narcissistic vulnerabilities. More often, the disability is not understood, and the child develops poor self-esteem and a tendency to avoid schoolwork. Thus, a parent might respond more than satisfactorily to a typical child but be unable to meet the needs of a special child. (p. 449)

Early interventions could prevent the problems that stem from unidentified learning disabilities. It could be so helpful if school personnel such as classroom teachers and school social workers could be trained to identify and help children with undiagnosed learning disabilities. Kohut (1985, p. 39) stated that although psychoanalytic principles cannot explain innate endowments, one cannot ignore their impact on the self's capacity for creativity. Innate deficits influence self-states.

Kohut's conceptualization of compensatory structures also offers considerable insight into the experiences of adults with innate deficits. Rather than being incapacitated by inadequate self-nurturing responses, many people with ULD (in and out of awareness) have creatively and ingeniously developed ways of compensating for their learning disabilities. Unfortunately, because no one knew, more adaptive compensations were not available. Though compensations often allow individuals to function adequately, they are probably nowhere near optimal, and in some circumstances they take a psychological toll. Perhaps, since 20 percent of adults suffer from ULD, Kohut was actually treating more people with undiagnosed learning disabilities than he may have appreciated.

Finally, the understanding of how individuals not only survive difficult and adverse conditions but go on to build fulfilling lives and careers is just beginning. This is because the ability to think and learn surely involves the self, and the self's relationship to learning is now coming under the microscope. One's innate capacity to think and learn, as well as the emotional consequences of this capacity, are surely issues of self.

Addendum 2

Historical Review

When so many people are affected, why has the topic of adults with ULD received so little attention? A brief historical overview may help clarify the cultural and political conditions that have helped create this dearth of information.

The field of learning disabilities was born of concern for intelligent children whose needs were not being met in school (Strauss and Lehtinen, 1947). It was assumed that children would outgrow their disabilities (Blakeslee, 1991; Bruck, 1987; Buchanan and Wolf, 1986; Gajar, 1992; Gerber, 1994; Vogel, 1989). Under that assumption, the literature focused only on children. It is now clear that many children retain their disabilities in adulthood (Frauenheim, 1978). Margaret Rawson (1977) followed a population of school-age children for twenty years and found that their dyslexia stayed with them. It took many years for anyone to realize that learning disabilities could be an adult affliction. Vogel (1989) states that "the manifestations of learning disabilities, though they may change, persist into adulthood, even among those who have above-average intelligence and who have completed advanced degrees" (p. 112).

In the 1970s, as the first generation of children identified as learning disabled grew up (Vogel, 1985), colleges began to take on the problem. Historically, colleges have taken the lead in research, but their purpose was practical: they wanted to test the knowledge and aptitude of students with LD to decide whether they should be admitted to college programs, and determine how to meet the educational needs of the students while maintaining the educational standards of the institution. Treatment was not their focus.

One factor that enhanced interest in adult LD was the passage of a federal law in 1973, Bill 504 (Vogel, 1985, p. 179), which mandates equal access to educational institutions for handicapped individuals. Colleges, therefore, were compelled to set up learning disability programs. This created a need for a literature of learning disabilities, because college counselors were now concerned with diagnosis and intervention. The focus was on identification, assessment, and educational interventions (Adelman and Taylor, 1986; Cohen, 1983; Vogel, 1985; Wren and Segal, 1985). These topics remained the focus of LD research throughout the 1980s.

Also in the 1980s, a literature developed that explained severe versus subtle pathology. The research subjects were psychiatric patients whose learning disabilities were discovered during diagnostic evaluation. Using a diagnosis of minimal brain damage, this literature created a medical model (Bellak, 1978, p. 75; Greenspan, 1978; Murray, 1979) in which the learning disabilities were viewed as tangential to the psychiatric diagnosis. Since these patients were often extremely troubled, this research gave no information about high-functioning people who suffer from subtle effects of ULD.

In addition, few professionals have written about severe learning disabilities in adults who have problems with functioning in life (Interagency Committee on Learning Disabilities, 1987; Gerber and Kelley, 1984; Gottesman, 1994; Rourke, Young, and Leenaars, 1989). Much of this research focuses on transitions to adulthood and problems involving lifestyle and vocation. Discussion centers on solutions and therapies (particularly occupational therapy) for practical problems such as inability to hold a job; but emotional variables are overlooked (White, 1992; Koziol, 1987).

In 1992 Gajar reviewed the research involving adults with learning disabilities. He concluded that literature about the emotional needs of LD adults was practically nonexistent and more research was needed. He spoke of a "paucity of articles addressing the adult with learning disabilities within the community setting" (p. 509).

WHY LD IS SO DIFFICULT TO SPOT

Why are so many people unaware that they are learning disabled? First, schools began identifying LD students twenty years ago. Public Law 94–142, which required schools to diagnose and address LD, did not pass until 1977. Any adult who finished school before that time had little opportunity for diagnosis and treatment (Gerber and Reiff, 1991; Ryan and Price, 1992; Cannon, 1996). Estimates that 10 to 15 percent of the U.S. population have LD are probably accurate (Malcolm, Polatajko, and Simons, 1990; Levin, 1991).

Second, diagnosing and understanding the interacting variables of ULD can be tricky. The group is extremely heterogeneous (Johnson and Blalock, 1987; Vogel, 1985). Important variables may include the patient's constitution, psychological state, environmental input, and stage of development, all interfacing and interacting with one another (Palombo, 1991; Buchholz, 1987). Furthermore, intelligent people learn how to compensate for their deficits, so though they may still feel that they are struggling, the LD remains invisible (Buchholz, 1987). The following are the subdivisions or categories of symptoms that indicate LD.

CATEGORIES OF SYMPTOMS

It is difficult to define LD and categorize LD sufferers because many have multiple handicaps that are invariably idiosyncratic (Patton and Polloway, 1982, p. 83; Pennington, 1991, p. 3). Furthermore, symptoms run the gamut from mild to severe (Ross, 1987) and may even vary within the individual from day to day (Vogel, 1985, p. 183).

How can the abstract, heterogeneous characteristics of LD be organized into practical categories that are useful in the context of adult life? The legal definition created in 1977 states:

> (10) *Specific learning disability*—(i) *General.* Specific learning disability means a disorder in one or more of the basic psychological processes involved in understanding or in using language, spoken or written, that may manifest itself in the imperfect ability to listen, think, speak, read, write, spell, or to do mathematical calculations, including conditions such as perceptual disabilities, brain injury, minimal brain dysfunction, dyslexia, and developmental aphasia.

> (ii) *Disorders not included.* Specific learning disability does not include learning problems that are primarily the result of visual, hearing, or motor disabilities, of mental retardation, of emotional disturbance, or of environmental, cultural, or economic disadvantage. (Now codified in the Code of Federal Regulations at 34 CFR 300.8(c)(10).)

However, there is little consensus on this issue, and academics and clinicians have categorized and defined LD in a number of different ways.

Generally, experts agree that learning disabilities are obstacles that constrict broad areas of adult functioning such as "(a) achievement; (b) language processing and cognitive deficits; (c) occupational adjustment; and (d) social adjustment" (Ross, 1987, p. 5). Affected individuals show mild to severe deficits in the areas of basic skills, language, memory, auditory processing, visual perception, and directionality (Gottesman, 1994). The problem with these general unevenness is that they create overly broad categories that are of limited explanatory usefulness.

Other clinicians use computer models of the brain to explain LD. Silver, in *The Gifted Learning Disabled Student* (1994), describes how the brain takes in information through the five senses. Learning is divided into steps that involve input, integration, memory, and output. According to Silver, learning disabilities primarily interfere with the process of creating meaning from the information taken in, storing this meaningful material, or outputting it.

Another strategy has been to divide learning disabilities into verbal and nonverbal disabilities. Verbal disabilities involve cognitive deficits in language, including symbols such as numbers. Such deficits are usually discovered in school (Lieberman, 1987) although their impact extends throughout the life span. Johnson and Blalock describe the different types of verbal disabilities; see their book *Adults with Learning Disabilities* (1987) for more detailed information.

To understand the verbal versus nonverbal distinction, it is important to note that some people do not communicate primarily through language. Language and meaning are not interchangeable. When verbal communication is disturbed, the result can be an inability to make friends and keep jobs, but people who have nonverbal strengths may enjoy success in fields that value nonverbal skills, such as the arts, graphic design, music, or athletics. For example, Einstein was apparently not such an excellent speaker but his power for conceptualizing nonverbally was obviously in a class by itself (Patten, 1973; Thompson, 1971).

Another verbal learning disability deals with expression. Some people have considerable trouble saying what they want to say. Either speech or writing can be affected. They can understand when they are listening, but when they talk, read, or write they run into obstacles. For others, the problem involves dyslexia, the inability to take in, decode, and perceive information visually because the sounds associated with language are not correctly processed in the brain (Pennington, 1991, p. 58). A person with dyslexia might not be able to correctly take down telephone messages or comprehend written instructions for using a VCR.

Nonverbal learning disabilities can be difficult to discern. They show themselves in disturbances of spatial orientation, body image, facial recognition, visual/spatial/motor organization, social interaction and analytic problem solving (Johnson, 1987b).

There is some agreement that nonverbal learning disabilities cause the greatest problems for adults in personal, social, and occupational realms (Patton and Polloway, 1982; Johnson, 1987b).

Apparently, these disabilities impact partly by disturbing comprehension of time and space (Ross, 1987).

What are some of the practical, day-to-day difficulties that adults with nonverbal learning disabilities encounter? Johnson and Blalock (1987, p. 44) describe people who are verbally adept, yet cannot organize their lives and frequently lose their way. Some people are unable to make appropriate plans for themselves because of an inability to prioritize. Some cannot self-monitor and therefore are unable to identify their own mistakes. Others cannot take in more than one kind of information at the same time and become frustrated and angry. Ross elaborates:

> Adults with learning disabilities of this type are likely to get lost easily, even in familiar places; to be either late or unusually early for appointments; or to lose track of time while absorbed in a task. They may also have trouble recognizing faces and interpreting nonverbal communication; making it more difficult for them to interact appropriately with others. (1987, pp. 5, 6)

When nonverbal learning disabilities interfere with normal interactions, social cues are bypassed. People may have trouble reading others' body language and facial expressions or they may not use their bodies well and end up looking clumsy. Setting a clock radio becomes difficult or impossible. Others who cannot organize or prioritize will have homes that are perpetually a mess. Thus, lack of organization skills can not only impede efficiency at work, it can damage relationships and quality of life. Those who are lucky have secretaries or efficient family members who can help them get organized.

Lastly, some researchers approach LD not by attempting to define or categorize it but through firsthand, subjective experiences of successful learning disabled adults (Butler, 1994; Mautner, 1984; Stein, 1987; Strauss, 1978). For example, the editors of the *Journal of Learning Disabilities* featured a moving personal account by N.L. Stein (1987). They prefaced the article by stating:

We publish articles *about* people with learning disabilities, but not often enough by people *with* learning disabilities. (p. 409, emphasis mine)

Far too often, LD literature tends not to consult the experts: the people with the disabilities. In their writings, Reiff, Gerber, and Ginsberg (1993) try to bridge this gap by focusing on the experiences of adults with LD. They say:

The voices of successful adults with learning disabilities are essential for understanding what *can* be accomplished and which kinds of approaches lead to success; in contrast, traditional perspectives have focused largely on what could *not* be achieved. (p. 124, emphasis mine)[*]

LIFE SPAN DEVELOPMENT

Although the literature on adults with ULD is scant (Gerber and Kelly, 1984; Kafka, 1984; Kaplan and Shachter, 1991) there is interest in learning disabilities and life span development (Polloway, Smith, and Patton, 1988). Researchers are beginning to look at the impact of learning disabilities over the course of a lifetime (Buchholz, 1987; Pickar, 1986; Orenstein, 1992). Goals seen through the lens of a life span will appear different than goals merely for academic achievement (Johnson and Blalock, 1987; Gerber and Kelly, 1984) or achievements in personal, social, and vocational competency (Gottesman, 1994; Basch, 1988; Lutwik, 1983; Patton and Polloway, 1982). Lieberman (1987) states:

Society at large tends to be more tolerant than school. Handicapped individuals are able to fade into the adult world and lead satisfactory and even fulfilled lives. They would abhor the idea of someone coming along and even suggesting that they were handicapped in some way. Their worst memories in life may be that being handicapped was thrust upon them in school. (p. 64)

Some individuals bypass or compensate for their learning disabilities and lead a "normal" life. As Lieberman (1987) says, "learning disabilities in adults is meaningful only if it helps people live"(p. 64). For others, learning disabilities are a source of suffering. Ryan and Price (1992) explain:

---

[*] Reiff, Gerber, and Ginsberg's thoughtful book Exceeding Expectations (1997) highlights the perseverance and difficulties experienced by successful adults with ULD.

> There are numbers of adults who are undiagnosed as hav-
> ing this handicap yet who now face problems of life adjust-
> ment without the knowledge that they are, indeed, bright
> enough to achieve, but are inefficient and ineffective when
> learning and applying knowledge. (p. 6)

Chronic failure leaves a developmental imprint that influences both internal perceptions and perceptions of the world (Buchholz, 1987; Gensler, 1993; Kafka, 1984; Koziol, 1987). Individuals can grow up experiencing the self as damaged (Buchholz, 1987; Garber, 1989), struggling with feelings of alienation, heightened self-exposure, serious self-esteem problems, feelings of humiliation, and fear of failure. The specter of these experiences creates anticipation anxiety, interfering with the capacity to try, which results in a loss of spontaneity (Gensler, 1993). Individuals learn to live with a chronic state of low-level anxiety and become increasingly withdrawn. Furthermore, if they cannot easily take in information in an organized way, interactions with others will be compromised (Buchholz, 1987; Malcolm, 1990). For example, an infant who does not have the capacity to organize visual input comfortably may not have an interactive smiling response, which enhances development and allows the infant to form ties with caregivers (Lichtenberg, 1983; Kraus, McGee et al., 1996).

MORE TO BE LEARNED

How are clinicians to understand the emotional ramifications of living with LD and ULD? More information is badly needed. So little is known (Johnson and Blalock, 1987; Bigler, 1992; Gerber, 1994; Kaplan and Shachter, 1991; Polloway, Smith, and Patton, 1988; Levin, 1991; Palombo, 1991; Vail, 1989). Even literature about adults with obvious, clearly diagnosed learning disabilities is sorely lacking—in part, because LD as a formal field of study did not emerge until the 1960s. The term "learning disability" was created specifically as an umbrella so that many disciplines could interface and interact with each other (Cruickshank and Johnson, 1975; Johnson and Myklebust, 1971; Lerner, 1981; Siegel and Gold, 1982). The fields of education, medicine, psychology, and language are all contributors. The youth of the field, coupled with its multidisciplinary nature, has complicated things enormously. For example, even the definition of learning disabilities has evoked controversy (Vogel, 1989). It took years for people from different disciplines to approach a consensus on a definition (Hammill, 1990).

Furthermore, there is a tendency to think of learning and emotions in different camps. Kirk and Gallaher (1979, p. 184) elaborate on this division. They observe that the medical profession identifies but does not necessarily cure severe problems, that psychologists study behavioral characteristics, and that educators provide interventions. This division has not created a backdrop amenable to the investigation of subjective experiences. It is difficult to justify researching the emotional consequences of learning disabilities when no firm definition of learning disability even exists. Reiff, Gerber, and Ginsberg cogently observe that the "insider's perspective" is missing when decision makers struggle with the definition of learning disabilities (1993, p. 115).

In introducing an article by Deci and Chandler (1986), Adelman and Taylor, as guest editors for the *Journal of Learning Disabilities*, observed that "basic psychological concepts [are] not widely discussed in the LD field" (1986, p. 399). Because the various disciplines (neurology, cognitive psychology, behavioral psychology, and socioemotional psychology) are unwilling to collaborate, LD sufferers, as well as those with other "interdisciplinary" psychological disorders, often do not receive adequate treatment (Deci and Chandler, 1986; Bartoli, 1990).

Kaplan and Shachter (1991) state that "virtually no research has dealt with adults with undiagnosed learning disabilities, whose problem often goes unrecognized by therapists" and that "such disabilities may represent a core issue in treatment, even when patients present with other difficulties" (p. 196). White (1992) reviewed the literature on adults with diagnosed LD and concluded that although it was clear that many adults have trouble adjusting, "of all the areas of adjustment that were investigated in the studies reviewed, social adjustment got the least amount of attention" (p. 454).

There are practical consequences of living with learning disabilities. The standards set by the world often cannot be easily and comfortably met. Cohen, an expert on college students with LD, states: "Although there are many children with learning problems who are not learning disabled, there are virtually no learning disabled children or adolescents who do not evidence significant psychological conflicts and concerns" (1985, p. 177). Adulthood does not guarantee resolution of these painful states. Gensler (1993) maintains that the influence of LD "continues into adulthood in a person's cognitive style, use of defenses, interpersonal relations, character, self-image, and career development" (p. 673).

Researchers and clinicians who listen to the experiences of LD adults are acutely aware of this emotional fallout (Haufrecht and Berger, 1984; Scheiber and Talpers, 1987). In their writing, these professionals repeatedly emphasize the need for mental health services for LD sufferers (Anderson, 1974; Blakeslee, 1991; Brier, 1994; Cox, 1977; Gajar, 1992; Gottesman, 1994; Johnson and Blalock, 1987; Malcolm, 1990; Palombo, 1985; Rawson, 1977; Rosenberger, 1988; Ross, 1987; Schechter, 1974; Shane, 1984; Vogel, 1989). The problem becomes more complicated when adults do not realize that they have learning disabilities (Ryan and Price, 1992; Schulman, 1984, Rothstein, 1988). In summary, many professionals have attested that LD in adults is a phenomenon that not only deserves more research, but calls for significantly more mental health services than are currently available.

Clearly, learning disabilities, whether diagnosed or undiagnosed, strongly influence the development of character and personality (Kafka, 1984; Garber, 1988). The individual's feelings of competence may be threatened (Basch, 1988). Other aspects of personality maybe negatively affected as well: independence (Kafka, 1984), the capacity to make choices that reflect one's interests, and the ability to compete without undue anxiety (Buchholz, 1987; Cohen, 1985).

EMOTIONAL FALLOUT: FRUSTRATION

Although many individuals with ULD suffer and learn how to survive, this invisible problem can have lasting effects on personality (Gensler, 1993; Gerber, Ginsberg, and Reiff, 1992) because order and logic seem out of reach (Palombo, 1991). What does it feel like to live with a cognitive deficit? Paul LeClerc, who wrote the foreword in the pamphlet *Dispelling the Myths: College Students and Learning Disabilities* (Garnett and LaPorta, 1991) explains the burden of living with learning disabilities:

Many of us are sometimes frustrated by our own inability to program a VCR, to sound knowledgeable when speaking to an auto mechanic or hardware sales person, or to fold a road map back to its original shape. All of us know couples that quarrel on trips because one of the pair always takes wrong turns but finds it painfully embarrassing to ask for directions. Such frustrations, though annoying, are insignificant—but would they be insignificant if our entire futures depended on our mastering that VCR, that map, that maze of highways? How would we feel if we had to achieve that mastery in one hour flat, while 20 people watched us—and if we thought that we alone could not finish the task in the set time? Like the beleaguered driver, would we be too embarrassed to ask for directions? Would we despair of our future?

That learning disabilities are often invisible to oneself and to others compounds emotional struggles (Ryan and Price, 1992; Schulman, 1984). White (1985) says "Millions of others [adults] struggle with the sometimes overwhelming trials of daily life without knowing why they are different from their friends and neighbors or how to overcome their problems" (p. 231). Furthermore, the later the diagnosis, the greater the chance for self-deficits (McGlynn, 1983). For example, if one has motor coordination problems or is clumsy, this problem can seriously affect self-esteem (Weil, 1978, p. 477). Deficiencies in language can interfere with social interactions and create barriers to empathically resonating with others (Gottesman, 1994).

Unless deficits such as these are understood within the context of an individual's overall intellect, expectations of high achievement can cause serious frustration. When expectations are thwarted, frustration follows, which may eventually lead to trauma. How does frustration manifest itself in intelligent but uneven learners? This frustration can include the following four discrete categories:

1. Working harder than others but achieving less
2. Uneven learning polarities: unexplained failures along with successes
3. Constricted potential: intelligence with no place to go
4. Character denigration

These four factors create the painful emotional ramifications of ULD. Others have written about these problems, and the following four sections introduce this literature to the reader.

Frustration from Working Harder and Achieving Less

Not surprisingly, it is frustrating to work much harder than others and accomplish much less. Wren and Segal (1985) write about the difficulties of living up to seemingly impossible standards without knowing why they are so impossible, when they seem easy for others.

Frustration from Uneven Learning: Unexplained Failures in the Face of Other Achievements

When people are used to success, an unexpected failure is confusing, frustrating, or even anguishing. Vogel (1985) discusses what she calls "Intra-Individual" differences and describes how difficult it can be to live with the polarities of cognitive discrepancies. Donna Shalala, when she was Chancellor of the University of Wisconsin-Madison in 1991, beautifully highlighted some of the problems discrepant learners face:

> Few lawyers are abashed because they are not invited to sing at the Met; few sculptors are concerned by their inability to

do statistics. And few of us think they should be. We take for granted that no one needs to do everything well. On the other hand, many people hold firmly to the idea that the college student—by virtue of being in college—should be omni-competent: able to learn with equal facility French, calculus, the elementary backstroke, English composition, and a lab science. And it is certainly true that most students can do this. But some students, despite their obvious intellectual competence, seem unable to . . . . In the past, those whose learning patterns were oddly discrepant—those who could learn some things well and other things only with great difficulty—were generally discouraged from continuing their education. (Shalala, 1991, p. ii)

Federal legislation has made it easier to cope in college. Yet intellectual discrepancies still pose difficult problems for students in college (Ryan and Price, 1992; Schulman, 1986; Wilson, 1993). Individuals with ULD write poignantly about this in self-reports (Stein, 1987; Mautner, 1984; Strauss, 1978; McMahill, 1993). Vogel (1985) elaborates:

Students with learning disabilities usually have areas of difficulty that contrast sharply with other areas where they excel. . . . Each LD student has a unique combination of strengths and weaknesses, but in every case the deficits make learning especially difficult. . . . Often, their learning disabilities are inconsistent or sporadic causing problems one day but not the next. Similarly, they may cause problems in only one specific area, or they may surface in many areas.

The striking unevenness of their [LD college student's] abilities . . . often tends to be exaggerated with maturity. . . . What they did well as children they seem to do even better, perhaps even exceedingly well as adults, while their functioning in areas of weakness becomes even more dramatically discrepant. (p. 183)

Frustration from Constricted Potential: Intelligence with No Place to Go

People with LD struggle with unexpressed intelligence. When people know they are bright but cannot achieve, they become very frustrated (Wren and Segal, 1985; Wren, Adelman, Pike, and Wilson 1987). Margaret Rawson (1977), comments on her 1968 study of fifty-six bright dyslexic boys. In this 1977 paper, she writes about the frustrations dyslexic children face when their language disabilities sabotage their potential. Rawson quotes a patient: "For years I've had this feeling that I've been able to use only a third of my mental powers. The other two-thirds just roll and tumble around in my head going nowhere . . . confusing, frustrating . . ." (p. 193). In 1968, Silver, reviewing Rawson's 1968 study concurred, saying, that "although the study is not scientifically rigorous, it clearly indicates that children with high scores on intelligence tests, coming from professional homes, are not exempt from the problems of language disability" (p. 220). Johnson and Blalock (1987) and Vail (1989) both conclude that more information is needed if we wish to help gifted LD students actualize their potential.

Frustration over Character Denigration

When ULD interferes with achievement, traumatic stereotypic denigration from others (being called lazy, stupid, etc.) can follow. Charles Madigan (1994) of the *Chicago Tribune,* although not speaking about LD, wrote an interesting article called "Welfare Finger-Pointing." He said that "society often determines stereotypes" and that "ever since the 19th Century . . . the assumption has been that those who don't make it in the USA were simply those who didn't try hard enough. . . . There remains an assumption that anyone who is good can achieve anything, even though that clearly is not true" (p. 1).

People with ULD can surely relate to these statements. Unexplained learning failures can cause individuals to be inappropriately judged and scrutinized (Wilson, 1983; Brazelton, 1980; Buchholz, 1987; Buchholz and Mishne, 1983). Bateman (1996) notes:

> The difficulties in identifying students who have learning disabilities include the persistent predisposition of some teachers to believe they could do it if only they would work harder (or if they had a better attitude, etc.). (pp. 37–38)

EMOTIONAL FALLOUT: TRAUMA

Individuals with ULD often grow up experiencing themselves as damaged (Buchholz, 1987; Cohen, 1985). When achievement falls far short of potential, the following psychological repercussions are common: alienation, heightened self-exposure, serious self-esteem problems, humiliation, fear of failure, and social problems (Lichtenberg, 1983; Buchholz, 1987; McGlynn, 1983; Cohen, 1985; Johnson and Blalock, 1987). This emotional fallout (Scheiber and Talpers, 1987, p. 13) can reflect anxiety, fear of discovery, depression, or anger. Cohen (1985) attests to the widespread nature of emotional fallout in LD children: "Although there are many children with learning problems who are not learning disabled, there are virtually no learning disabled children or adolescents who do not evidence significant psychological conflicts and concerns" (p. 177).

Gensler (1993) wrote a very thoughtful paper about the impact of ULD on defenses, interpersonal relations, character, self-image, and career development. When fear of humiliation and exposure makes LD sufferers afraid to try, spontaneity is inhibited, and motivation is sabotaged. Shame and withdrawal render them bored with life and increasingly reliant on others (Kafka, 1984).

Not surprisingly, the continual experience of these painful emotional states leaves the LD sufferer prone to depression. Often, school failures impact negatively on students' self-esteem (Kaplan and Shachter, 1991). Cohen (1983) describes why college students with LD are so often clinically depressed: although the students could compensate to some degree, they struggled with foreign languages, math, reading too slowly, sloppy handwriting, spelling discrepancies, and lack of organization.

Galatzer-Levy (1993) believes that many of the devastating emotional effects of LD can be attributed to cognitive difference. The LD brain is simply not structured in the same way as a non-LD brain, which creates "primary variations in the organization of experiences [that] range from the construction of body image to the sequencing of ideas which may be extraordinary in ways that may be evaluated *as maladaptive or creative or both*" (emphasis mine). He elaborates:

> These primary variations in experience take on added personal meaning as the person finds it difficult to negotiate a world largely designed for people whose cognitive organization differs from his own. Depending on the environment's response, the variation is commonly experienced as a defect and may come to symbolize other feelings of defectiveness, incompleteness, or vulnerability. (Galatzer-Levy, 1993, p. 181)

Perhaps "variations in experience" might also explain some of the personality disorders associated with LD. Rhodes and Jasinski (1990), Wood et al. (1976), and Wood, Wender, and Reimherr (1983) address the interface between learning disabilities and substance abuse. Another more sizable literature examines the interface between learning disabilities and personality disorders (Christman, 1984; Eisen, 1993; Mautner, 1984; Koziol, 1987; Vail, 1989; Cohen, 1983; Kafka, 1984; Levin, 1991; Wilson, 1993).

EMOTIONAL ENHANCEMENT: RESILIENCE

Resilience is a word that evokes the capacity to learn *how* to learn as one grows and develops. It's is a hopeful concept. It implies the capacity to learn, over time, to make changes, to adapt, and to better adjust to the world around us so that life can be more manageable (Basch, 1988). *Time* magazine quotes Arthur Reynolds, who says, "there is a sort of chain reaction that leads to resilience later, and that chain reaction begins with children who are very young" (2005, p. A53). Consider Rutter's statement, "There is now a much greater appreciation that few life events are random occurrences. Rather, they need to be seen as the outcome of what has gone before" (1994, p. 375).

Culture influences how we learn to adapt and protect ourselves. For example, the United States provides a context for the growth of resilience through its emphasis on individualism and entrepreneurship (Rigby, 1994). Take the American cowboy or early settlers whose rugged individualism, coupled with the ingenuity to solve seemingly impossible problems, surely made resilience an admirable trait for Americans.

But, resilience is still a difficult concept to define (Cohler, 1987; Garmezy, 1994; Rutter, 1994; Miller, 1997). The defintion can vary from person to person and from context to context (Masten, 1994). The war hero who is resilient on the battlefield may not be able to adapt to risk factors after he returns home.

How did resiliency as a focus of study evolve? The study of resiliency came about because researchers interested in developmental psychology were surprised by outcomes. It was first observed in the longitudinal studies of children in the now famous Kauai study. Many of the children growing into adulthood became contributing members of their culture despite severe risks in their environment (Werner, 1993; Anthony and Cohler, 1987). Researchers' predictions about what happens to children who experience difficult lives growing up didn't always turn out as expected (Rutter, 1994; Miller, 1996; Anthony and Cohler, 1987). So questions about why and how people who grow up in highly stressful situations are able to navigate through a stressful childhood and mature into successful adults.

Researchers wanted to learn more. Clearly one's difficult environment did not always lead to maladjustment. As researchers began to wonder how people learned to adapt to the risks in their lives; they began to explore the issues of the developmental implications of risk and resiliency. They questioned how at-risk individuals somehow protect themselves against the vulnerabilities in their lives and succeed anyway (Miller, 1997; Felsman and Vallaint, 1987; Wang and Gordon, 1994). Why was there was psychopathological absence in the face of undue stress in one's environment? How does the "active process of endurance, self-righting, and growth in response to crisis and challenge" evolve? (Seccombe, 2002, p. 385). What are the cultural, biological, psychological, and environmental influences?

The study of resilience is complicated. Because physical, psychological, and cultural factors all play a role (Garmazy 1994;

Rigby, 1994; Wang and Gordon, 1994), inquiry demands an interactively multidiscipline approach. The fields of psychology, sociology, medicine, and psychiatry are all necessary in order to best serve individuals with LD. An interdisciplinary approach respects the contrasts between vulnerability and invulnerability risk factors, and stressful life events (Werner and Smith, 1992; Anthony and Cohler, 1987).

An example of this kind of multidisciplinary inquiry can be seen in the work of the Center for Advanced Study in the Behavioral Sciences (Garmazy, 1994). In 1982, this center formed an interdisciplinary consortium that looked at chronic illness and stress in children. Over time, their focus turned to longitudinal studies of development and adaptive and maladaptive responses to stress. The concept of risk factors, or what prevents people from achieving, and resiliency factors, or what allows people to achieve despite risk, became a focus of inquiry. Their perspective has now been incorporated into educational philosophies in the popular literature (Masten, 1997).

Inquiry into protective factors that enhance resilience and deter against vulnerabilities and stress leads to questions about biologically based issues of temperament versus environmental input (Fajardo, 1991). Gore and Eckenrode looked at personal traits which have biological derivatives from environmental resources. They struggled to distinguish between (1) what a person brings to an encounter with their environment, and (2) the objective features of that environment (1996, p. 34).

In regard to what a person brings to an encounter with their environment, Werner, Bierman, and French's 1971 long-term study found core commonalities in temperament and in a support system (the people who rewarded their competencies). Other factors involving temperament are intact self-esteem, intelligence, confidence, mastery, verbal skills, and the capacity to care for others (Gorman, 2005; Morrison and Cosden 1997).

Researchers also began looking at temperamental characteristics that elicited positive social responses from parents, peers, and teachers. These characteristics included efficacy, planfulness, ability to plan well, and self-esteem. The people supporting resilient individuals include all of those who foster trust and a sense of coherence or faith. "Second chance" opportunities in society at large (at school, at work, in church, in the military) enable high risk youths to have the opportunity to acquire competence and confidence (Werner and Smith, 1992).

"Second chance" environmental factors interact, modulate, and can actually change characteristics (Levin, 1991; 2003). The influence of such factors as family functioning, school activity, peer relationships, and work situations influence in a major way one's capacity to adapt or not to stressors (Brooks and Goldstein, 2004; Morrison and Cassen 1997; Gore and Eckenrode, 1996).

But although resiliency is generally depicted as reactive, the capacity to protect against risk and harm (Werner and Smith, 1992), it also has another function. Resiliency can be *proactive* and involve the capacity to *look for and take* risks (Panksepp, and Biven 2010). Therefore, it can also be seen as an enhancer and a predictor for success (Vogel, Hruby, Adelman, 1993; Vogel and Adelman, 1993). Successful people who have learned to adapt also learn to be risk takers. Not being afraid to struggle with risk enhances flexibility and adaptability and such risk-taking is mandated in educational circles (Reiff, Gerber, and Ginsberg, 1997, pp. 68–69; 77–78). Certainly, there is risk in tackling what one doesn't know. The risk involves the shame of failure (Orenstein, 2000).

Furthermore, resiliency can be seen from an interactive viewpoint. Jordon talks of "Relational Resilience," which is the capacity to connect with others. She contrasts Rutter's protective model with her own transformational perspective (1992, p. 3). Her paper on resiliency suggests that the capacity for enhanced interaction with others is a developmental process going from isolation to relatedness and which changes people permanently. These transformations happen when individuals have the capacity to positively engage with others (Hartling, 2003). The resiliency involved in learning how to build relationships includes: (1) an awareness that disconnects have occurred, and (2) a flexible capacity to find ways of reconnection (Jordon, 1992). Jordon enforces the importance of having mentors (noting especially grandparents) who believe in you.

Resiliency builds on itself. Success breeds success. Gerber's (2002) empowerment model is interesting. He suggests that the all-encompassing factor for achieving success is a sense of control. This sense of control includes three components: Self-awareness, self-determination, and self-advocacy. Gerber describes the individual's capacity for recognition, understanding, and acceptance of problems coupled with a plan of action that one can put into effect.

In looking at resilience in people with LD, it's clear that both biologically and psychologically based experiences are major influences in the growth or hampering of resilience. Miller (1997) asks very important questions: How do people with LD become resilient, and is there a way to learn from them and then teach what we know to others? Surely it's clear from the participants' experiences discussed in the first part of this book that resilient people with LD can and do overcome the serious obstacles that learning disabilities pose. Countless people with LD achieve— some are very high achievers. Thomas Edison, Bruce Jenner, and Cher are examples of individuals who overcame serious obstacles in learning by persevering until success was forthcoming (Miller, 1997).*

Some researchers question how resilient people with LD succeed; they look at concepts of risk and protective factors (Miller, 2002; Reiff, 1997; Brooks and Goldstein, 2004; Cohler, 1987; Garmezy, 1994; Keogh and Weissner, 1993; Masten, 1997; and Spekman, Goldberg, and Herman, 1993, cited in Morrison and Casden, 1997). Others look at the capacity for adaptation and the ability to make appropriate adjustments (Levin et al., 2005; Morrison and Casden, 1997; Spekman, Herman, and Vogel, 1993 [cited in Morrison and Casden, 1997]). Jayne Green-Black (2002) cites Betsy Morris's article that appeared in *Fortune* magazine that

---

* Many successful people are discussed in the web site ldonline.com.

underscores the traumatic past experiences that many successful people with LD endure. Greene-Black cites Morris (2002) quoting individuals with LD: "If you could survive childhood, dyslexia was a pretty good business boot camp." Or people with LD "are always expecting a curve ball" (p. 62). In other words, no one asks for traumatic experiences, but many people do learn from them.

This capacity for adaptation and good judgment is discussed by Gerber (2002), who underscores the ability of resilient individuals with LD to find and use social supports without becoming dependent. They also have the capacity to learn and use new technologies (such as a spelling checker) to help them overcome intrinsic learning gaps (Greene-Black, 2002; Gorman, 2005).

Furthermore, the capacity to effectively find others to help bridge learning gaps has been explored. Morrison and Cosden (2002) suggest that the characteristics of a child, which include factors of self-awareness and self-esteem, actually influence how families adapt to LD problems.

In ending this section I cite a website produced by the Israel Center for the treatment of psychotrauma, located at www.traumaweb.org. This is a website for lay people, and one of the articles found there, "Improving Resilience" (2005), includes the following advice: work at relationships, be knowledgeable about problems, talk about feelings, enjoy humor, exercise hope, and try to be optimistic. Many of these approaches can be taught (Brody, 2005; Miller, 2002) and schools are taking up the challenge of LD (Masten 1997; Brooks and Goldstein, 2004).

This historical review is one way of categorizing the literature about adults with learning disabilities. Hopefully, in the future, much more will be learned and others will continue to fill in the gaps.

Recommended Reading

Brooks, R. and Goldstein, S. (2004). *The Power of Resilience: Achieving Balance, Confidence, and Personal Strength in Your Life.* New York: Mc-Graw-Hill.

Gerber, P.J. and Reiff, H. B. (1991). *Speaking for Themselves: Ethnographic Interviews with Adults with Learning Disabilities.* Ann Arbor, MI: University of Michigan Press.

Goleman, D. (1995). *Emotional Intelligence.* New York: Bantam Books.

Lelewer, N. (1994) Something's *Not Right: One Family's Struggle with Learning Disabilities.* Action, MA: VanderWyk and Burnham.

Mooney, J. and Cole, D. (2000). *Learning Outside the Lines.* New York: Fireside Press.

Reiff, H., Gerber, P. J., and Ginsberg, R. (1997). *Exceeding Expectations: Successful Adults with Learning Disabilities.* Austin, TX: Pro-Ed.

Schmitt, A. (1992) *Brilliant Idiot: An Autobiography of a Dyslexic.* Intercourse, PA: Good Books.

Schwartz, J. (1992). *Another Door to Learning: True Stories of Learning Disabled Children and Adults, and the Keys to Their Success.* New York: Crossroad Publishing Company.

Vogel, S.A. (2005). *College Students with Learning Disabilities: A Handbook for College Students, Faculty, Administrators, and Disability Service Providers,* eighth edition. Pittsburgh, PA: LDA of American Bookstore.

Wren, C. and Einhorn, J. (2000). *Hanging by a Twig: Understanding and Counseling Adults with Learning Disabilities and ADD,* New York: W.W. Norton.

Bibliography

Abrams, J.C. (1980). "A Psychodynamic Understanding of the Emotional Aspects of Learning Disorders," in B. Keogh, ed., *Advances in Special Education: A Research Annual. Perspectives on Applications* 2. Greenwich, CT: JAI Press, pp. 29–50.

Adelman, H. and Taylor, L. (1986). Introduction to the *Importance of Motivation for the Future of the L.D. Field* by E.L. Deci and C.L. Chandler, *Journal of Learning Disabilities* 19(10), p. 399.

Adelman, P.B. and Vogel, S.A. (1990). "College Graduates with Learning Disabilities: Employment Attainment and Career Pattern," *Learning Disability Quarterly* (13), Summer.

American Psychiatric Association, (1994). *Desk Reference to the Diagnostic Criteria from DSM-IV,* Washington, DC: American Psychiatric Association.

Anderson, C. (1974). "The Brain-Injured Adult: An Overlooked Problem," in R.E. Weber, ed., *Handbook on Learning Disabilities: A Prognosis for the Child, the Adolescent, the Adult.* Englewood Cliffs, NJ: Prentice-Hall, pp. 217–241.

Anthony J.E. and B.J. Cohler, eds. (1987). *The Invulnerable Child.* New York: Guilford Press.

Baker, H.S. (1987). "Underachievement and Failure in College: The Interaction Between Intrapsychic and Interpersonal Factors from the Perspective of Self Psychology," in S.C. Feinstein, ed., *Adolescent Psychiatry* 14. Chicago: The University of Chicago Press, pp. 441–460.

Baker, H.S. and Baker, M.N. (1987). "Heinz Kohut's Self-Psychology: An Overview," *American Journal of Psychiatry* 144(1), pp. 1–9.

Bartoli. (1990). "On Defining Learning and Disability: Exploring the Ecology," *Journal of Learning Disabilities* 23(10), pp. 628–631.

Basch, M.F. (1980). *Doing Psychotherapy.* New York: Basic Books.

———. (1988). *Understanding Psychotherapy: The Science Behind the Art.* New York: Basic Books.

———. (1992). *Practicing Psychotherapy: A Casebook.* New York: Basic Books.

Bateman, B. (1996). "Legal Definitions and the Juvenile Delinquency-Learning Disability Linkage," *LDA Newsbriefs* 31(1), 37–38.

Baum, S., Renzulli, J., and Hebert, T. (1994). "Reversing Underachievement: Stories of Success," *Educational Leaderships,* 52(3), pp. 47–52.

Bellak, L. (1978). *Psychiatric Aspects of Minimal Brain Dysfunction in Adults.* New York: Grune and Stratton.

Bigler, E.D. (1992). "The Neurobiology and Neuropsychology of Adult Learning Disorders," *Journal of Learning Disorders* 25(8), pp. 488–506.

Blakeslee, S. (1991). "Study Ties Dyslexia to Brain Flaw Affecting Vision and Other Senses," *The New York Times* September 15, p. 1.

Bogen, J.E. (1969). "The Other Side of the Brain: An Appositional Mind," *Bulletin of the Los Angeles Neurological Societies* 34(3) (July), reprinted in Ornstein, R. *The Nature of Human Consciousness.* San Francisco: Freeman, 1973.

———. (197X). Statement at Conference in Chicago in Approximately 1977–78. Approximate Topic of Conference: "The Psychology of Consciousness."

Bollas, C. (1983). "Expressive Uses of the Countertransference: Notes to the Patient from Oneself," *Contemporary Psychoanalysis* 19(1), January, pp. 1–34.

Brazelton, B.T. (1980). "Neonatal Assessment," in S.I. Greenspan and G.H. Pollock, eds., *The Course of Life: Psychoanalytic Contributions Toward Understanding Personality Development.* Adelphi, MD: National Institute of Mental Health, pp. 203–205.

Bresslau, N. (1990). "Does Brain Dysfunction Increase Children's Vulnerability to Environmental Stress?" *Archives of General Psychiatry* 47(1), pp. 15–21.

Brier, N. (1994). "Psychological Adjustment and Adults with Severe Learning Difficulties: Implications of the Literature on Children and Adolescents with Learning Disabilities for Research and Practice," *Learning Disabilities: A Multidisciplinary Journal* 5(1), pp. 15–27.

Brody, J.E. (2005). "Get a Grip: Set Your Sights Above Adversity," *The New York Times*, March 1, Science Times Section, D7.

Brooks, R. and Goldstein, S. (2004). *The Power of Resilience: Achieving Balance, Confidence, and Personal Strength in Your Life.* New York: McGraw-Hill.

Bruck, M. (1987). "The Adult Outcomes of Children with Learning Disabilities," *Annals of Dyslexia: An Interdisciplinary Journal of the Orton Dyslexia Society* 37, pp. 252–262.

Buchanan, M. and Wolf, J.S. (1986). "A Comprehensive Study of Learning Disabled Adults," *Journal of Learning Disabilities* 19(1), pp. 34–38.

Buchholz, E.S. (1987). "The Legacy from Childhood: Considerations for Treatment of the Adult with Learning Disabilities," *Psychoanalytic Inquiry* 7(3), pp. 431–452.

Buchholz, E. and Mishne, J. (1983). *Ego and Self Psychology: Group Interventions with Children, Adolescents, and Parents.* New York: Jason Aronson.

Buchsbaum M.S., Haier, R.J., Sostek, A.J., Weingartner, H., Zahn, T.P., Siever, L.J., Murphy, D.L., and Brody, L. (1984). "Attention Dysfunction and Psychopathology in College Men," *Archives of General Psychiatry* 4(42), pp. 354–360.

Butler, W.D. (1994). "Learning Disabilities Information," reproduced in the *National Networker: Quarterly Newsletter for Adults Who Have a Learning Disability*, PO Box 32611, Phoenix AZ 85064-2611.

Cannon L., ed. (1996). "Learning Disabilities and Juvenile Justice: Evidence of Failure for Persons with Learning Disabilities," Report of the Summit on Learning Disabilities, 1994, *LDA Newsbriefs* 31(1), p. 21.

Christman, D.C. (1984). "Notes on Learning Disabilities and the Borderline Personality," *Clinical Social Work Journal* 12(1), pp. 18–30.

Chuaeoan, H. (1997). "He Was My Hero," *Time Magazine*, January 27, p. 25.

Cohen, J. (1983). "Learning Disabilities and the College Student: Identification and Diagnosis," *Adolescent Psychiatry: Developmental and Clinical Studies* 11, pp. 177–198.

———. (1985). "Learning Disabilities and Adolescence: Developmental Considerations," *Adolescent Psychiatry: Developmental and Clinical Studies* 12, pp. 177–196.

Cohler, B.J. (1987). "Adversity, Resilience, and the Study of Lives," in Anthony J.E. and Cohler B.J. eds. (1987).

Cox, S. (1997). "The Learning-Disabled Adult," *Academic Therapy* 13(1), pp. 79–86.

Cozolino (L.) (2002). *The Neuroscience of Psychotherapy.* New York and London: W.W. Norton and Company.

Cruickshank, W. and Johnson, G.O. (1975). *Education of Exceptional Children and Youth.* Englewood Cliffs, NJ: Prentice-Hall.

Darwin, C. (1859/1995). *The Origin of the Species.* Gramercy Books.

Deci, E.L. and Chandler, C.L. (1986). "The Importance of Motivation for the Future of the L.D. Field," *Journal of Learning Disabilities* 19(10), pp. 587–594.

Deikman, A. (1982). *The Observing Self: Mysticism and Psychotherapy.* Boston: Beacon Press.

Einhorn, J. (2004). "Adults with Learning Disabilities," presentation to the professional group Professionals in Learning Disability, Winnetka, IL.

Eisen, M.R. (1993). "The Impact of the Learning-Disabled Child on the Family," in K. Field, E. Kaufman, and C. Saltzman, eds. (1993), pp. 126–138.

Ekman, P. (2003). *Emotions Revealed: Recognizing Faces and Feelings to Improve Communication and Emotional Life.* New York: Henry Holt and Co.

Elson, M. (1986). *Self Psychology in Clinical Social Work.* New York: W.W. Norton.

Engel, S. (1999). *Context Is Everything.* New York: Freeman.

Fajardo, B. (1991). "Analyzability and Resilience in Development," *Annual of Psychoanalysis* 19, pp. 107–126

Felsman, J.K. and Vaillant, G.E. (1987). "Resilient Children As Adults: A 40 Year Study," in E.J. Anthony and B.J. Cohler, eds. (1987), pp. 289–324.

Field, K., E. Kaufman, and C. Saltzman, eds. (1993). *Emotions and Learning Reconsidered: International Perspectives.* New York: Gardner Press.

Frauenheim, J.G. (1978). "Academic Achievement Characteristics of Adult Males Who Were Diagnosed As Dyslexic in Childhood," *Journal of Learning Disabilities* 11(8), pp. 21–28.

Friedman, Thomas L. (2014). "It Takes a Mentor," op-ed, *The New York Times,* Sept. 9.

Freud, S. (1891). *On Aphasia* (E. Stengel, trans.). New York: International Universities Press.

———. (1917). "Mourning and Melancholia," in E. Jones, ed., and J. Riviere, trans., *Sigmund Freud: Collected Papers. The International Psychoanalytical Library* 10, Vol. 4. New York: Basic Books, pp. 152–170.

Fuqua, P.B. (1993). "A Model of the Learning Process Based on Self Psychology," in K. Field, E. Kaufman, and C. Saltzman, eds. (1993), pp. 13–33.

Gajar, A. (1992). "Adults with Learning Disabilities: Current and Future Research Priorities," *Journal of Learning Disabilities* 28(8), pp. 507–519.

Galatzer-Levy, R.M. (1993). "When You're Stupid and Things Don't Work Right: Notes from the Analysis of an Adolescent Boy with a Learning Disability," in K. Field, E. Kaufman, and C. Saltzman, eds. (1993), pp. 171–186.

Garber, B. (1988). "The Emotional Implications of Learning Disabilities: A Theoretical Integration," *The Annual of Psychoanalysis, a Publication of the Institute for Psychoanalysis* 16. Madison, CT: International Universities Press, pp. 111–128.

———. (1989). "Deficits in Empathy in the Learning-Disabled Child," in K. Field, B. Cohler, and G. Wool, eds., *Learning and Education: Psychoanalytic Perspectives*. New York: International Universities Press, pp. 617–637.

Gardner, H. (1983). *Frames of Mind: The Theory of Multiple Intelligences*. New York: Basic Books.

Garmezy, N. (1993). "Children in Poverty: Resilience Despite Risk," *Psychiatry* 56, pp. 127–136.

———. (1994). "Reflections and Commentary on Risk, Resilience, and Development," in Haggerty, R.J., Sherrod, L.R., Garmezy N., and Rutter, M., eds. (1994).

Garnett K. and Laporta, S. (1991). "Dispelling the Myths," *College Students and Learning Disabilities*. Hunter College/National Center for Learning Disabilities, 99 Park Avenue, Sixth Floor, New York, NY 10016.

Gedo, J. (1999). *The Evolution of Psychoanalysis: Contemporary Theory and Practice*. New York: Other Press.

Gensler, D. (1993). "Learning Disability in Adulthood: Psychoanalytic Considerations," *Contemporary Psychoanalysis* 29(4), pp. 673–691.

Gerber, P.J. (1994). "Researching Adults with Learning Disabilities from Adult-Development Perspective," *Journal of Learning Disabilities* 27(1), pp. 6–9.

————. (2002). "Navigating the Beyond-School Years: Employment and Success for Adults with Learning Disabilities," Careertrainer: the Career Practitioner's Website, www.Careertrainer.Com.

Gerber, P.J., Ginsberg, R., and Reiff, H. (1992). "Identifying Alterable Patterns in Employment Success for Highly Successful Adults with Learning Disabilities," *Journal of Learning Disabilities* 25(8), pp. 475–487.

Gerber, P.J. and Kelley, R.H. (1984). "Learning Disabilities and Social Skill Development: Research-Based Implications for the Developmental Life-Span," in W.M. Cruickshank and J. M. Kliebhan, eds., *Early Adolescence to Early Adulthood: Selected Papers from the 20th International Conference of the Association for Children and Adults with Learning Disabilities.* Syracuse, NY: Syracuse University Press, pp. 69–77.

Gerber, P.J. and Reiff, H.B. (1991). *Speaking for Themselves: Ethnographic Interviews with Adults with Learning Disabilities.* Ann Arbor, MI: University of Michigan Press.

Gladwell, M. (2005). *Blink: the Power of Thinking Without Thinking.* New York: Little, Brown.

Goldberg, A. (1990). *The Prisonhouse of Psychoanalysis.* Hillsdale, NJ: Analytic Press.

————. (1994). *The End of Inquiry.* Presentation given at the meeting of the Chicago Psychoanalytic Society, September 27, 1994.

Goldberg. C. (1991). *Understanding Shame.* Northvale, NJ: Jason Aronson, Inc.

Goldberg, E. (2001). *The Executive Brain: Frontal Lobes and the Civilized Mind.* New York: Oxford University Press.

Goleman, D. (1995). *Emotional Intelligence.* New York: Bantam Books.

Gore, S. and Eckenrode J. (1994). *Context and Process in Research on Risk and Resilience,* in Haggerty, R.J., Sherrod, L.R., Garmezy N., and Rutter, M., eds. (1994).

Goreman (2005). "The Importance of Resilience," *Time,* January 17, pp. A52–A55.

Gottesman, R.L. (1994). "The Adult with Learning Disabilities: An Overview," *Learning Disabilities: A Multidisciplinary Journal* 5(1), pp. 1–14.

Greene-Black, J. (2002). "Having a Learning Disability Can Be a Career Asset," Contact Point, Summer 2002 (at contactpoint.ca).

Hartling, L.M. (2003). "Strengthening Resilience in a Risky World: It's All About Relationships," Work in Progress No. 101. Wellesley Centers for Women, Wellesley College, MA.

Greenspan, S. (1978). "Principles of Intensive Psychotherapy of Neurotic Adults with Minimal Brain Dysfunction," in L. Bellak, ed., *Psychiatric Aspects of Minimal Brain Dysfunction in Adults*. New York: Grune and Stratton, pp. 161–175.

Haggerty, R.J., Sherrod, L.R., Garmezy N., and Rutter, M., eds. (1994). *Stress, Risk, and Resilience in Children and Adolescents: Processes, Mechanisms, and Intervention*. Cambridge: Cambridge University Press.

Hammill, D. (1990). "On Defining Learning Disabilities: An Emerging Consensus," *Journal of Learning Disabilities* 23(2), pp. 74–84.

Harmon, A. (2004). "How About Not 'Curing' Us, Some Autistics Are Pleading," *New York Times*, National Edition, December 20, p. 1.

Hartling, L.M. (2003). *Strengthening Resilience in a Risky World: It's All About Relationships*. Work in Progress No. 101. Wellesley Centers for Women, Wellesley College, Massachusetts, pp. 1–12.

Haufrecht, B. and Berger, P.C. (1984). "Adult Psychosexual Disorders: An Integrated Approach," *Social Casework* 65(8) (October), pp. 478–485.

Hinshelwood J. (1917). *Congenital Word Blindness*. London: H.K. Lewis.

Horowitz, F.D. (1989). "Using Developmental Theory to Guide the Search for the Effects of Biological Risk Factors on the Development of Children," *American Journal of Clinical Nutrition* 50, pp. 589–597.

Interagency Committee on Learning Disabilities (1987). *Learning Disabilities: A Report to the U. S. Congress*. Washington, DC: U.S. Department of Health and Human Services.

International Dyslexia Association. (2005). Web Page on Learning Disabilities, www.Interdys.Org/Servlet/Compose?Section_Id=47, citing work by Paula Tallal.

———. (2005). Citing work by Albert Galaburda and Associates.

Israel Center for the Treatment of Psychotrauma (2005). "Improving Resilience," www.traumaweb.org/improving_resiliency.shtml.

Johnson, D. (1987a). "Principles of Assessment and Diagnosis," in D. Johnson and J. Blalock, eds. (1987).

———. (1987b). "Nonverbal Learning Disabilities," *Pediatric Annals* 16(2), pp. 133–141.

Johnson D.J. and Blalock, J.W. (1987). *Adults with Learning Disabilities*. New York: Grune and Stratton.

Johnson, D. and Myklebust, H. (1971). *Learning Disabilities: Educational Principles and Practices*. New York: Grune and Stratton.

Jordon, J.V. (1992). "Relational Resilience," Work in Progress No. 57, Jean Baker Miller Training Institute, Stone Center. Wellesley College, Wellesley, MA, pp. 1–12.

Kafka, E. (1984). "Cognitive Difficulties in Psychoanalysis," *Psychoanalytic Quarterly* 53(4), pp. 533–550.

Kagan, J., and Snidman, N. (2004). *The Long Shadow of Temperament*. Cambridge, MA: Belknap Press/Harvard University Press.

Kaplan C.P. and Shachter. (1991). "Adults with Undiagnosed Learning Disabilities: Practice Considerations," *Families in Society: The Journal of Contemporary Human Services* 72(4), pp. 195–201.

Kaufman, R. (1989). "The Inability to Learn in School: The Role of Early Developmental Deficiencies in Learning Disabilities," in K. Field, B. Cohler, and G. Wool (Eds.), *Learning and Education: Psychoanalytic Perspectives*. Madison, CT: International Universities Press, pp. 559–615.

Keogh, B. (1988). "The Future of the Learning Disability Field," in S. Chess, A. Thomas, and M. Hertzig, eds., *Annual Progress in Child Psychiatry and Child Development*. New York: Brunner/Mazel, pp. 207–219.

Kirk, S. and Gallagher, J. (1979). *Educating Exceptional Children*. Boston: Houghton Mifflin.

Kohut, H. (1971). *The Analysis of the Self*. New York: International Universities Press.

———. (1977). *The Restoration of the Self*. New York: International Universities Press.

———. (1984). *How Does Analysis Cure?* Chicago: the University of Chicago Press.

———. (1985). *Self Psychology and the Humanities: Reflections on a New Psychoanalytic Approach*. C.B. Strozier, ed. New York: W.W. Norton and Co.

Kohut, H. and Wolfe, E.S. (1978). "The Disorders of the Self and Their Treatment: An Outline," *International Journal of Psychoanalysis* 59(4), pp. 413–423.

Kosarych-Coy, J.M. (1984). "A Study of the Self-Concepts of Community College Students Identified As Learning Disabled," *Dissertation Abstracts International* 45(5), p. 1299A.

Kozoil, L.F. (1987). "Learning Disorders—Food for Clinical Thought," *Clinical Review* 1(2), pp. 1–2.

Kraus, N., McGee, T. J., Carrel, T.D., Zecker, S.G., Nicol, T.G., and Koch, D.B. (1996). "Auditory Neurophysiologic Responses and Discrimination Deficits in Children with Learning Problems," *Science* 273(5277), pp. 971–973.

Krystal, H. (1988). *Integration and Self Healing.* Hillsdale, NJ: Analytic Press.

Landers, A. (1997a). "The Streets Are Full of Easily Lost People," *Chicago Tribune,* January 6, Tempo Section 5, p. 3.

———. (1997b). "No Clue When it Comes to Some Faces," *Chicago Tribune,* March 25, Tempo Section 5, p. 3.

Ledoux, J. (1998). *The Emotional Brain: The Mysterious Underpinnings of Emotional Life.* (See diagram p. 164, Fig. 6–3, of the "High Road [through the cortex]" and "Low Road" [underneath the cortex] from the sensory thalamus to the amygdale.)

Lerner, J. (1981/2003). *Learning Disabilities: Theories, Diagnosis, and Teaching Strategies.* Boston: Houghton Mifflin.

Levin, F.M. (1991). *Mapping the Mind.* Hillsdale, NJ: London Analytic Press.

———. (1995). "Psychoanalysis and Knowledge: Part 1. The Problem of Representation and Alternative Approaches to Learning," in J.A. Winer, ed. *The Annual of Psychoanalysis.* Hillsdale, NJ: The Analytic Press, pp. 95–116.

———. (1997). "Some Thoughts on Attention," *Samiksha, Journal of the Indian Psychoanalytic Society* 51, pp. 23–30.

———. (1998). "Mind and Brain: Attempting to Bridge Our Understanding of Conscious and Unconscious Processes," *Samiksha, Journal of the Indian Psychoanalytic Society* 52, pp. 39–48.

———. (2003–2004). "Mind and Brain Interactions: A Neuro-Psychoanalytic Perspective on Emotional Attention, Cytokines, and New Long-Term Memory," *Samiksa: Journal of the Indian Psychoanalytical Society* 57, pp. 13–23.

———. (2005). "Dreaming Enhances Survival by Facilitating Learning About Dangers: A Neuro-Psychoanalytic (NP) View of Deferred Action Plans As a 'Missing' Adaptive Part of Dreaming," presented to the International Neuro-Psychoanalytic Congress, Rio De Janeiro, July 27, 2005.

———. (2003). *Psyche and Brain: The Biology of Talking Cures.* Madison, CT: International Universities Press.

———. (2005). Book Review of *Neuro-Psychoanalysis of Revolutionary Connections: Psychotherapy and Neuroscience* (2003), J. Corrigall and H. Wilkinson, eds., London: Karnac Press, *Neuro-Psychoanalysis* 7(1), pp. 107–111.

Levin, F.M. and Kent, E.W. (1995). "Psychoanalysis and Knowledge: Part 2. The Special Relationship Between Psychoanalytic Transference, Similarity Judgment, and the Priming of Memory," in J.A. Winer, ed., *The Annual of Psychoanalysis*. Hillsdale, NJ: The Analytic Press, pp. 117–130.

Levine, M. (2002). *A Mind at a Time*. New York: Simon and Schuster.

Lewin, T. (1996). "College Toughens its Stance on Learning Disabilities Aid," *The New York Times National*, February 13, p. 1.

Lichtenberg, J. (1983). "The Psychoanalytic Situation and Infancy," in J. Lichtenberg, ed., *Psychoanalysis and Infant Research*. Hillsdale, NJ: The Analytic Press, pp. 183–214.

————. (1988). "Infant Research and Self Psychology," in A. Goldberg, ed., *Frontiers in Self Psychology: Progress in Self Psychology*. Hillsdale, NJ: The Analytic Press, pp. 59–64.

Lieb, P. (1990). "The Origins of Ambitions," in A. Goldberg, ed., *The Realities of Transference: Progress in Self Psychology*. Hillsdale, NJ: The Analytic Press.

Lieberman, L.M. (1987). "Is the Learning Disabled Adult Really Necessary?" *Journal of Learning Disabilities* 20(1), p. 64.

Lutwik, N. (1983). "Countertherapeutic Styles When Counseling the Learning Disabled College Student," *Journal of College Student Personnel* 24(4), pp. 321–324.

Madigan, C.M. (1994). "Welfare Finger-Pointing: Society Often Determines Stereotypes," *Chicago Tribune*, February 20, Perspective, p. 1.

Malcolm, C.B., Polatajko, H.J., Simons, J. (1990). "A Descriptive Study of Adults with Suspected Learning Disabilities," *Journal of Learning Disabilities* 23(8), pp. 518–520.

Masten, A.E. (1994). "Resilience in Individual Development: Successful Adaptation Despite Risk and Adversity," in M.C. Wang and E.W. Gordon, eds., *Educational Resilience in Inner-City American: Challenges and Prospects*, Hillsdale, NJ: Lawrence Erlbaum Ass. Publishers, pp. 3–25.

————. (1997). "Resilience in Children At-Risk," *Carei: Center for Applied Research and Educational Improvement* (Spring Issue) Http://Education.Umn.Edu/CAREI/Reports/Rpractice/Sprig97/Resilience.Htm.

Mautner, T.S. (1984). "Dyslexia—My 'Invisible Handicap'," *Annals of Dyslexia: An Interdisciplinary Journal of the Orton Dyslexia Society* 34, pp. 299–311.

McGlynn M.J. (1983). "Differences in Self-Concept in Learning Disabled Versus Non-Learning Disabled Adults," *Dissertation Abstracts International* 44(3), p. 711–A.

McMahill, V. (1993). "Learning Disabilities and Self-Esteem," *LDA Newsbriefs* 26(6), p. 22.

Miller, M. (1996). "Relevance of Resilience to Individuals with Learning Disabilities," *Internal Journal of Disability: Development and Education* 43(3), pp. 255–269.

————. (1997). "Resilience in University Students Who Have Learning Disabilities," *Learning Disabilities* 8(2), pp. 89–95.

————. (2002). "Resilience Elements in Students with Learning Disabilities," *Journal of Clinical Psychology* 58(3), pp. 291–298.

Modell, A. (2003). *Imagination and the Meaningful Brain.* Cambridge, MA: MIT Press.

Mooney (J). (2000). *Learning Outside the Lines.* New York: Fireside Press

Moore B.E. and Fine, B.D. (1990). *Psychoanalytic Terms and Concepts.* New Haven and London: American Psychoanalytic Association and Yale University Press.

Morris, B. (2002). "The Dyslexic CEO," *Fortune.* May 16, pp. 53–70.

Morrison, G.M. and Cosden, M.A. (1997). "Risk, Resilience, and Adjustment of Individuals with Learning Disabilities," *Learning Disability Quarterly* 20 (Winter), pp. 43–60.

Murray, M. (1979). "Minimal Brain Dysfunction and Borderline Personality Adjustment," *American Journal of Psychotherapy* 33(3) (July), pp. 391–403.

Muslin, H.L. and Val, E.R. (1987). *The Psychotherapy of the Self.* New York: Brunner/Mazel Publishers.

National Center for Learning Disabilities. "Attention and Learning Problems: Which Came First?" at www.ncld.org.

Nathanson, D. (1987). "A Timetable for Shame," in D.L. Nathanson, ed., *The Many Faces of Shame.* New York: The Guilford Press, pp. 1–64.

Navarez, D., Panksepp, J., Shore A.N., Gleason, T.R., eds. (2013) *Evolution, Early Experience and Human Development.* Oxford: Oxford University Press.

Orenstein, M. (1992). "Imprisoned Intelligence: The Discovery of Undiagnosed Learning Disabilities in Adults," *Psychological Abstracts,* AAD98-16334, 58–11, p. 6243.

————. (2000). "Picking Up the Clues: Understanding Undiagnosed Learning Disabilities, Shame, and Imprisoned Intelligence," *Journal of College Student Psychotherapy* 15(2), pp. 35–46.

Orenstein, M, and Levin, F.M. (2003). "Thoughts on Traumatic Learning Failure," *Educational Therapist* 14(2).

Ornstein, R. (1997). *The Right Mind: Making Sense of the Hemispheres.* New York: Harcourt Brace.

Palombo, J. (1979). "Perceptual Deficits and Self-Esteem in Adolescence," *Clinical Social Work Journal* 7(1), pp. 34–61.

————. (1985a). "The Treatment of Borderline Neurocognitively Impaired Children: A Perspective from Self Psychology," *Clinical Social Work Journal* 13(2), pp. 117–128.

————. (1985b). "Depletion States and Selfobject Disorders," *Clinical Social Work Journal* 13(1), pp. 32–49.

————. (1988). "Adolescent Development: A View from Self Psychology," *Child and Adolescent Social Work* 5(3), pp. 171–186.

————. (1991). "Neurocognitive Differences, Self Cohesion, and Incoherent Self Narratives," *Child and Adolescent Social Work* 8(6), pp. 449–472.

————. (2001). *Learning Disorders and Disorders of the Self in Children and Adolescents.* New York: W.W. Norton.

Panksepp, J. (1998) *Affective Neuroscience: The Foundations of Human and Animal Emotions.* New York: Oxford University Press.

————. (2010). "Affective Neuroscience of the Emotional BrainMind: Evolutionary Perspectives and Implications for Understanding Depression," *Dialogues in Clinical Neuroscience* 12(4), pp. 533–545.

Panksepp, J., and Biven, L. (2010). *The Archeology of Mind: Neuroevolutionary Origins of Human Emotions.* New York: W.W. Norton.

Panksepp J., and Watt, D. (2011). "Why Does Depression Hurt? Ancestral Primary Process Separation-Distress (Panic/Grief) and Diminished Brain Reward (Seeking) Processes in the Genesis of Depressive Affect," *Psychiatry* 74(1), pp. 5–14.

Patten, B.M. (1973). "Visually Mediated Thinking: A Report of the Case of Albert Einstein," *Journal of Learning Disabilities* 6(7), pp. 415–420.

Patton, J.R. and Polloway, A.A. (1982). "The Learning Disabled: the Adult Years," *Topics in Learning Disabilities* 2(3) (October), pp. 79–87.

Pennington, B.F. (1991). *Diagnosing Learning Disorders: A Neurological Framework.* New York, London: The Guilford Press.

Person, E.S. (2002). *Feeling Strong: The Achievement of Authentic Power.* New York: Harpercollins.

Pickar, D. (1986). "Psychosocial Aspects of Learning Disabilities: A Review of Research," *Bulletin of the Menninger Clinic* 50(1), pp. 22–32.

Pollock, G.H. (1961). "Mourning and Adaptation," *International Journal of Psychoanalysis* 42, pp. 341–361.

Polloway, E.A., Smith, J.D., and Patton, J.R. (1988). "Learning Disabilities: An Adult Developmental Perspective," *Learning Disability Quarterly* 7(2), pp. 265–272.

Poznanski, E. (1979). "Handicapped Children," in S. Harrison and J. Noshpitz, J., eds., *Basic Handbook of Child Psychiatry.* New York: Basic Books, pp. 641–650.

Raskind, M.H., Goldberg, R.J., Higgins, E.L. and Herman, K.L. (1999). "Patterns of Change and Predictors of Success in Individuals with Learning Disabilities: Results from a Twenty-Year Longitudinal Study," *Learning Disabilities: Research and Practice* 14(1), pp. 35–40.

Raven, J. (1984). *Competence in Modern Society: Its Identification, Development and Release.* London, H.K. Lewis and Co.

Rawson, M. (1968). "Developmental Language Disability: Adult Accomplishments of Dyslexic Boys," Paper. Baltimore, MD: Johns Hopkins Press.

———. (1977). "Dyslexics As Adults: The Possibilities and the Challenge," *Bulletin of the Orton Society: An Interdisciplinary Journal of Specific Language Disability* 27, pp. 193–197.

Reiff, H., Gerber, P.J., and Ginsberg, R. (1993). "Definitions of Learning Disabilities from Adults with Learning Disabilities: The Insiders' Perspective," *Learning Disability Quarterly* 16(2), pp. 114–125.

———. (1997). *Exceeding Expectations: Successful Adults with Learning Disabilities.* Austin, TX: Pro-Ed.

Rhodes, S. and Jasinski, D.R. (1990). "Learning Disabilities in Alcohol-Dependent Adults: A Preliminary Study," *Journal of Learning Disabilities* 23(9), pp. 551–556.

Rigsby, L.C. (1994). "The Americanization of Resilience: Deconstructing Research Practice," in Wang, M.C. and Gordon, E.W., eds., *Educational Resilience in Inner-City America: Challenges and Prospects.* Hillsdale, NJ: Lawrence Erlbaum Associates.

Rosenberger, J. (1988). "Self Psychology As a Theoretical Base for Understanding the Impact of Learning Disabilities," *Child and Adolescent Social Work* 5(4), pp. 269–280.

Ross, A.O. (1977). *Learning Disability: The Unrealized Potential.* New York: McGraw-Hill.

Ross, J.M. (1987). "Learning Disabled Adults: Who Are They and What Do We Do with Them?" *Lifelong Learning: An Omnibus of Practice and Research* 11(3), pp. 4–8.

Rothstein, A. (1998). "Neuropsychological Dysfunction and Psychological Conflict," *The Psychoanalytic Quarterly* 67(2), pp. 218–240.

Rothstein, A., Lawrence, B., Crosby, M., and Eisenstadt, K. (1988). *Learning Disorders: An Integration of Neuropsychological and Psychoanalytic Considerations.* Madison, CT: International Universities Press.

Rourke, B.P., Young, G.C., and Leenaars, A.A.A. (1989). "Childhood Learning Disability That Predisposes Those Afflicted to Adolescent and Adult Depression and Suicide Risk," *Journal of Learning Disabilities* 22(3), pp. 169–175.

Rutter, M. (1994). "Stress Research: Accomplishments and Tasks Ahead," in Haggerty, R.J., Sherrod, L.R., Garmezy N., and Rutter, M., eds., (1994).

Ryan, A.G. and Price, L. (1992). "Adults with LD in the 1990s," *Intervention in School and Clinic* 28(1), pp. 6–20.

Schechter, M.D. (1974). "Psychiatric Aspects of Learning Disabilities," *Child Psychiatry and Human Development* 5(2), pp. 67–77.

Scheiber, B. and Talpers, J. (1987). *Unlocking Potential: College and Other Choices for Learning Disabled People—A Step-By-Step Guide.* Bethesda, MD: Scheiber and Adler.

Schulman, S. (1984). "Psychotherapeutic Issues for the Learning Disabled Adult," *Professional Psychology: Research and Practice* 15(6), pp. 34–39.

————. (1986). "Facing the Invisible Handicap," *Psychology Today* 20(2), February, pp. 58–61.

Schwartz, J. (1992). *Another Door to Learning: True Stories of Learning Disabled Children and Adults, and the Keys to Their Success.* New York: Crossroad Publishing Company.

Schwartz, M., Gilroy, J., and Lynn, G. (1976). "Neuropsychological and Psychosocial Implications of Spelling Deficit in Adulthood: A Case Report," *Journal of Learning Disabilities* 9(3), pp. 144–148.

Seccombe, K. (2002). "'Beating the Odds' Versus 'Changing the Odds':

Poverty, Resilience and Family Policy," *Journal of Marriage and Family* 64, pp. 384–394.

Shah, I. (1998). *The Lion Who Saw Himself in the Water.* Cambridge, MA, Hoopoe. www.hoopoekids.com.

Shalala, D. (1991). Foreword, in K. Garnett and S. Laporta, *College Students and Learning Disabilities.* New York: Hunter College National Center for Learning Disabilities, p. ii.

Shane, E. (1984). "Self Psychology: A New Conceptualization for the Understanding of Learning Disabled Children," in P. E. Stepansky and A. Goldberg, eds., *Kohut's Legacy.* Hillsdale, NJ: The Analytic Press, pp. 191–201.

Shapiro, J., Loeb, P., and Bowermaster, D. (1993). "Separate and Unequal," *U.S. News and World Report,* Dec. 13, 1993, pp. 46–60.

Siegel, E. and Gold, R. (1982). *Educating the Learning Disabled.* New York: Macmillan.

Silver, L. (1968). "More Than Twenty Years After: A Review of Developmental Language Disability. Adult Accomplishments of Dyslexic Boys," *The Journal of Special Education* 3(2), pp. 219–222.

————. (1979). "Minimal Brain Dysfunction Syndrome," in J. D. Noshpitz, ed., *Basic Handbook of Child Psychiatry,* Vol. 2. New York: Basic Books.

————. (1981). "The Relationship Between Learning Disabilities, Hyperactivity, Distractibility, and Behavioral Problems," *Journal of the American Academy of Child Psychiatry* 20, pp. 385–397.

————. (1984). "Emotional and Social Problems of Children with Developmental Disabilities," in R. Weber, ed., *Handbook on Learning Disabilities.* Englewood Cliffs, NJ: Prentice-Hall, pp. 97–120.

————. (1989a). "Learning Disabilities," *Journal of the American Academy of Child Psychiatry* 20, pp. 309–313.

————. (1989b). "Psychological and Family Problems Associated with Learning Disabilities: Assessment and Intervention," *Journal of the American Academy of Child and Adolescent Psychiatry* 28(3), pp. 319–325.

————. (1994). "What Are Specific Learning Disabilities?" in *The Gifted Learning Disabled Student.* Baltimore, CT: CTY Publications and Resources, pp. 25–28.

Silver, L. and Brunsetter, R.W. (1987). "Learning Disabilities: Recent Advances," in J.D. Noshpitz, ed., *Basic Handbook of Child Psychiatry,* Vol. 5. New York: Basic Books, pp. 354–361.

Smaller, M.D. (2012). "Psychoanalysis and the Forward Edge Hit the Streets: The Analytic Service to Adolescents Program (ASAP)," *Psychoanalytic Inquiry* 32, pp. 136–148.

Snarey, J.R., and Vaillant, G.E. (1985). "How Lower- and Working-Class Youth Become Middle-Class Adults: The Association Between Ego Defense Mechanisms and Upward Social Mobility," *Child Development* 56, pp. 899–910.

Spekman, N.J., Goldberg, R.J., and Herman, K.L. (1993). "An Exploration of Risk and Resilience in the Lives of Individuals with Learning Disabilities," *Learning Disabilities: Research and Practice* 8(1), pp. 11–18.

Stein, L.K., Mendel, E.D., and Jaboley, T. (1981). *Deafness and Mental Health.* New York: Grune and Stratton.

Stein N.L. (1987). "Lost in the Learning Maze," *Journal of Learning Disabilities* 20(8) August/September, pp. 409–441.

Stern, D. (1985). *The Interpersonal World of the Infant.* New York: Basic Books.

Sternberg, R.J., and Grigorenko, E.L. (1999). *Our Labeled Children.* New York: Perseus/Harpercollins.

Strauss, A.A. and Lehtinen, L.E. (1947). *Psychopathology and Education of the Brain-Injured Child.* New York: Grune and Stratton.

Strauss, R. (1978). "Richard's Story," *Bulletin of the Orton Society: An Interdisciplinary Journal of Specific Language Disability* 18, pp. 181–185.

Thompson, L. (1971). "Language Disabilities in Men of Eminence," *Journal of Learning Disabilities* 4(1), pp. 113–121.

Time Magazine. (2005). "The Importance of Resilience," January 17, pp. A52–A55.

Tolpin, M. (2002). "Doing Psychoanalysis of Normal Development: Forward Edge Transferences," in A. Goldberg, ed., *Progress in Self Psychology* 18, pp. 167–190.

Tomkins, S. (1987). "Shame," in D L. Nathanson, ed., *The Many Faces of Shame.* New York: The Guilford Press, pp. 133–161.

Trevarthen, C. (2003). "Neuroscience and Intrinsic Psychodynamics: Current Knowledge and Potential for Therapy," Chapter 2 in J. Corrigall and H. Wilkinson, eds., *Revolutionary Connections: Psychotherapy and Neuroscience.* London: Karnac Books, pp. 53–78.

U.S. Government Code of Federal Regulations. "Learning Disability," (34CFR300, 7(C)(107).

U.S. Office of Education. (1977). "Definition and Criteria for Defining Students As Learning Disabled," *Federal Register* 42(250), 65083, Washington, DC: U.S. Government Printing Office.

Vogel, S. (1985). "Learning Disabled College Students: Identification, Assessment, and Outcomes," in D. Duane and C. Leong, eds., *Understanding Learning Disabilities: International and Multidisciplinary Views.* NY: Plenum Press.

————. (1989). "Special Considerations in the Development of Models for Diagnosis of Adults with Learning Disabilities," in L.B. Silver, ed., *The Assessment of Learning Disabilities: Preschool Through Adulthood.* Boston: College Hill, pp. 111–134.

Wang, M. C., and Gordon, E.W., eds. (1994). *Educational Resilience in Inner-City America: Challenges and Prospects.* Hillsdale, NJ: Lawrence Erlbaum Associates.

WBEZ. (1996). Commercial for Epson Printers, May 3, National Public Radio.

Webster's New Collegiate Dictionary (1981). Springfield, MA: G. & C. Merriam Co.

Weil, A.P. (1978). "Maturational Variations and Genetic-Dynamic Issues," *Journal of the American Psychoanalytic Association* 26(3), pp. 461–491.

Weintraub, P. (2012) "Discover Interview: Jaak Panksepp Pinned Down Humanity's Primal Emotions," *Discover* (May), (http://discovermagazine.com/2012/May/11-Jaak-Panksepp-Rat-Tickler-Found-Humans-7-Primal-Emotions#.Uzqmhtyhgpe).

Werner, E.E., Bierman, J.M., and French F.E. (1971). *The Children of Kauai.* Honolulu: University of Hawaii Press.

Werner, E.E. and Smith, R.S. (1992). *Overcoming the Odds: High Risk Children from Birth to Adulthood.* Ithaca, NY: Cornell University Press.

Werner, E.E. (1993). "Risk and Resilience in Individuals with Learning Disabilities: Lessons Learned from the Kauai Longitudinal Study," *Learning Disabilities: Research and Practice* 8(1), pp. 28–34.

White, W.J. (1985). "Perspectives on the Education and Training of Learning Disabled Adults," *Learning Disability Quarterly* 8(3) Summer, pp. 231–235.

————. (1992). "The Postschool Adjustment of Persons with Learning Disabilities: Current Status and Future Projections," *Journal of Learning Disabilities* 25(7), pp. 448–456.

Wilson, N.O. (1993). "Learning Disabilities and the General Public," *LDA Newsbriefs* 28(4), LDA, 4156 Library Road, Pittsburgh, PA 15234.

Wines, M. (2005). "In South Africa, Yachting Erases a Racial Barrier," *New York Times*, February 1, p. 1.

Wolf, E. (1988). *Treating the Self: Elements of Clinical Self Psychology.* New York: The Guilford Press.

Wood, D., Reimherr, F.W., Wender, P.H., and Johnson, G.E. (1976). "Diagnosis and Treatment of Minimal Brain Dysfunction in Adults: A Preliminary Report," *Archives of General Psychiatry* 33(12), pp. 1453–1460.

Wood, D., Wender, Ph. H., and Reimherr, F.W. (1983). "The Prevalence of Attention Deficit Disorder, Residual Type, or Minimal Brain Dysfunction, in a Population of Male Alcoholic Patients," *American Journal of Psychiatry* 140(1), pp. 95–98.

Wren, C. and Segal, L. (1985). *College Students with Learning Disabilities: A Student's Perspective,*" Carol T. Wren, Director, Project Learning Strategies, DePaul University, 2323 Seminary, Chicago, IL 60614.

Wren, C., Adelman, P., Pike, M.B., and Wilson, J.L. (1987). *College and the High School Student* with *Learning Disabilities: The Student's Perspective.* Project Learning Strategies, DePaul University, 2323 Seminary, Chicago, IL 60614.

Wren, C. and Einhorn, J. (2000). *Hanging by a Twig: Understanding and Counseling Adults with Learning Disabilities and ADD,* New York: W.W. Norton.

Wurmser, L. (1987). "Shame: The Veiled Companion of Narcissism," in D.L. Nathanson, ed., *The Many Faces of Shame.* New York: The Guilford Press, pp. 64–92.

Index

Made in the USA
San Bernardino, CA
06 August 2019